نام انسان

Intellectual
Studies on
ISLAM

Sketch of Martin Bernard Dickson by Sandra Assasnik Anderton

Intellectual Studies on
ISLAM

ESSAYS WRITTEN
IN HONOR OF
MARTIN B. DICKSON
Professor of Persian Studies,
Princeton University

Edited by
Michel M. Mazzaoui
and
Vera B. Moreen

UNIVERSITY OF UTAH PRESS
SALT LAKE CITY, UTAH

Library of Congress Cataloging-in-Publication Data

Intellectual studies on Islam : essays written in honor of Martin B.
Dickson / edited by Michel M. Mazzaoui and Vera B. Moreen.
   p. cm.
Includes bibliographical references and index.
ISBN 0-87480-342-X
1. Civilization, Islamic. I. Dickson, Martin Bernard.
II. Mazzaoui, Michel M., 1926–   III. Moreen, Vera Basch.
DS36.86.I48 1990   90-52746
909'.097671—dc20   CIP

CONTENTS

PART III

PART IV

Preface

"Myself when young did eagerly frequent/Doctor and saint, and heard great argument/About it and about; but evermore/Walked out from the same door as in I went." This might be true of Omar Khayyam in the poetic rendering of Edward Fitzgerald. But it most certainly is not true of Martin B. Dickson, a latter-day "doctor and saint," professor of Persian history and literature at Princeton; teacher, colleague, and friend, in whose honor this volume of essays has been written and published.

When you sit and listen to Martin Dickson talking on virtually any subject, you simply do not walk out from the same door as in you went! For his conversation, serious or trivial, commonplace or profound, opens to the listener a hundred doors from which he or she may choose to walk out to a new and different world. The originality of his ideas, the intensity of his views, the openness of his mind, and many more of such and other rare qualities, make of him the ideal *ustad* (master). He is a living example of how, in classical Islamic times, the partaking of knowledge and learning is described: the student "sat between the hands" of the master (*jalas-a bayn-a yaday-hi*).

Professor Dickson has been occupying the chair of Persian studies at Princeton for the past thirty years. During this period, inside and outside the classroom, he has left an indelible mark on his numerous students and on everyone who came in contact with him. Many of those who graduated "at his hands" occupy important positions in the field of Near Eastern studies in various American universities. He is also widely known in the Middle East and Europe including the Soviet Union. May he continue to enjoy a long and productive life.

Except for the opening essay by Stuart Cary Welch—an eloquent testimony to his long association with Martin Dickson in their magisterial edition of *The Houghton Shahnameh*, published by Harvard University Press in 1981—the articles more specifically cover four major approaches within the overall intellectual tradition of Islam that reflect the particular scholarly interests of the authors:

Part I. *Historical-Biographical*

This is represented by the contributions of Professors Haarmann, McChesney, Mazzaoui, Moreen, Roemer, Woods, and al-Imad. Roemer's article on the Qizilbash Turcomans, Moreen's on two Judaeo-Persian texts, and Mazzaoui's on Shah Isma^{c}il II, deal with aspects of Persian history of the Safavid period—one of the most important dynastic breakdowns of the history of Iran. McChesney's article on the anthology of Central Asian poets and Woods's biography of Timur fill in and update significant gaps in the biographical literature of Islamic history that goes hand in hand with purely historical investigations and is indispensable for the proper understanding of the progress and development of the history of the Middle East. Haarmann's article on the Law of the Turks and al-Imad's on women and religion during the Fatimid period treat important political and social topics of the Muslim medieval tradition.

Part II. *Sufi-Mystical*

Two articles in the collection—Hamori's on the great Muslim Sufi master, Junayd, and Annemarie Schimmel's on an aspect of Sufism in the Indian subcontinent—deal with the great Muslim tradition of mysticism (Sufism), perhaps the most meaningful and humane dimension of Islam. While Hamori stresses the literary side of the tradition, Schimmel is recognized as one of the leading authorities on the subject of Islamic mysticism.

Part III. *Philosophical*

Peter Heath's analysis of a treatise by Ibn Sina (Avicenna), one of the greatest Muslim minds in the Middle Ages, and Peters's contribution on the roots of Arabic-Islamic occultism, represent two discourses on Muslim philosophy and the occult sciences which, although they had their roots in the ancient Greek tradition, witnessed tremendous impetus and development at the hand of celebrated Muslim thinkers.

Part IV. *Artistic*

Finally, two articles plus Cary Welch's opening "Salute to a Coauthor" deal with the celebrated Muslim tradition of miniature painting. Thackston's annotated translation of a treatise on calligraphic arts explains the use of ink, color, brush, paper, etc., at the ateliers of Muslim miniaturists; Marlow's article on the Peck Shahnameh describes manuscript production and the distinctive style of painting of the school of Shiraz in central Iran.

In their totality, the fourteen articles of this volume cover significant achievements of the Muslim intellectual and cultural tradition in history, biography, mysticism, philosophy, and art—achievements which in themselves demonstrate the high caliber attained by Islamic societies in medieval and early modern times. The tradition was still resourceful, inventive, and vibrant. The desuetude that befell the tradition in more recent times (say, after 1800) should not keep us blind to the great accomplishments of the past. In fact, modern Western as well as Eastern intelligent and curious readers continue to be fascinated by the tremendous strides in the realms of thought and culture of the common Islamic heritage. On the one hand, the West wants to know more about the not-anymore-so-mysterious East; and the Muslim East, undergoing nowadays an exciting resurgence, wants very much to unfold and expose to the thoughtful world its intellectual and cultural treasures and build on the glorious past a more meaningful and brighter future.

Due to the complexity of rendering Arabic, Hebrew, Persian, and Turkish (and other) words and terms in English, it was decided to keep the transliteration systems used by the various authors as they had originally used them. Also—except for the ʿayn and the hamzah—no other diacritical marks have been shown in the text. All these and other meticulous points, however, have been used throughout the Bibliographies and Index, with proper cross-references.

The editors wish to express their thanks to all the authors who contributed their essays to this volume. Without them this endeavor would have been impossible. Special thanks go to Shohreh Gholsorkhi, graduate research assistant, for her editorial work on the various essays and her attention to details, and to Christine Elkington and Tessa Hauglid for their work in preparing the entire manuscript for the press. The Princeton Department of Near Eastern Studies assisted us financially in the final preparation of the manuscript for which we are duly thankful.

Special thanks must also got to Sandra Assasnik Anderton for her artistic talents in making the sketch of Martin Bernard Dickson for the frontispiece.

Most of all we would like to thank the University of Utah Press and its director, Dr. David Catron, and his staff for their cooperation and encouragement and for including this volume among their publications. In particular we thank Norma Mikkelsen for her editorial assistance and for her invaluable suggestions throughout.

Both editors have worked as carefully and diligently as possible in producing this volume honoring their most esteemed teacher and friend. They can only describe it as a true labor of love.

Michel M. Mazzaoui
Vera B. Moreen

Intellectual
Studies on
ISLAM

(From the *Shahnameh*)

S. CARY WELCH

Fogg Museum
Cambridge, Massachusetts

Salute to a Coauthor: Martin Bernard Dickson

MARTIN DICKSON'S intense, soaring quickness of mind impressed me when we first met in Beirut in June 1954. Most of the characteristics remembered from his traveling years still apply to this determinedly Princeton-bound savant. His sharp black pupils dart and smoulder circled by radiant whites, under a rounded brow combed over with a thinning arc of Chinese-black (now grisaille) hair. Scholar-pale, with a gently eagleish nose sensitively marbled by capillaries at the nostrils, he has thinker's hands that rustle, alert as cockatoos. This bird-man is wiry in build, and although he cants sideward while ambling (swift of mind, his body rarely hurries), he seems well coordinated. From a distance, he resembles statues of another quiet innovator: long-bellied Akhenaten. Martin smiles, teeth flashing, as he speaks; and unlike many academics— it is a delight to note—he never lectures at you. Instead of drubbing you with words and ideas, he stimulates them. Talking with Martin is comparable to participating in an orientalist Marx Brothers film, or rallying with an agile squash opponent. Whatever the game, he plays it animatedly; whatever the conversation, he is keen to join in, often with startling, usually controversial (if not shocking) insights and refreshingly quirky, sometimes comical opinions. Whatever the definition of "genius," Martin strikes me—a visually oriented illiterate—as being its embodiment.

Friendship with Martin began when my wife, Edith, and I set out on a year-long wedding trip. Our travels had linked with an ambitious motor cavalcade in the East planned by a close friend, John Goelet. Martin was one of several people invited by John to share in the journey from Cairo to Bhutan. Our inspired entrepreneur had acquired two Jeep trucks and a Jeep automobile for the trip. They were outfitted with many thoughtfully chosen "essentials": a phonograph to waft chamber music into the desert night while we bedded down; a shower *cum* water tank; and a quaintly capacious milk can attached to a truck's running board. This was brim-full of the secret defense against tourist-killing amoebas—yogurt. Although John was responsible for most of the equipment, including the musical repertoire, Yettalil Fanner, his most charming guest (and now Mrs. Goelet), deserves credit for the latter. Having grown up in Cairo, capital of "Gypsy tummy," she insisted that daily swallows of its wholesome bacteria turned travelers' stomachs into battlefields where good bugs vanquished bad ones.

John and Yettalil assembled the *dramatis personae*: Marie Melas, daughter of the Greek ambassador to Egypt; James Harvey, an American artist and John's fellow recipient of a Fulbright grant, who later designed the Campbell's soup tin that made Andy Warhol famous; "Farouk," a young Copt, who knew Jeeps inside and out and developed a yen for Iranian caviar; and Martin, a last-minute addition introduced by a mutual friend, Richard Mitchell, whom Martin was visiting in Cairo. To these veterans of eastern living Edith and I contributed little more than questionable respectability. Although we had settled into staid marital bliss not quite two weeks before, we were deemed responsible chaperons for an otherwise unmarried clutch of young vagabonds.

The proposed itinerary (courtesy of our host *cum* "Man from Cook's") was comprehensive and exciting. The caravan had set off from Cairo, and after Beirut it was to visit Baalbek, Damascus, Palmyra, Homs, Hama, Aleppo, Iskanderun, Nigde, Urgup, Kayseri, Sivas, Erzincan, Erzurum, Tabriz, Sultaniyeh, and Teheran, as well as many other lesser places. The ultimate destination, after crossing Iran and Afghanistan into India, was Bhutan. Although the traveling library included a stack of grammars and dictionaries (John Goelet's favorite bedside reading), only Martin could cope aloud with most of the tongues of the route.

The group lingered for several days in Beirut, staying in a pleasingly located waterfront hotel, with views of a sprawling beach, used more often as a public latrine than for bathing. Food and document gathering and museumry went on by day; evenings were spent roaming, chattering, and enjoying Beirut's excellent Franco-Arab food—memorable prawns, houmus, kebabs, and the flat bread that conquered America and thirty-five years later is enjoyed at every U.S. barbecue.

Martin soon became a particular friend. Down the years I recall our first evening together in a modest *boite de nuit* that brought to mind

Isherwood's Berlin, without—alas—any traces of real vice. Attracted by its emptiness and quiet, we walked in, seeking nothing more than drinks and chitchat. Only our masochistically old-fashioned manners kept us from fleeing when peace and quiet were threatened by a sinister announcement. A cabaret was to be perpetrated by "renowned danseuses just arrived from Paris." Brave and determined as they were unwelcome and hairy, the ever-smiling little troupe sang, pranced, and sweated through a cycle as endless as the Ring, first as *apaches*, then as Carmens and toreadors, and finally, we supposed, as "arabesques" and legionnaires. Martin and the Welches could survive almost anything.

Palmyra was our first major encampment. After a long day on the road, we stopped several miles short of the site. Bach and Mozart leavened the desert air as we unrolled sleeping bags, brushed teeth, and prepared for the first night on the sand. John's novice girl and boy scout pack had made the grade—or so it seemed. On awakening to yogurt, Marie biscuits, and instant coffee, we discovered that the agreeably flat ground on which we had slept was the main road. Wondering what might have happened if trucks rather than camels had broken the still night, we drove off to inspect the majestic temples, palaces, fallen columns, and classicistic, big-eyed sculptures. By midmorning, the heat was intense, but eager to explore and photograph the site, we darted back and forth at ten-minute intervals between the cool of the archaeological guesthouse and museum and what seemed the hottest, brightest, most desiccated monuments in the world.

On the road, Martin usually sat in the back seat of the Jeep while I drove. Distances were often long between stops, but there was no tedium. "Dr. Dickie" was a man of parts, and the parts were not only polylingual but polymusical. However extraordinary Martin had seemed at first, he gained further luster in our eyes as we crossed scrub, desert, and mountain. From his back-seat revelations, a Dickson legend grew. The facts often shamed such nonlinguists as ourselves. While studying Turkish and Ottoman history at the University of Istanbul, for instance, Martin heightened the challenge by taking notes in Chinese! (His recent summer diversions were comparing Japanese and Russian uses of participial clauses and learning Hungarian.) Particularly arduous drives were lightened by music: Martin's renderings of arias from Chinese operas. He also performed entire scenes by Verdi and warbled Milanese nightclub ballads. Occasionally, his falsetto, tenor, and basso voices gave way to baritone, as when he serenaded Marie Melas with politically alarming songs of the Greek guerrillas. Martin could be naughty, and he knew exactly which raw nerve to tweak.

As we traveled, Martin's modesty and self-effacingness occasionally yielded to self-revelation, meted out in enticing snippets. His oriental interests, we learned, had developed during World War II, after being drafted into the army and given a battery of examinations. "You test as a linguist, or a truck driver," he was told. Unable to drive a car, Martin chose languages. Intensive training followed, during which he studied *Farsi* with Richard Ettinghausen. By the end of the war, Martin's future in scholarship was assured. Chinese Turkestan became his area of specialization until political changes banned traveling there. He shifted to Turkish history of the Ottoman and pre-Ottoman periods and enrolled at the University of Istanbul. He studied with Dr. Zeki Velidi Togan and became friends with a fellow student from a village near Urgup, a gifted young man whose agriculturalist family proudly sacrificed every luxury to further his studies.

This friendship led to a particularly enjoyable evening. When our cavalcade of Jeeps reached Urgup to see the moonlike erosion-scape and Christian wall paintings in the rock-cut caves, Martin called upon his friend's family. All of us were invited for dinner. Bedraggled and famished, we straggled into a subtly proportioned, immaculately whitewashed house, with a "throne platform" at one end. Simple but elegant benches edged the walls, and geometric, flat-woven carpets covered the floor. In our topsy-turvy world aristocratic ways were best maintained, it seemed, by so-called "peasants," such as our village hosts. This notion was further supported by a warmly sensitive yet formal welcoming by the impressively distinguished elders of the household and by the arrival moments later of food that would have delighted Escoffier. We were reminded that Turkish cuisine—of which we were enjoying a provincial but delicious survival—ranks with French and Chinese. Even after we had gorged to the full, twenty more courses were served by the talented ladies of the household. Pleasure gave way to poignancy, however, when Martin explained that his friend's "one-cow family" had lavished upon us a third of their food for the year. More than three decades later, we regret not yet having been able to return their heartfelt hospitality.

The mid-1950s were glorious times for Middle Eastern travel. Tourism—most pernicious of *isms*—had not yet broadcast its infections. Magnificent mosques, caravanserais, and tombs could be experienced unhampered by soda pop hawkers, souvenir stands, or hard-topped parking lots often associated with cultural progress. "Five star" hotels of the sort that homogenize cultures in the name of hygiene existed only in major cities. But the traditional, humbler ones were friendly, enjoyably atmospheric, and adequately, often picturesquely, comfortable. Recollections compact into kaleidoscopic vignettes. Still vivid to me is a large, festively crowded central hallway at Aleppo ("It looks like a bordello,'' whispered Martin) from which small bedrooms were entered through beaded string curtains that tickled. There, we spoke with a stocky Palestinian refugee, polite but embittered by America's role in forcing his people from the houses and orange groves where they had prospered for centuries. The moldering grandeur of Erzerum's nineteenth-century hotel springs to mind, with its wide, red-carpeted hallways into which one's feet sank as though into a bog. Nigde stands out not only for its marvelous architectural facades, alive with arabesques and inscriptions, but because of one of our party's misadventures in a public lavatory. If the spiritually elevating Blue Mosque and massively rounded brick city walls of Tabriz spring to mind, so does a comical episode in a hotel: a supposedly private bedroom and w.c. invaded through a long, odoriferous night by parades of staggering perpetual fountains, the patrons of the hotel's bar.

If hotels are remembered, landscape and architecture left far more vivid traces in the mind. Desert sunsets outshone their orientalist portrayals; delightfully cool, lushly forested mountains in eastern Turkey recalled Switzerland without the chocolate. John had planned an instructive and captivating survey of many periods of Islamic architecture, as represented by the imposing citadel of Aleppo, Seljuk tombs, mosques, and caravanserais, and the majestic Il Khanid tomb at Sultaniyeh. We also recall pleasurable encounters with local people, as at the river of Hama, near the waterwheels, where joyous, naked Syrians simultaneously rode and bathed horses, incarnating my recollection of one of Picasso's liveliest blue period pictures. Another incident still haunts: an old villager in an eastern Turkish teahouse gathering courage to slit the throat of a pet lamb, his offering for a feast. This biblical sacrifice was being carried out while we drove off, not daring to look back.

Unforgettable, too, was our one-thirty A.M. arrival at Iskanderun's art deco hotel. The dark silence of the streets was shattered by the only American words—other than our own—heard in weeks, four-letter ones jubilantly shouted by sailors on liberty. After driving day and night we were so exhausted that we shuffled zombielike into a warm and airless bedroom. Too tired to undress, I turned down the sheets, sighted a symposium of bedbugs big as watermelon seeds, and jumped in without brushing them away. (They did not bite.)

During another night drive, near the border between Turkey and Iran, we chose the more promising fork of a road, and bumped merrily along until the headlights beamed on a dazzlingly energetic silhouette—a soldier in long underwear, shaking a rifle in the air. We were headed in the wrong direction, and had the nocturnal ballet not stopped us, we should have crossed the Soviet border and contributed a tiny footnote to the annals of the Cold War.

Another nocturnal drive took us to overcrowded Teheran. After being turned away by several hotels, we telephoned the U.S. embassy and were told by a kind Marine guard to try the Pension *Majcen*, a hospitable, sprawling, shadowy place of flowerpot gardens and muted conversations where all of the other guests resembled Peter Lorre. Teheran was our longest stopover. With Martin, we explored the city, parts of which reminded me of the wide streets and stony facades in provincial French cities. Although suffering from stomach trouble—a souvenir from the delicious water buffalo iced cream of Tabriz—we explored the rich collections of the archaeological museum, enjoyed teahouses, and were gladdened by Caspian caviar, after a German doctor had prescribed tincture of opium that transmuted agonizing fluids into painless "concrete" by arresting peristaltic action.

At last there was time to present one of a series of letters of introduction generously given by Prince Sadruddin's father, the Aga Khan. It was addressed to Colonel Shah Khalili, whose cars and chauffeurs henceforth arrived daily to whisk us to dinner parties. Had it not been for long days of bazaar-hopping and museum-visiting, these feasts would have been even more enjoyable. On at least one evening, most of us were too exhausted to speak. Perhaps we were recovering from a visit to the Gulistan Library, where diplomacy, cajolery, and patience were rewarded by being led into a small room, sat round a table, and shown a splendid Qajar manuscript. Innocent Marie Melas turned its pages while modest Yettalil and stainless Edith looked on. Over their shoulders, Martin's and my worldlier eyes sparkled at the sight of altogether remarkable illustrations to the Arabian Nights—all of them pornographic!

For the Welches, the pleasures of Teheran were soon nullified. Cables from home reported the death of my grandmother and my father's heart attack. But there was also happier news. The cause of Edith's queasiness was not gastronomic. Dr. Shaybani, her examiner, became the angel of the annunciation. Our wedding trip had been all too successful! Instead of driving on with the others to Afghanistan and India (they did not reach Bhutan), we wended our way homeward. Many months later, John became a godfather.

The Goelet eastern caravan lingers as a happy memory, associated with several warm friendships. Although Jim Harvey died in New York a few years later, and we have seen neither Marie Melas nor "Farouk" since the trip, Martin became—and remains—a key figure in our lives. Mutual interest in Turko-Iranian art and culture, as well as "good chemistry," inevitably caused our paths to converge. Martin's grounding in both Central Asian and Turkish studies drew him in turn to the Safavis. His intriguingly detailed accounts of the poison plot against Shah Tahmasp, the great patron of Safavi painting, doubtless increased my understanding of Safavi art. In the aftermath of shared travels, our dialogue continued.

After returning to the U.S., we soon settled in Cambridge, where Eric Schroeder, Honorary Keeper of Islamic Art in the Fogg Art Museum, invited me to be his honorary assistant. As a sophomore at Harvard, I had met Eric through Arthur Young, his brother-in-law. As friendly as he was brilliant, Eric became an exciting mentor. Like him, I was drawn to the arts from a painter's rather than from a historian's point of view. Stopping by at Eric and Marn Schroeder's house on Follen Street to discuss pictures and objects over tea and currant cake baked by the master himself was an educational pleasure. Although Eric was always eager to look at such things, his responses often differed from mine. Defending oneself against Eric's friendly but barbed critiques was a test of mettle; and formidably literary Eric's example of expressive but clear argumentation sharpened wits.

Because no courses in Persian or Indian painting were given at Harvard (or elsewhere) during the early 1950s, my path to knowledge was autodidactive, through travel and study of collections. This enjoyable program was catalyzed by building an archive of 35mm Kodachrome slides, oddly an innovative practice at that time. Although several friendly colleagues, such as B. W. Robinson and Robert Skelton, welcomed this invaluable tool and began to develop their own sets of slides, others were unenthusiastic. When I gave full views and details of miniatures from the Gulistan Library to another notable specialist, he spurned their use as not quite honorable, akin to cheating at cards. Nevertheless, we spent years on end studying and photographing collections not only in the U.S. but in Paris, London, Dublin, Istanbul, and other centers of Turko-Iranian art.

Except for Eric Schroeder's insightful and brilliantly written catalog of the Fogg Art Museum's Persian miniatures, printed in 1942, publications on Persian and Indian painting were few between the 1930s and 1950s. Virtually unique among his generation in England is B. W. Robinson, a devoted scholar of Persian painting, whose passion for it began at the great Persian art exhibition at Burlington House in 1931 where he was taken as a schoolboy. After serving in the Pacific during World War II, he returned to England and began to write his invaluable shelf of books and articles on Persian painting. I am especially grateful for his characteristic generosity in lending me his learned and insightful notes to the Beatty, Kevorkian, and Bibliotheque Nationale collections.

In the 1940s and 1950s, few institutions or individuals in the world more than casually collected Persian, Turkish, or Indian pictures. Most of the prewar collectors had either died or become inactive; and prices even for "masterpieces" were ludicrously low. The inheritors of the major

French collections assembled in the early 1900s by Louis J. Cartier, Barons Edmond and Maurice de Rothschild, and Henri Vever banished their miniatures, drawings, calligraphies, and manuscripts to library closets or bank vaults. Neither they nor their friends were much interested; and once eager Sir Chester Beatty of Dublin lacked ardor. Modest new gatherers such as myself, who bought his first Safavi miniature for seventy dollars at the age of twelve, pined for the glorious material known from books published during the earlier decades of the century, when wealthy connoisseurs vied with one another for the treasures brought from Persia, Turkey, and India by adventurous Armenian *negotiants*. While at boarding school and college, I was in touch with the few dealers in New York with "old stocks"—Adrienne Minassian, Nasli and Alice Heeramaneck, Hagop Kevorkian, and Dikran Kelekian. I acquired whatever I could afford, and in the early 1950s better endowed friends, such as John Goelet, Prince Sadruddin Aga Khan, and William P. Wood began to do likewise.

By 1954, each of us had formed modest but good collections, and a long-neglected field was returning to life. Auction houses whose sale catalogs rarely illustrated such material, began to print better documented ones. Other friends and acquaintances, including Edwin Binney III, joined the small circle of buyers. All of us vied with a few English connoisseurs to acquire in the sale rooms or from dealers such as Maggs Brothers and Quartich of London and Soustielle, Injoudjian, and Henri Kevorkian of Paris. Excellent Persian, Mughal, Deccani, and Rajput pictures could be found in London for less than one hundred pounds. Visits to Paris were always rewarded by the discovery of thrilling miniatures, sometimes in the flea market.

One day in Cambridge, Eric lamented that the Fogg collection—nurtured by him with the support of Edward Forbes—sorely lacked outstanding examples from one of the great periods of Persian art, that of the Safavis. While scrutinizing such books as *Marteau and Vever* (1913) or *Binyon, Wilkinson, and Gray* (1933), I remembered his words. I also remembered a school acquaintance, Claude Cartier, the son of Louis J. Cartier, the creative art deco jeweler and greatly discerning Parisian connoisseur whose Safavi pictures ranked with those of the British Museum and the Rothschild collection. Coincidentally, Claude Cartier's inherited jewelry firm was in a fiscal lull at the very time when he needed money to marry. When I asked if he would part with his father's Persian and Indian miniatures, his encouraging reply led to weeks of art-fantasizing insomnia.

John Goelet—the friend, lover of works of art, and benefactor who introduced Martin to me in 1954—was also instrumental in Martin's and my work in the field of Safavi art. When John and I first met in the later 1940s at Harvard, he stood out as a remarkably innovative, knowledgeable, and enjoyable undergraduate whose studies included Arabic. Although he was a few years junior to me, John and I regularly played squash together and lengthily discussed Islam, Islamic art, and related matters. Although he then firmly believed that works of art belonged in museums rather than at home, John shared my pleasure in unfashionable Persian and Indian miniatures and drawings and encouraged and abetted the stalking of the Cartier and of other old—mostly French—collections of Islamic art. Indeed, it was after he had examined the Cartier Persian miniatures during a trip to Europe that he spontaneously offered to acquire most of them for the Fogg; and it was he who located and got in touch with Monsieur Mautin, the charmingly nomadic and mysterious heir (with his sister) to the Vever collection. Decades later, John's enthusiasm for oriental miniatures inspired him to divulge M. Mautin's name and address to the London dealer through whom it was sold recently to the Sackler Museum in Washington, D.C.

In the meantime, I had met with the Cartier representatives in their Fifth Avenue office. The negotiations were lengthy and conducive to further sleepless nights. Eventually, however, a year-long stay in London was interrupted by a visit to Paris to collect the pictures and bring them to our Earl's Court mews. One day, to show it to Basil Gray at the British Museum, I packed most of the Cartier collection—which would now be protected by a bombproof truck and armed guards—into a battered briefcase. A few weeks later, the treasure was tucked away in the same casual fashion for a penny-pinching Icelandic Airlines flight to Boston. Due to John Goelet's generosity, Harvard now owned one of the major collections of Safavi art.

We now reach the second phase of John's and my explorations of great French collections, the phase in which Martin was to play a major role. During the same London visit, I read an obituary notice in the *Times*. Baron Maurice de Rothschild (1881–1957), a great collector and son of an even greater collector, Baron Edmond (1845–1934), had died. Knowing that he had inherited Shah Tahmasp's own copy of the *Shahnameh*, illustrated with nearly three hundred miniatures, and also knowing that Persian miniatures were still neglected by "serious" art collectors, I cabled John Coolidge. Unrealistically, I had supposed that Harvard might want to pluck more Safavi plums, and I was unperturbed when there was little response.

Less than two years later, however, in Cambridge, John Coolidge invited me for luncheon. Between sips of tomato juice he asked if I knew of a major work of art that could be bought. "I have a friend," he added, "who wants one; and he does not care what it is." At once, I suggested the Rothschild *Shahnameh*, then being offered for sale in New York by

Baron Edmond de Rothschild (b. 1926), grandson and namesake of Baron Edmond who had acquired it before 1903.

Within the month, I showed the Cartier miniatures to John Coolidge's "friend," Arthur A. Houghton, Jr., who admired them. I also told him about the Rothschild manuscript. He reacted swiftly. "My imagination has been wildly stirred by the conversations," he wrote John Coolidge on December 9, 1958. He and I soon stood side by side in a paneled room at the gallery of Baron Rothschild's agents, Rosenberg and Stiebel of New York. A large, unpainted wooden box was brought out and placed atop a marble-topped Louis Quinze console table. I opened it and took out a hefty volume, bound in leather stamped with gold arabesques. More cautiously than Marie in Teheran, I began to turn its pages.

This copy of Firdawsi's *Shahnameh* ("The Book of Kings") was then a legend of a book, never exhibited after 1903, and not seen for countless decades (centuries?) by anyone profoundly aware of Safavi art. The Swedish scholar-diplomat-collector F. R. Martin, who is unlikely to have examined it, published a few of its lesser miniatures in 1912. Unaccountably, he described it very unenthusiastically, as, in 1930, did Basil Gray, who later wrote me that he had not in fact seen it. My high regard for this controversial manuscript was based upon a few splendid miniatures published by Edgar Blochet and Georges Migeon in 1903 and upon the better of those reproduced by Martin. These established it in my eyes as the watershed volume created for Shah Tahmasp and described in the preface to a noble album (now in Istanbul) commissioned by the shah's brother and assembled by Dust-Muhammad, one of the royal artist-calligraphers. Heart in mouth, I opened the *Shahnameh*, eager for proof in the form of a masterpiece by Sultan-Muhammad specifically described by Dust-Muhammad in his introduction to the album.

After leafing past a stunningly illuminated rosette, an inventively rich double-page frontispiece, and several superb miniatures by other court artists, we reached folio 20 verso, the overwhelming painting I sought. Seeing its flickering flame-shaped composition centered by Iran's first ruler, Shah Gayumars, attended by animals and courtiers dressed in leopard skins, was breathtaking. According to a faulty translation (later corrected by Martin) of Dust-Muhammad's praise, Sultan-Muhammad's rival artists "hung their heads in shame" before this glorious picture. Neither Mr. Houghton nor I, awed as we were, bowed ours. Exhilarated, we wanted to see more. Wondering what could follow it without seeming anticlimactic, I turned the page—and laughed. For it held Sultan-Muhammad's *Hushang Slays the Black Div*, a romp of a picture, combining joy with heroism to the point of ecstasy, painted *con brio* to beguile Tahmasp, the princely boy-patron. After an hour and a half of viewing vividly colorful shahs, demons, heroes, heroines, dragons, and phoenixes in paradisaical landscapes and palaces, Arthur Houghton was convinced that he must buy the manuscript. I hoped—even assumed—that he would give it to Harvard as the "crown jewel" of his earlier gift, the Houghton Library. Although I was not privy to the negotiations, it was satisfying to learn a week later (before November 20, 1959) that terms had been reached. To delight in the volume and expound upon its significance, I met again soon with Mr. Houghton, to whom I proposed that if he were interested in publishing it I would be honored to do so. He reacted enthusiastically. The *Shahnameh* project was initiated.

The prospect of writing a book about such a great work of art was exciting but humbling. An impassioned "connoisseur" who enjoyed writing about art, I was nevertheless profoundly unqualified to deal with matters literary, historical, or epigraphical. Aware that Martin would be the ideal collaborator, I telephoned him at once. Within minutes occurred the first of a series of almost miraculous coincidences. On our separate paths, Martin and I had come to the same fresh conclusions about the formation of Safavi culture, conclusions that would have been seen by most scholars as revolutionary but which to us were self-evident. The cognoscenti saw Safavi poetry and art as slightly tired echoes of classic Timuri idioms. To us, Safavi art, literature, poetry, and all else exemplified an exciting new synthesis derived both from the Turkmans of Tabriz (western Iran) and from the Timuris of Herat (eastern Iran). Martin realized this through slow, scholarly work, whereas I saw it via a pleasurable pictorial route. It had come to me "in a flash" while scrutinizing two key pictures: the British Museum's great *Sleeping Rustam* and *Worldly and Otherworldly Drunkenness* from the Cartier Hafiz, one of two signed paintings by the greatest Safavi artist, Sultan-Muhammad. Both, I realized, were by the same artist, and both owed more to the visionary, earthy, fervidly expressive, wildly illogical mode of Aq-Qoyunlu Turkman Tabriz than to the classically restrained, logical, more naturalistic style associated with master Behzad of Timuri Herat. Excited by our mutual discovery—and no more aware than I of the horrendous labor ahead—Martin agreed to help.

Still willing to travel, Martin came to Cambridge, a daring step for a bachelor-scholar. By now, there were six Welches, four of them barely beyond "the age of criminal insanity," when bric-a-brac is fondled, hefted, and often hurled to test its fragility. Even more threatening to one set in his ways might have been the bald observations associated with those the Bible describes as "very babes and sucklings." One of ours, on sighting a notably tall, exceedingly distinguished friend ice skating while wearing his elegant kilt, squealed: "Who's that man showing off in a skirt?" Nevertheless, Martin's Cambridge visit—like the others over the *Shahnameh* years—scattered pleasure throughout the household. He survived childish sermons on the hazards of cigarette smoking, and the young Welches, already tolerant of an eccentric father, warmed to Martin's electric smiles, invariable good humor, and generosity. His month-long visits (never long enough) were welcome festivals.

The first stay was professorial, spent sharing information. Martin underwent trial by color slides; I took notes (not in Chinese) on Safavi history, Sufism, and court gossip. We reveled in the ways that our very different kinds of evidence meshed. As I had expected, one plus one—one Dickson and one Welch—added up not to two but to two squared.

We outlined the structure of the book. After the front matter, there would be a chapter on the manuscript's peregrinations, from Shah Tahmasp's to the Ottoman sultan's courts, as a royal gift not long before the patron died, through its flight in about 1900 to the Rothschilds (as a gift to his art loving bankers from the railroad building sultan?), and the purchase by Mr. Houghton. This chapter would also paraphrase the curiously damning opinions of earlier specialists.

Since Martin and I agreed that this book about a book was intended not only for a handful of "experts" and students but for intelligent general readers such as Mr. Houghton, we wanted to provide enough technical, historical, and art-historical background to enable them to appreciate its beauty and significance. In a chapter entitled "The Creation of the Book," we described the way manuscripts were planned and carried out by royal calligraphers, painters, illuminators, paper handlers, and binders at a Turko-Iranian court, with particular relevance to the Houghton volume. The fruits of Martin's painstaking, fulsome readings of Iranian literature, poetry, books of history, and chronicles appear on every page of the other introductory chapters, "A Tradition and Its Artists," "Timuri and Turkman Roots of Safavi Art," and "The Safavi Synthesis." Using Martin's extraordinary documentation culled from Dust-Muhammad, ᶜAli, Qadi-Ahmad, and many other sources, I was to write separate monographs on each of the court artists who worked on Shah Tahmasp's grandest volume (fifteen as it turned out). These included discussions of all the other miniatures and drawings known to me by the early Safavi court painters of the *Shahnameh*. It was also my task—with Martin's ever-generous help—to write an epilogue, describing the impact of this major early Safavi monument upon later painting in Iran, Turkey, and India. Throughout volume one, illustrations of related material as well as details from the manuscript's miniatures would enlighten and please.

Volume two was to contain a complete set of black-and-white reproductions of the *Shahnameh*'s miniatures, major illuminations, and binding. Each was to be faced by an account of the action (with Martin's direct quotations when required), translations of inscriptions, attributions to artists, and color descriptions, which I checked for accuracy with the help of a kind and promising graduate student, Everett Fahy. Inasmuch as Martin had prepared new translations from every significant source, these were to be included in appendices.

Once Martin's and my schema was clear, a meeting took place in New York City on April 12, 1961, with Mr. Houghton and an impressive array of designers and publishers, a 1960s gathering that must have resembled those assembled by the 1520s Safavi patrons. Round the spacious oval table in the board room of the Steuben Glass Company sat Arthur Houghton, his assistants Sally Walker and Betty Howe, John Coolidge, Thomas J. Wilson, the president of the Harvard University Press, Joseph Blumenthal of the Spiral Press, Peter Oldenburg, the distinguished book designer, Harold Hugo of the Meriden Gravure Company, and me. It soon became evident that Mr. Houghton wanted not only a book commensurate with the importance of his manuscript, but he also wanted one that would exemplify the highest standards of American design, typography, printing, and binding. Those of us who aspired to create a book perhaps less opulently beautiful but more comfortably readable and affordable to scholars and libraries politely deferred to more ambitious bibliophiles. The authors' quaint notions of handleable volumes on the scale of Phaidon Press productions—with many color illustrations reproduced in offset and footnotes printed at the bottom of the page—were of little concern to the dedicated lovers of books for their own sakes. The far higher cost of richly produced volumes, printed in "hot type" on specially commissioned paper, with color and black-and-white collotype as opposed to offset illustrations, gilded fore-edges, and magnificent bindings stamped in gold leaf did not dampen the patron's contagious enthusiasm.

Ignoring such aesthetic considerations, Martin and I pursued our work. Angelica Rudenstein, a very bright and scrupulous editor, was appointed on my suggestion to help. Although contemporary painting was her field, her eyes were open to all art, including Islamic. We welcomed her sympathetic intelligence.

Martin and I took over the Welch dining and drawing rooms. Wherever we settled, we improvised minimalist still lifes. Dog-eared, plastic-bound notebooks created a spritely chaos of aniline blues, pinks, and acid-yellows, deftly accented by chipped glass ashtrays, half-empty (cold) coffee cups, cookie-crumbed and ash-stained saucers, and crunched cigarette packets. The academic clutter gained architectonic solidity from arrangements of framed miniatures and photographs leaning against legs of chairs. Cigarette smoke clouded the air, and cushions and curtains took on chic Martinesque *bouquet de Chesterfields*.

If our labors sometimes tormented Edith and a younger generation of Welches, whose husband and father was lost to the Safavis for many years, they also sorely tested Mr. Houghton. He pined to see and read the volume whose production he supported. Years later, it is clear that neither he nor the authors fully understood the scale of the project. Nor did any of us realize the sacrifices it forced upon us. At the outset, aware that much—but not *that* much—time and effort would be expended, I asked John Coolidge if people were paid for such work. "No," he replied, "it is in the tradition of American scholarship to work on such projects without payment." As a second-generation volunteer in the Fogg Art Museum's department of Islamic art, this did not surprise me; and Martin—the personification of academic poverty—was oblivious to all worldly concerns. We pushed ahead. When asked how much time our work would require, wanting neither to lie nor to offend, I prevaricated. Would any of us have pursued the project had we known that as many years would be spent studying and discussing the *Shahnameh* as were required to create it?

John Coolidge arranged for us to have complete sets of prints of the miniatures, binding, and important illuminations; and Martin also received a full set of photocopies of the text. In June 1962 the manuscript was made available for an extensive period of study in the Houghton Library at Harvard, and on November 11, 1963, the Board of Syndics of the Harvard University Press met and approved the arrangements whereby they would publish the book.

In Philip Hofer's study in the Houghton Library, I scrutinized the manuscript and took thousands of color slides, as many as thirty enlarged details in addition to full views of especially beautiful—or important—pictures and illuminations. On trips to London, Paris, Dublin, and many other centers, I also photographed all of the related material that had previously escaped my lens. To discourage interruptions, part of our Channing Street basement was rebuilt. Rough stone walls were covered with panels of Japanese grass fiber, and the concrete floor was paved with Welsh tile. A niche behind my desk held slide projectors facing a matte white wall on which slides could be compared or studied with a magnifying glass while I wrote.

Once during a July storm, while Martin and I sat in the subterranean study speculating upon Master Dust's waywardness, we were startled by a horrific crack of lightning. Supposing that the house had been struck, I scurried up the spiral staircase to the front hall, where I nearly collided with the children's aged nanny emerging from the dining room. "A flash of light came down the back stairs and knocked me flat in front of the refrigerator!" she croaked. Simultaneously, I heard water coursing down the front stairs. Three steps at a time, I ran to the top floor. Lightning through an open window had struck and shattered the toilet bowl. I summoned plumbers and insurance agents. Thrilled by my announcement, they joined Martin and myself within minutes to inspect proof of nature's might—in fact a dreary arrangement of ceramic sherds, without a trace of fire or brimstone.

Except during Martin's occasional Cambridge visits, and my few trips to Princeton, each of us studied and wrote at home. Daily telephone calls kept us in touch, calls of such length that had the project footed our expenses we would have been embarrassed to present them. For both of us, the work was lonely as well as challenging and stimulating. I recall the disciplining moment in the *"Shahnameh* Lounge" when, seated cross-legged on a six-foot-square platform, I began to sort photographs of the manuscript's 258 miniatures according to hands, an engrossing, sometimes frustrating game of solitaire that went on for years. Although only two of the manuscript's paintings are signed (one of them in tiny gold calligraphy that went undiscovered until long after I had attributed it [correctly]), some of them were quickly separated by style into tidy piles.

Easiest to attribute were those by one of the senior artists, Mir Musavvir, whose unevolving style, with its gloriously idiosyncratic palette and gracefully calligraphic linearism, was immediately recognizable. His small stack of pictures reminded me at first sight of a portrait in the British Museum inscribed with his name. Rather harder to single out were Sultan-Muhammad's paintings. Prolific and vital as Picasso, he changed his constantly growing style according to mood, sometimes almost splashing pigment with inspired vigor, and at others working with a jeweler's finesse. But whether he painted an accurately observed, almost illusionistic world, or dashed off visionary scenes from imagination, his essential character and habits of draftsmanship could be recognized. One by one the *Shahnameh*'s painters emerged as separate artistic personalities. When they emerged from anonymity, I shared the exciting news with concerned friends and students.

Especially hard to identify was the work of Aqa-Mirak, one of the three senior painters, whose pictures fell into two groups. The first was recognizable through similarities to inscribed miniatures in the British Library's *Quintet* of Nizami, also illustrated for Shah Tahmasp. The second, more troublesome group, painted in a broader manner with figures larger and bolder in scale, I assigned initially to another artist, dubbed glibly as "The Big Figure Painter"—until it came to me that these exemplified Aqa-Mirak's way of painting less slowly. Inasmuch as major pictures required many months or years to complete, it was necessary for each master artist to develop a simplified mode, without sacrificing artistic quality. I hastened to test my discovery. Would fellow specialists see what took me so long to find? Others were more likely to accept Aqa-Mirak's dual styles, it seemed, if I could convince Eric Schroeder. I invited him to come for a viewing. In sphinxlike silence he listened to my barrage of words and examined hundreds of slides before accepting—with dramatically enthusiastic gestures—my theory. Another dependable critic of my continuing attributions was B. W. Robinson, to whom I sent many letters and packets of slides. His spirited espousal of my theories on Sultan-Muhammad, Mir Musavvir, Mirza-cAli, and other Safavi artists sustained faith in the value of our effort.

It became clear that Martin and I were in effect moving a desert with teaspoons. Although it would have been easier and less time consuming to produce a pleasing picture book with a text of the usual sort—one that avoided problems of attribution and discussions of the relationships between patrons and artists and ignored other Safavi manuscripts illustrated by the same circle of artists—we chose to write the first comprehensive study not only of a great Persian manuscript but also of early Safavi painting. Fanatically determined to learn all that I could about Shah Tahmasp's artists, I resolved not only to understand and explain the characters of the major artists but also to do so for their assistants. And when both a master and an assistant had worked on a picture, I wanted to identify what each had done. Once we had decided to advance our understanding far beyond the usual safe limit in our field, Martin prophesied—accurately, it appears—that twenty-five years would pass before our fellow specialists would fully comprehend what we had achieved. We were obsessed.

On emerging at dawn from our Cambridge cellar with a bleeding eye caused by ten hours of staring at slides, it was comforting to know that Martin at Princeton struggled comparably. For days and nights on end he faced far worse challenges, such as translating Safavi flights of wit. Some of these, he explained, required finding the *mots justes* for triple puns.

To maintain our spirits, I often telephoned Martin in disguised voices, claiming on one occasion to be a roaming Indian scholar "friend of Mister Welch, arriving in one hour with joint family—wife and five little ones—all vegetarian, for two months' stay only, no trouble." Such playfulnesses were welcome. Only once did I offend, when I sent him a fat envelope of "Shahnameh by-products"—confetti made by punching holes in typewriter paper. If opening it produced a terrible "snowstorm," I felt no qualms, knowing that Martin always kept a vacuum cleaner next to his desk.

If Martin and I usually enjoyed our research and writing, others were less pleased. At Princeton, after the first year or two of Martin's perpetual and monomaniacal labor, his colleagues became restive. By then, both of us, to avoid distractions, had turned night into day and seemed antisocial.

I as a volunteer teacher-curator at Harvard was beyond harassment, but he the Princeton professor consumed by a labor of love was not. One sympathizes somewhat with the departmental chairs whose distresses were signaled by a sequence of incidents that grew from harrumphs to what struck me at the time as devious plots. One of these, verbal poison intended to create friction between coauthors, reached me when a Harvard colleague snickered that he had heard at Princeton that Martin claimed to be writing our entire book. I laughed, and when I recounted this machination to Martin, we guffawed. Although many pages could be written about these trollopian drolleries, one more suffices—a venomous insinuation that our book was in fact a sham, conjured up to avoid "serious" work. Although this speck of malice amused us by its similarity to Henry James's story of the artist whose masterpiece was revealed posthumously to be a blank canvas, it was given sufficient credence to be investigated officially.

One also sympathizes with the eager but frustrated Mr. Houghton, who had hoped to see the grand fruits of his project many years before its eventual publication in 1981. A log of reasons for his dismay can be reconstructed through records kept by Mrs. Horace "Miggie" Frost, another volunteer who served the project long and devotedly. In June 1968, Angelica Rudenstein, the first editor, was "confident that Cary's work would be ready for editing by early September." In January 1970, however, Angelica was "feeling very gloomy about all of this . . . it has now dragged on for so long." And in December 1974, Mrs. Daniel Robbins, the second editor, who had replaced Angelica who had accompanied her husband to Princeton, wrote that "we are trying desperately to get it off to the press this year." On March 10, 1978, Seymour Slive, then director of the Fogg Art Museum, and I informed Arthur Houghton that "the galleys would be in by the end of the month"; and in June, Seymour Slive assured Harvard University Press that "the completion of the project is finally in sight." Another expression of distress, nevertheless, emerged from Sydney Freedberg—the third Fogg director whose responsibilities included shepherding our time-consuming project—who told Arthur Houghton in March 1979 that "[the press] reassures me that . . . they will hold to their resolve not to accept a single other editorial amendment."

For the determined authors, however, the ultimate quality of the book was even more crucial than the shorter term goodwill of either long-suffering Mr. Houghton or of their fellow strugglers at Harvard. Ever more appreciative of the great *Shahnameh*, which had become for them an expanding historical and art-historical cornucopia, they valued the freedom that came from working without compensation, freedom that enabled them to rediscover the personalities and accomplishments of wondrous long-dead artists and patrons without the work being cut short by rigid deadlines.

Although the project entailed months of dreary work, our spirits usually were zestful, especially encouraging when seemingly dubious aperçus found support. On one occasion, after a lengthy "meditation" on Sultan-Muhammad and Mir Sayyid-ᶜAli's *The Execution of Zahhak*, when I sensed the artists' seemingly inappropriate sympathy for the tyrant, he cited contemporary literary equivalents to their antinomianism. Another exhilarating example of mutual support occurred after a night spent scrutinizing slides of Dust-Muhammad's signed *Haftvad and the Worm*. Two conclusions were startling. On the basis of a Mughal painting I attributed to him, the painter must have emigrated to India; and on grounds of the composition's sagging forms, trees dug in against a deluge, and alarmingly disturbed characterizations of people, animals, and hidden grotesques, I suspected that he had been an alcoholic or drug addict. Realizing that one should not publish such slander, even about the dead, I nevertheless wrote down my thoughts. Martin was intrigued. After a few days, he telephoned with exciting news. He had found and translated a chronicle that quoted a letter from Master Dust himself confessing that because of his addiction to wine he had left the Safavi court, where alcohol was banned by the now puritanical shah, and he had joined the Mughal court!

As the work progressed, it was occasionally necessary to travel in order to test discoveries. B. W. Robinson had called my attention to an illustrated copy of ᶜArifi's *Guy u Chawghan* ("The Ball and the Polo Mallet") for which the scribe was the boy patron of the *Shahnameh*, Shah Tahmasp himself. Excited by this, I asked John Coolidge if it might not be possible—in this instance alone—for the project to pay my expenses. He agreed, and I flew to Leningrad, where fellow scholars were most helpful. Although I was not permitted to make slides of the manuscript's small miniatures, it was possible to attribute each of them to artists known from the *Shahnameh*.

Other travels were equally productive. At Martin's suggestion, I studied a small catalog of manuscripts in the Topkapi Serayi Museum Library written by his late distinguished mentor, Professor Zeki Velidi Togan, whose historical and literary expertise surpassed his awareness of painting. One of the hundreds of manuscripts listed by him, a *Quintet* of Nizami copied "at Tabriz" in 1481 for the Aq-Qoyunlu rulers, was crucially important to our work. Here was the long-sought proof that a series of miniatures and drawings I had ascribed to Turkman Tabriz were indeed from there.

While in Istanbul, I was also able to examine and photograph the splendid album gathered by Dust-Muhammad for Shah Tahmasp's brother, Bahram Mirza. It contained not only Master Dust's introduction, in which he referred to Shah Tahmasp's *Shahnameh* containing Sultan-Muhammad's court scene, but it also included pictures by many of the court painters. Especially enlivening finds were a painting and drawing by Shah Tahmasp himself that engagingly amplified one's understanding of his introspective personality. Created when he was young and ardent, they comically— but fondly—spoof his household staff, particularly a jolly gentleman nick-named "Mellon-sultan," the pot-bellied court butler.

Our work revived many "ghosts" of extraordinary, long-lost artists and courtiers. Through Martin's interpretations of texts and my gatherings of pictures, vivid personalities leapt back to life. Shah Isma^cil, founder of the dynasty, for instance, emerged as a tempestuously energetic founding father, the perfectly attuned patron of Sultan-Muhammad, whom we found to be an equally visionary painter-saint.

The intense but at times strained devotion felt by Shah Tahmasp for his nephew and son-in-law, Sultan Ibrahim Mirza, emerged from Martin's documentation and from the paintings of Mirza-^cAli and Shaykh-Muhammad. Both artists moved to the nephew's court at Mashhad after Shah Tahmasp had forsaken painting in the aftermath of a series of ter-rible, guilt-inspired dreams. Even now, the tragedy is so vividly haunting that I turn away from it as I did during the sheep killing in eastern Turkey. Fortunately, the troubled friendship that led to Sultan Ibrahim's banishment to Sabzivar—where he was accompanied by the devoted artists—warmed again toward the end of Shah Tahmasp's life. At least one more manuscript, now scattered, was created by shared patronage. But horror followed. When the shah died, his successor ordered Sultan Ibrahim's execution, and lest the victim's favorite album fall into the mur-derer's hands, his widow, Shah Tahmasp's daughter, dipped it into a stream and washed away the paintings and calligraphies.

During the many years of our collaboration, Martin's intimate knowledge of the Safavi court and mine of pictures, including many in-scribed portraits, reattached faces to anecdotes. Out of the blue one day the postman delivered a photograph showing an inscribed portrait of a slightly sinister youngish man holding a sheet of paper while standing as though before the shah. Dateable to about 1540, it appeared to be by one of our artists, perhaps the one then known to me as "Painter D." I for-warded it to Martin, who translated the inscriptions which identified the subject as Mirza-Muhammad Qabahat, the favorite page boy of the shah, about whose scandalous behavior I had been writing. Moreover, the por-traitist was ^cAbd ul-^cAziz (eventually identified as "Painter D"), who had absconded with the page after counterfeiting the royal seal for their forged passport. The culprits were caught and brought before the shah, who imprisoned the boy, whom he later forgave. ᶜAbd ul-ᶜAziz was sentenced to death, after being denosed. But his life was spared. He returned to work—after carving and polychroming himself a new and better beak.

Martin and I were only once out of touch. The lengthy and bewildering break of communication occurred when the work neared completion. Thousands of typed pages had gone off to the last of our editors, Anne-Louise McLaughlin, and in due course galleys had been sent to us, mine to Cambridge, Martin's to Princeton. Seeking relief from the work, I had gone *en famille* to Europe. On returning, eager for Martin's news, I telephoned him. There was no reply. Repeated attempts to call him over several months were equally disappointing. I fretted about his health and made inquiries at Princeton.

Finally, he answered the telephone, perhaps unintentionally. For the first time, his voice was unfriendly, almost disagreeable. Fearing dire news, I mustered every diplomatic skill I possessed. An explanation emerged. He was profoundly upset. The galleys had rubbed salt in wounds suffered over the years by authors of a book on a subject that, to put it gently, never fully engaged the publishers' interest. Indeed, Martin and I often felt isolated in our devotion to the Safavis and their art. From the beginning, we sensed greater concern with our pace than with our subject or accomplishment. When the decision was made to lump footnotes inaccessibly at the back of the book, we realized that design held priority over content. And when early in the production of the color collotype plates I was told by the master printer, whose work was deplorable, that he had "made an interpretation, not a mere reproduction[!]," it seemed that grandeur outranked accuracy.

Martin's darkest, silencing moments came when he read the galleys and found that extensive, crucial passages of text and footnotes were missing. Bitterly disillusioned, he washed his hands of our project. Sympathetic as I was to his position, so much had been accomplished by a small army of photographers, designers, typographers, color block makers, collotype printers, and many others that it seemed incumbent upon us to adjust to circumstances, however infuriating. Were our aches and pains worse than those endured for the sake of the *Shahnameh* by squads of Safavi craftsmen, or by ᶜAbd ul-ᶜAziz the noseless? And should one not sympathize with Arthur Houghton's frustrations? I wondered if in some respects his echoed those of Shah Tahmasp, who may have been comparably outraged by apparent dillydallying! How could we desert the great spirits who had created the *Shahnameh*, spirits that, after years of intense concern for them, had come to life as friends?

Martin recovered from his justifiably dark mood, and we began the aggravating task of sorting out and reassembling our wounded chapters. Because the typographical design was by now so advanced, few replacements could be made within the body of the text. Most of the scrapped material was jammed into footnotes, sometimes in telegraphic brevity.

At last, in 1981, *The Houghton Shahnameh* was published. After years of delight, struggle, horror, and anticipation, its bright blue buckram and gold-stamped presence loomed more as a monument than as the book we had written. This typically cynical author wondered who—other than very rich and aesthetically inclined weight lifters—could both afford to buy and have the strength to handle it. In fact, a friendly enthusiast of Safavi art bought five copies, while another acquired one for each of his houses. Generous Mr. Houghton presented copies to several worthy scholars and to a list of institutions deemed too poor to buy them. Touchingly, on December 16, 1981, he wrote the authors that "your labor over the long years has produced a work that is unequalled in every respect. I salute you."

Others were also appreciative. B. W. Robinson wrote a sensitive and laudatory review, as did Walter Denny, a former student at Harvard. Less Safavi-minded art historians approached the massive volumes like trout anglers confronted by whales. After issuing a few blandishments—or taking a few jabs—they backed off. At least one exceptionally keen collector, three Russian scholars, an emigre Iranian artist, one or two students, and a few others have impressed me over the years as having read it.

To herald the event in 1979 and 1980, an exhibition—*Wonders of the Age,* which included many superb folios from the *Shahnameh* as well as much of the finest related material—was held in the British Museum, the National Gallery of Art (Washington, D.C.), and at the Fogg Art Museum. But during the many years of writing and book production, the world had changed. The shah, who had reserved a royal number of copies, no longer held sway. Symbolically, the request was canceled. Once-admired Iran was in low repute. Just before the Washington opening, American hostages were taken in Teheran. In the aftermath, putting at risk most of the world's great Safavi pictures was so worrying that the exhibition was very nearly canceled.

Another significant change had taken place since Mr. Houghton acquired his manuscript. Along with most other nonwestern art, Persian pictures had gained a far larger following. Iranian collectors spent huge sums reacquiring examples of their cultural heritage that had been sold by earlier generations to Europeans and Americans. Mr. Houghton's marvelous manuscript—acquired at a time when most connoisseurs were unaware not only of Sultan-Muhammad but of the Safavi dynasty—increased enormously in value. In 1970, he gave seventy-nine of its miniatures to the Metropolitan Museum of Art, where an exhibition centering upon the manuscript was held two years later. A sudden request from the museum resulted in my writing—in two weeks!—a greatly condensed account of the *Shahnameh* (*A King's Book of Kings*, New York, 1972) to which Martin generously contributed information. Following the gift to the Metropolitan Museum of Art, a number of miniatures were sold to private collectors and museums.

Martin and I could lament that major parts of our lives were devoted to a great work of art that has since been dismembered and scattered, partly because our investigations established its importance. Instead of deploring this, we try to sympathize with Mr. Houghton in the belief that even for him the responsibility of possessing such a glorious work of art was excessive. We could cite, moreover, miniatures intended for the manuscript that were separated from the rest and mounted in royal albums, as well as countless instances of great manuscripts torn apart by Timuri and Safavi patrons for page-by-page delectation. Martin and I, therefore, focus upon our good fortune in having been encouraged by Arthur Houghton to learn about and publish a manuscript that transported us into the fascinating world of the Safavi court. Its patrons and artists still live in our thoughts. Charismatic Shah Isma^{c}il, troubled Shah Tahmasp, mystical Sultan-Muhammad, and dozens more are at least as close to us as our own aunts and uncles. Martin often adds freshly discovered information to the same colorful notebooks that once brightened smoky Channing Street. I occasionally find unrecorded pictures by "my friends" the Safavi artists, and I am now planning a series of one- and two-man exhibitions of their work, each to be accompanied by a well-illustrated book—to be written with Martin's help.

A few days ago, I telephoned Martin the Sage, who continues to nibble at TV dinners near his vacuum cleaner and is now learning Georgian. "I could never speak it, of course," he joked, "because healthy Georgians were all taken to Turkey and the people who stayed home and developed the language must have stammered or had hare lips. How can you pronounce something spelled 'splkrz'?" (Completed, July 4, 1988.)

I

1

HANS R. ROEMER

Albert-Ludwigs-Universität, Freiburg im Breisgau
Federal Republic of Germany

The Qizilbash Turcomans: Founders and Victims of the Safavid Theocracy

THE MILITARY POTENTIAL which constituted one of the most important conditions, if not the decisive one, for the establishing of the Safavid reign, consisted of troops whose elements were called Qizilbash. The great majority of these troops was composed of Turcoman tribal warriors, whose origin was so little known that some fifty years ago Richard Hartmann[1] could consider the elucidation of their provenance as a task of Oriental studies. In the meantime, this problem of considerable significance has found many authors who have by and large succeeded to solve it, though questions still remain open. The state of research has been summed up by the Turkish historian Faruk Sümer in his book on the role of Anatolian Turks in the founding and consolidation of the Safavid empire.[2]

This was in 1976, a rather fruitful year for Turcoman studies. In this very year, John Woods also submitted his dissertation on the Aq-Qoyunlu,[3] whereas I myself contributed to the Walther Hinz Festschrift,[4] a general survey of the "Turcoman Intermezzo." A few years ago, Robert D. McChesney,[5] in his comments on an article by James J. Reid,[6] gave credit for Qizilbash history to the achievements some time ago of the late Il'ja Pavlovič Petrushevskii[7] (1949) and Martin B. Dickson[8] (1958).

As a matter of fact, not only recent, but also older Qizilbash contributions offer certain difficulties, even to specialists, because of their polyglot character and their publication in scattered places. Thus, a new resumé of the state of the art may claim our attention.

──────────── I ────────────

The Qizilbash are mostly descendants of Turcoman tribes who lived in smaller or bigger unions or federations, mainly as cattle-breeding nomads in Asia Minor, Armenia, Transcaucasia, and Syria, where they had arrived during the Oğuz migrations.[9] These tribal formations, which also include single representatives of Turcoman tribal aristocracy, suffered badly during the rise of the Ottomans as well as during the formation of the numerous post-Mongolian petty states in Anatolia.[10] They seem to have lost their bases precisely through the breakdown of such dominions in Anatolia and elsewhere and were in search of new political and military careers. Furthermore, and this is no settled question,[11] they were associated with remnants of forces set free as a result of the decline or fall of the bigger Turcoman principalities which had been formed by the Qara Qoyunlu and the Aq-Qoyunlu federations. All these elements were tied together not only by ethnic origin and a common language,[12] but much more so by their way of living, namely nomadic features peculiar to their vast majority. These, however, were already changing into a kind of seminomadism, when Shah Isma⁽c⁾il began establishing his empire. Of course, the common tradition, as preserved in the Book of Dede Qorqut,[13] played a role in their sense of solidarity.

Vladimir Minorsky, who dealt with the striking phenomenon of Turkish and Turcoman eastward migrations,[14] speaks in this context of three waves of Turkish emigrants who moved from Asia Minor toward East Anatolia and Northwest Persia, then toward the Iranian plateau, namely, a Qara Qoyunlu wave, an Aq-Qoyunlu one, and finally that of the Safavids.[15]

──────────── II ────────────

We know at present, not in full detail but in broad outline, which were the tribes who took part in the Safavid wave, where lived the tribes they dissociated from, and what were the destinies they had by then gone through.

Among the tribes which the sources repeatedly mention, the first place during Isma⁽c⁾il's rise belongs to the Rumlu, Ustajlu,[16] Shamlu, Dulgadir,[17] Tekelu, and the Qajar,[18] as well as to the, only later, less frequently mentioned Versaq, Turġudlu, Chapni, Baiburdlu, and Ispirlu. Thus, it is difficult to find in the early sources equally strong tribes such as the Turkman, the Afshar[19] and also smaller tribes, or subtribes, or clans like the Gündüzlü or the Purnak.[20]

Obviously, the appearance and success of the Qizilbash are primarily to be related to the Turcomans. Immediately the question arises whether the masters of the Safavid Order (particularly Isma^{c}il, as the most successful and the state founder) were themselves Turcomans.[21] The question may be answered affirmatively, considering that one of his grandfathers was the Aq-Qoyunlu king Uzun Hasan. That his family, besides, goes back to landowners in Gilan[22] is a fact to be dealt with later. At any rate, Isma^{c}il's Turkish or Turcoman descent is beyond any question.

Yet, this does not justify characterizing the Qizilbash movement as an exclusively Turkish phenomenon. Not every member of Turkish ancestry was ipso facto Qizilbash. The name was applied to the warrior who acknowledged his belonging to the Qizilbash movement and was officially admitted as a member by way of bestowing upon him the red headgear—a privilege not necessarily reserved for men of Turcoman origin. There were also Qizilbash who were not Turkish (e.g., Najm-i sani, Isma^{c}il's famous *vakil*, or Kurds like the Chigani tribe). However, on the whole, the non-Turkish Qizilbash were not only in the minority, but were even rare exceptions.[23]

III

First of all, the Safavid state, founded by Shah Isma^{c}il, was a Turcoman achievement. Since its founder was descended from Uzun Hasan, the Safavid state can be considered as a direct continuation of the Aq-Qoyunlu principality, which in turn had already replaced another Turcoman regime, that of the Qara Qoyunlu, thirty-five years before. Those two Turcoman states[24] had been characterized by an undoubted instability, and their shaky systems, which in both cases led to a remarkably short-lived existence, had much in common with many other Turkish states, namely the Anatolian beyliks of post-Mongolian times, and also the Timurid successor states on Persian territory.[25] Quite different was the Safavid state: it lasted more than two centuries and somehow survived up to modern times in several successive states which adopted and preserved a good deal of its characteristics. What saved the Safavids from the instability of other Turkish states?

Of course, the relatively fast breakdown of those pre-Safavid Turkish states can be connected with the "chronic disease"[26] of the thirteenth through fifteenth centuries, that being the weakness of economic and social life, resulting from the Mongol invasion and rule, followed later by Timur's campaigns. However, the Safavid empire itself still had to face similar problems. A further resemblance is due to the nomadic character of the state's fundamental ethnic components, that is, the Turcoman tribes. Yet here a certain difference can be noticed, namely the transition of the Qizilbash tribes toward sedentarization occurring already under Isma^{c}il's reign.

Other reasons may have been of greater importance. First of all, the Iranian participation in the state's administration gave the government a considerable degree of stability. Thus, the sedentary element of the population, with its tendency toward continuity, enjoyed a dominant influence in the bureaucracy, sometimes even in the military hierarchy. This development is, of course, closely linked to the Safavids' centralized Iranian monarchy.[27]

Furthermore, the efficient introduction of Shi^{c}ism[28] as the new state religion helped in consolidating Safavid rule. Until then the Shi^{c}a had been only sporadically dominant in Iran. Through the political and military victories of the Safavid order Shi^{c}ism acquired a special attractiveness and, at least temporarily, even the vehemence of a fascinating ideology.

Last but not least, the introduction by the Safavids of a succession rule guaranteed an acceptable transition from one shah to the next. This system cut the ground from under the old Turkish concept that understood state power as family property which, upon the death of the ruler, was submitted to partition, exactly like any other piece of estate—a concept which quite frequently triggered endless and often pernicious disputes and civil wars.

IV

Military potency, a modus vivendi between heterogeneous population groups, and the introduction of a reasonable succession rule—are these sufficient prerequisites for the achievement of such unusual victories as accomplished by the Qizilbash? Certainly not. Two other decisive factors might be added: a charismatic leader and an exciting concept. Both elements are closely connected with the personality of the young Isma^{c}il.

If we first examine the ideological background, we come upon Shi^{c}ism, which Isma^{c}il declared as the official creed in the summer of 1501, immediately after his arrival in Tabriz, which up until then was a predominantly Sunni capital. Yet, what he understood by "Shi^{c}ism" was far from the principles of Shi^{c}ite theologians. The heterodox conceptions developed in his poetic *divan*[29] are well known. Striking examples are not only the acknowledgment of ^{c}Ali and the other eleven imams, but also the stress on God's manifestation in human form (*tajalli*) and on metempsychosis (*tanasukh*), according to which he himself was a reincarnation of ^{c}Ali and a manifestation of God.[30]

Let us now have a glance at the religious situation of the Turcomans. Their ancestors, the Oğuz, had already accepted Islam in the tenth century when they had set out from central Asia for the west. Yet, it must have been a more or less superficial conversion. Many among them were still attached to inherited shamanist concepts, thinly covered with an Islamic veneer. Also, in later generations, the situation would certainly not have been very different.

This might be the reason why Isma^{c}il had a drinking cup made out of the skull of a conquered enemy, and why the Qizilbash would roast the flesh of a fallen opponent and eat it, hoping to acquire his toughness.[31] In studying the religious attitudes of both the Qara Qoyunlu and Aq-Qoyunlu, Jean Aubin came across a striking opportunism as the background for their oscillating between the Sunna and the Shi^{c}a.[32] By referring to the religious views and customs of contemporary, modern, Islamic sects in East Anatolia and North Iran, Irène Mélikoff has maintained that explicitly non-Islamic doctrines were practiced in the Turcoman milieu under the first Safavid leaders.[33] Here we meet with the aforementioned belief in God's incarnation (*tajalli*) and metempsychosis (*tanasukh*). She considers these religious concepts as specifically Turcoman ones which had been given their Sufi, and subsequently Shi^{c}i, character only by Safavid propaganda. Supposing Mélikoff's argumentation is right, we would have to conclude that Isma^{c}il's followers, at the time of his proclaiming Shi^{c}ism, had been aware that his doctrine did not agree with Shi^{c}i dogma. This is not impossible, but not very probable. Even less convincing is the thesis that Isma^{c}il acted in full consciousness of the heretic character of his teachings. Good faith, at least, should not be denied so enthusiastic a young man.

V

On the whole, the fifteenth century displays the image of a rather doubtful orthodoxy, not only from the Sunni point of view, but also from the Shi^{c}i one. We understand better such extravagances if we remember that Islamic theologians, whose power had been annihilated by the Mongols, had not yet been able to restore their older influence at that time and were obliged to witness in frustration how an uncanny popular religiosity was sprouting everywhere. A real folk Islam arose,[34] containing all the aspects of what had always been a thorn in the flesh of the orthodox: belief in miracles, soothsaying, oneiromancy, worship of saints, popular pilgrimage centers, and mighty orders with mystical practices.[35]

Wherever Sufi orders appear in Islam, doubts about their Sunni orthodoxy will be appropriately noted. This is in particular justified in a milieu like that of the Safavid order during the second half of the fifteenth century, when the leaders of the order increasingly surrounded themselves with Turcoman disciples (*muridan*). Indeed, under Sheikh Junaid and his son, Sheikh Haidar, the order's propaganda acquired a missionarily organized structure.[36] Simple people like the Turcoman tribal warriors, especially in view of their rather superficial bonds to Islam and their apparent ties to the shamanist spiritual world, may well be regarded as an exceptionally fertile soil for popular religiosity, concepts of folk Islam, and pseudo-Shi^ci heresies. To the love of adventure and the desire for booty was added the attractiveness of young Sufi masters along with their spirit of enterprise and gallantry. So charged an atmosphere did not change after the failure of three masters—Sheikh Junaid, Sheikh Haidar, and Sultan ^cAli, all of whom died in action. On the contrary, were they not martyrs for the Safavid cause?

VI

At any rate, this is how the situation presented itself to the young Isma^cil and his adherents as he set out at the dawn of the century in order to gain political power. Although there are many indications that the thirteen-year-old leader was backed by certain Turcoman emirs[37] to whom most of the operative ideas and decisions have to be ascribed, success and victories he was to gain henceforth go undoubtedly back to his personal credit. He was the one who knew how to implant into his Turcoman warriors and to preserve in them enthusiasm for his cause, readiness for struggle, courage to face death, and unrestricted loyalty. The magnet which attracted masses of new adepts was the young God-king Isma^cil. Dancing and singing, the Turcoman tribal warriors came to meet him,[38] and he led them from triumph to triumph until, little more than a decade later, the whole Iranian plateau lay at his feet. As an explanation of such unusual achievements much credit has been given to Isma^cil's charismatic personality whose emanation, indeed, must have been very strong, in view of the widespread messianic expectations cherished among the Turcomans.

Along with the conquest of Iran, the building of a sacred state,[39] a theocracy, was taking place, though it was of a basically different kind compared to the one created by the Prophet Muhammad in Medina. Isma^cil did not waive the claim of kingship, a heritage of his grandfather Uzun Hasan. Yet also as shah he still remained the master of the Safavid order from which the military Qizilbash aristocracy had started to develop. In the Janus-faced organism that the Safavids had presented since the middle of the fifteenth century, the military features were now becoming more and more distinct. This dualistic position of the young shah still prevailed under his first successors. As reincarnation of ^cAli and manifestation of God, Isma^cil intrinsically had so strong a position that the question why he should have tried to strengthen it by claiming genealogical descent from ^cAli[40] is not easy to answer.

Iranians played a substantial part in the new theocracy. They were appointed holders of higher and highest nonmilitary court and state offices. They constituted the third fundamental pillar of the state—the bureaucracy.

The Qizilbash emirs occupied the military positions of the court and of the provinces. They were appointed provincial governors, and they moved at the head of their tribal contingents to the regions[41] assigned to them, thus starting a specific Safavid feudal system. With the economic and political influence that they acquired, the first step was also taken toward the formation of a praetorian class, which was earnestly striving for the preservation and strengthening of its personal power.

When Ismaᶜil was defeated by the Ottomans at the battle of Chaldiran (1514), he lost his aura of invincibility and presumably his charismatic gifts as well.[42] The attempt to balance or diminish the increasing power of the Qizilbash emirs by strengthening the Iranian element—attempts at first undertaken by Ismaᶜil, then repeated by Tahmasb I—was bound to fail: three out of five unsuccessful Iranian candidates for the influential office of viceroy (*vakil*) were to pay for their ambition with their lives.[43]

As a consequence of the persistent decline of royal authority and monastic discipline, the Qizilbash fell back into their tribal mischief, and when, upon Ismaᶜil's death in 1524, the supreme power was nominally given to Tahmasb, then ten years old, but de facto exercised by certain emirs, tribal particularism raised its head again. Qizilbash rivalries and coalitions led to a civil war which Shah Tahmasb was able to quell only in the tenth year of his reign. But state authority was so much bound to his personality that some forty years later, when he was about to die, the quarrel between the tribes broke out anew in all its bitterness.

The intertribal chaos lasted for years and almost brought the Safavid state to ruin. Two of Tahmasb's successors proved to be impotent against the intrigues of the Qizilbash. Even the Shahiseven institution[44] turned out to be rather unsuccessful. Only Shah ᶜAbbas I was capable of imposing his will on them. In 1587, on the eve of his succession, he used a revolt as pretext to eliminate the Qizilbash, not only by playing off one tribe against the other,[45] but by brutally crushing his most dangerous opponents. His grand scale military reforms brought about lasting success.[46] These consisted mainly of the formation of new arms and contingents, based on ethnic elements different from the until then almost exclusively Turcoman troops, thus canceling their traditional monopoly on leadership as well as the principle that the commander of one or the other tribal unit must be a member of the same tribe. Even though loyal emirs were allowed to keep their positions, the Turcoman privilege was abolished forever. Not only Georgian, Cherkes, and Armenian officers made their entry, but also warriors of rank and file of such descent. Many of them were previous prisoners of war converted to Islam or their sons who had already grown up in Iran.

If in Ismaᶜil's time all his followers were members of the Safavid Order, this "personal union" was no longer compulsory under Shah Tahmasb.[47] There were more and more Qizilbash who did not belong to the order, and order members who were not Qizilbash. Indeed, Shah ᶜAbbas still laid stress on his position as Sufi master, but the respect for and authority of the Sufis were rapidly declining. This obviously happened under the influence of the Shiᶜi theologians,[48] who, in the meantime, had become stronger. They were no longer willing to tolerate the vagaries of the Sufi orders. As a matter of fact, these were finally assigned only lower services and at the end banned from the capital.[49]

With the stabilization of the Safavid empire under Shah ᶜAbbas, the formative role of the Qizilbash was over.[50] As a result of their tribal interests, which turned out to be stronger than their originally very close solidarity with the Safavid order and state, they finally fell victims to their divergent goals.

Notes

[1] *Deutsche Literaturzeitung* 61 (1940): col. 561.

[2] *Safevi Devletinin Kuruluşu ve Gelişmesinde Anadolu Türklerinin Rolü* (Şah İsmail ile halefleri ve Anadolu Türkleri) (Ankara, 1976). Mehrdad Torabi-Nejad's Hamburg dissertation of 1979, "Die Problematik der autochthonen Genesis der modernen Wirtschaftsweise in Iran, Vergleich zwischen der sozio-ökonomischen Struktur des safawidischen Persiens und des vormodernen Westeuropa," shows the gaps in economic history still to be filled so far as the Qizilbash Turcomans are concerned.

[3] *The Aq Qoyunlu: Clan, Confederation, and Empire,* (Minneapolis, 1976).

[4] "Das turkmenische Intermezzo—Persische Geschichte zwischen Mongolen und Safawiden," *AMI NF* 9 (1976): 263–97. I have also touched on the subject in my article "Historische Grundlagen der persischen Neuzeit," *AMI NF* 10 (1977): 305–21.

[5] "Comments on 'The Qajar Uymaq in the Safavid Period, 1500–1722'," *Iranian Studies* 14 (1981): 87–105.

[6] "The Qajar Uymaq in the Safavid Period, 1500–1722," *Iranian Studies* 11 (1978): 117–43. The article seems to be an enlarged extract of an until then unpublished UCLA dissertation under the title "Tribalism and Society in Islamic Iran, 1500–1629" (1978), subsequently published under the same title by Udena Publications, Malibu, Calif., 1983.

[7] Očerki po istorii feodal'nikh otnoshenii v Azerbajdžane i Armenii v XV-nachale XIX vv. (Leningrad, 1949), esp. 89–110.

[8] "Shah Tahmasb and the Uzbeks (The Duel for Khurasan with ᶜUbayd Khan 930–946/1524–1540)," unpublished Ph.D. dissertation, Princeton University, 1958.

[9] P. B. Golden, "The Migrations of the Oğuz," *Archivum Ottomanicum* 4 (1972): 45–84.

¹⁰ İsmail Hakkı Uzunçarşılı, *Anadolu Beylikleri ve Akkoyunlu, Karakoyunlu devletleri. Siyasi, fikri, iktisadi hayat: ilmi ve içtimai muesseseler: halk ve toprak* (Türk Tarih Kurumu yayinlarindan VIII seri-No. 2) (Ankara, 1937), ²1969.

¹¹ Even though Sümer ends his book with the remark that the founders of the Safavid state had been "Anatolian Turks, completely different from the Kara-Koyunlu and the Ak-Koyunlu confederations," he elsewhere (e.g., *EI²* [French ed.], 1 [1960]) speaks of members of the Aq-Qoyunlu federation who had entered Safavid service. Oktaj Efendiev, "Le rôle des tribus de langue turque dans la création de l'état safavide," *Turcica* 6 (1975): 24–33, enumerates even groups of Qara Qoyunlu and Aq-Qoyunlu tribes under the Qizilbash.

¹² The affinity of language may, for instance, be documented by the poems of the Qara Qoyunlu ruler Jihanshah and those of Shah Ismaᶜil I, who, in his language, belongs to the Aq-Qoyunlu, cf. Minorsky, "Jihan-shah Qara-qoyunlu and his Poetry" (*Turcmenca* 9) and "The Poetry of Shah Ismaᶜil I," *BSOAS* 10 (1939–42): 1006a-1053a, and Tourkhan Gandjei, ed., *Il Canzoniere di Šah Ismaᶜil* (Napoli, 1959), and Cahit Özteli, "Les oeuvres de Hatâyi," *Turcica* 6 (1975): 7–10.

¹³ Cf. Ettore Rossi, *Il "Kitab-i Dede Qorqut"* (Rome, 1952). For an exhaustive bibliography see Fahir İz, "Dede Ḳorḳut," *EI²* 2 (1965): 206 ff.

¹⁴ "The original form of the name Türkmän is nothing but a derivation of Türk, to which the suffix -män gives an intensified meaning, which in our days might be rendered as 'hundred percent Turks'." Minorsky, "The Middle East in the 13th, 15th, and 17th Centuries," *JRCAS* 27 (1940): 439. The origin of the term may go back to the second half of the tenth century, cf. İ. Kafesoğlu, "Türkmen adı, manası ve mahiyeti," *J. Deny Armağani* (Ankara, 1958), 121–33.

¹⁵ Minorsky, ed., *Tadhkirat al-muluk* (London, 1943) (reprint Cambridge, 1980), 188. For details see my articles "Das turkmenische Intermezzo—Persische Geschichte zwischen Mongolen und Safawiden," *AMI NF* 9 (1976): 263–97, and "Historische Grundlagen der persischen Neuzeit," *AMI NF* 10 (1977): 305–21.

¹⁶ Jean-Louis Bacqué-Grammond, "Une liste d'émirs Ostağli révoltés en 1526," *Studia Iranica* 5 (1976): 25–35 and "Un document sur la révolte des Ostağlu," *Studia Iranica* 6 (1976): 169–84.

¹⁷ The frequently used Arabized *Dhu 'l-qadr* is a popular etymology. Annemarie von Gabain (*Der Islam* 31 [1953]: 115) takes the secondary Tulġadir to suppose an original *tilga* + *dar* "Helmträger." Details about the tribe and its origin are in ᶜArifi pasha, "Zu-l-kadir (Dulġadir) oğullari hükûmeti," *TOEM* 5 (1915): 541, J. H. Mordtmann and M. H. Yinanç, "Dulkadırlılar," *İA* 3 (1945): 654–62, F. Sümer, "XVI. asırda Anadolu, Suriye ve Irak'ta yaşayan Türk aşiretlerine umumi bir bakış," *İktisat Fak. Mecm.* 11 (1949–50): 509–23 (Dulgadirlar, 512 ff.), Bacqué-Grammond, "Un 'fetiḥname' Ẕu-l-ḳadiride dans les archives Ottomanes," *Turcica* 2 (1970): 138–50.

¹⁸ As to the Qajar we may refer to M. Longworth-Dames and B. Darkot, "Kaçar (Ḳacar)," *İA* 6 (1955): 33–39; F. Sümer, "Ḳadjar," *EI²* 4 (1978): 403 ff.; James J. Reid, "The Qajar Uymaq in the Safavid Period, 1500–1722," *Iranian Studies* 11 (1978): 117–43; also Robert D. McChesney, "Comments on 'The Qajar Uymaq in the Safavid Period, 1500–1722,'" *Iranian Studies* 14 (1981): 87–105.

[19] Few Qizilbash tribes have been treated by so many authors as the Afshar were: Ahmad Kasravi, "Afsharha-yi Khuzistan," *Ayanda* 1 (1925, reprint 1352): 241–48, and "Il-i Afshar," *Ayanda* 2 (1926, reprint 1352): 596–603; B. Nikitine, "Les Afšars d'Urumiyeh," *JA* 214 (1929): 112 ff.; Fuad Köprülü, Avşar," *İA* 2 (1944): 28–38; F. Sümer, "Avşarlar'a dair," *Fuad Köprülü Armağani* (Istanbul, 1953), 453–78; M. F. Köprülü, "Afshar," *EI²* 1 (1960): 247 ff.; Georg Stöber, Die Afshar: Nomadismus im Raum Kerman (Zentraliran) (*Marburger geographische Schriften* 76) (Marburg, 1978).

[20] Only some references out of the numerous publications on minor Qizilbash tribes can be given here: F. Sümer, "Bayatlar," *Türk Dili ve Edebiyati Dergisi* 4 (1952): 373–98, and "Bayat," *EI²* 1 (1960): 1150 ff.; V. Minorsky, "Aynallu/Inallu," *RO* 17 (1951–52): 1–11; also James J. Reid, "The Qaramanlu: The Growth and Development of a Lesser Tribal Elite in Sixteenth and Seventeenth-Century Persia," *Studia Iranica* 9 (1980): 195–209. Besides, for composition and structure of the Qizilbash tribes Minorsky's comments in *Tadhkirat al-muluk*, 16 ff., to Iskandar Munshi's explanations are still valid. Further important details are given by Efendiev, *Turcica* 6 (1975): 24–33.

[21] A detailed study on Isma^cil's ancestry may be found in Walther Hinz, *Irans Aufstieg zum Nationalstaat im 15. Jahrhundert* (Berlin and Leipzig, 1936), 74 ff.

[22] Many authors deal with Isma^cil's rural Iranian ancestors, mostly quoting Ibn Bazzaz, *Safvat as-safa*, e.g., Michel M. Mazzaoui, *The Origins of the Safawids* (*Freiburger Islamstudien* 3) (Wiesbaden, 1972), 51 ff., or Jean Aubin, "La propriété foncière en Azerbaydjan sous les Mongols," *Le Monde Iranien et l'Islam* 4 (1976–77): 123 ff.

[23] O. Efendiev, "Le rôle des tribus de langue turque," *Turcica* 6 (1975): 24–33, and Hans R. Roemer, "Historische Grundlagen der persischen Neuzeit," *AMI NF* 10 (1977): 316.

[24] Details in Hans R. Roemer, "Das turkmenische Intermezzo—Persische Geschichte zwischen Mongolen und Safawiden," *AMI NF* 9 (1976): 263–97.

[25] Hans R. Roemer, "Die Nachfolger Timurs—Abriss der Geschichte Zentral— und Vorderasiens im 15. Jahrhundert," in Richard Gramlich, ed., *Islamkundliche Abhandlungen Fritz Meier zum sechzigsten Geburtstag* (Wiesbaden, 1974), 226–62.

[26] As formulated by M. H. Yinanç, "Akkoyunlular," *İA* 1 (1941): 266.

[27] The integration of both Iranians and Turcomans as fundamental partners in the very same state may be considered as a specifically Safavid achievement of high merit, so much more as Iranians and Turks intrinsically "did not mix freely . . . like oil and water," cf. Minorsky, ed., *Tadhkirat al-muluk*, 188.

[28] In pre-Safavid Iran, Shi^ci adherents could only be found in a few places, such as Qum, Kashan, Sava, and Rayy, cf. I. P. Petrushevskii, *Islam v Irane v 7–15 vekakh* (Leningrad, 1966), 351 (according to Hamdallah Mustaufi Qazvini, *Nuzhat al-qulub*).

[29] See note 12 above. Even though Jean Aubin's postulation (*JESHO* 2 [1959]: 55), that, first of all, it was necessary to find out the real significance of the Shi^ci phenomenon in fifteenth-century Iran, is still waiting to be answered, Isma^cil's concept of Shi^cism is incompatible even with a very bold Shi^ci definition. A general outline of the religious situation in Iran at the moment of Isma^cil's accession to

the throne is given by Erika Glassen, "Schah Isma^cil und die Theologen seiner Zeit," *Der Islam* 48 (1972): 254–68.

[30] Irène Mélikoff, "Le problème qizilbaş," *Turcica* 6 (1975): 49–67, has recently studied the terms "incarnation" (*tajalli*) and "metempsychosis" (*tanasukh*), occurring in Isma^cil's *divan*, in the context of contemporary heterodoxies of East Anatolia and Northwest Persia.

[31] Jean Aubin, "La politique religieuse des Safavides," *Le Shi^cisme imamite* (*Travaux du Centre d'Études Supérieures spécialisé d'Histoire des Religions de Strasbourg*) (Paris, 1970): 235–44. Röhrborn (p. 38 of his book indicated in note 47 below) cites even a quotation according to which Isma^cil's men had eaten the flesh of living traitors with his consent.

[32] Repeatedly in Jean Aubin, e.g., "Notes sur quelques documents Aq Qoyunlu," *Mélanges Massignon* 1 (Damascus, 1956): 132.

[33] Aubin, "Notes," 65.

[34] Franz Babinger, "Der Islam in Kleinasien, neue Wege der Islamforschung," *ZDMG* 76 (1922): 126–52 (*Aufsätze und Abhandlungen* 1 [Munich, 1962]: 52–75). V. A. Gordlevski in Theodor Menzel, "Russische Arbeiten über türkische Literatur und Folkloristik (Gordlevski, Zavarin, Olesnijicki)," *Der Islam* 4 (1913): 123 ff. Ahmed Refik, *On altinci asirda Rafizilik ve Bektaşilik* (Istanbul, 1932), passim. Klaus E. Müller, *Kulturhistorische Studien zur Genese pseudo-islamischer Sektengebilde in Vorderasien* (Wiesbaden, 1967), passim. Michel M. Mazzaoui, *The Origins of the Safawids* (*Freiburger Islamstudien* 3) (Wiesbaden, 1972), 58–63.

[35] Jean Rypka, *Iranische Literaturgeschichte* (Leipzig, 1959), 215 ff. N. D. Miklukho-Maklaji, "Shiizm i ego sotsial'noe litso v Irane na rubeže XV-XVI vv," *Pamjati . . . Krchkovskogo* (Leningrad, 1958): 221–34. Hossein Nasr, "Religion in Safavid Persia," *Iranian Studies* 7 (1974): 271–86. Irène Mélikoff, "L'Islam hétérodoxe en Anatolie," *Turcica* 14 (1982): 142–54.

[36] Hanna Sohrweide, "Der Sieg der Safaviden in Persien und seine Rückwirkungen auf die Schiiten Anatoliens im 16. Jahrhundert," *Der Islam* 41 (1965): 95–229. Roger M. Savory, "The Office of Khalifat al-Khulafa under the Safawids," *JAOS* 85 (1965): 497 (b). Sohrweide, "Gelehrte Scheiche und sufische Ulama," *Studien zur Geschichte und Kultur des Vorderen Orient (Festschrift Spuler)* (Leiden, 1981), 376, mentions the book of a Khalvatiya sheikh, *Kitab at-tabyin fi bayan-i millat-i Shah ^cAbbas al-la^cin*, written between 1626 and 1629, which merits attention in our context. Jean-Louis Bacqué-Grammond's dissertation "Ottomans et Safavides au temps de Šah Isma^cil et Tahmasp," Sorbonne (June 11, 1980), has not been accessible to the present author.

[37] Suppositions and allusions in this sense have been uttered from both Anglo-Saxon and Soviet scholars: I. A. Gusenov et al., eds., *Istorija Azerbajdžana* 1 (Baku, 1958): 224 ff., I. P. Petrushevskii, *Islam v Irane* (Leningrad, 1966), 370, and *expressis verbis*—R. M. Savory, "Some Reflections on Totalitarian Tendencies in the Safavid State," *Der Islam* 53 (1976): 61–69, and O. Efendiev, *Turcica* 6 (1975): 29.

[38] Erika Glassen, *Die frühen Safawiden nach Qaži Ahmad Qumi* (*Islamkundliche Untersuchungen* 8), (Freiburg, 1970), 93.

[39] Certain references are given by Röhrborn, "Staatskanzlei und Absolutismus im safawidischen Persien," *ZDMG* 127 (1977): 313–43.

⁴⁰ This question has not been discussed by Ahmed Z. V. Togan, "Sur l'origine des Safavides," *Mélanges Massignon* 3 (Damascus, 1957), 345–57.

⁴¹ In general, the provinces remained in the hands of those Qizilbash tribes to whose emirs they had once been assigned—changes being limited to grave causes only. The situation on the eve of the accession of Shah ᶜAbbas I is illustrated by a sketch in Roemer, *Der Niedergang Iran nach dem Tode Ismaᶜils des Grausamen 1577–1581* (Würzburg, 1939), 22. So far, there is no study on the formation of tribal groups within the Safavid order which must have taken place prior to Ismaᶜil's rise to power. For the time being we have to go back to publications such as Paul Wittek, "Le rôle des tribus turques dans l'empire ottoman," *Mélanges Georges Smets* (Brussels, 1952). Abdülbaki Gölpinarlıı, "Kizilbaş," *İA* 6 (1955): 779–95. Michel M. Mazzaoui, "The Ghazi Background of the Safavid State," *Iqbal Review* 12 (1971): 79–90. Certain details are also given by Röhrborn, "Provinzen und Zentralgewalt Persiens im 16. und 17. Jahrhundert" (*Studien zur Sprache, Geschichte und Kultur des islamischen Orients* 2) (Berlin, 1966).

⁴² In their reports European travelers have spoken of divine veneration also toward Safavid kings after Shah Ismaᶜil I, cf. Aubin, "Politique religieuse," 237. The fact that Ismaᶜil did not take part in any further campaign after his Chaldiran defeat in the remaining ten years of his life indicates a serious identity crisis.

⁴³ R. M. Savory, "The Significance of the Political Murder of Mirza Salman," *Islamic Studies* 3 (Karachi, 1964): 181–91. Cf. also Aubin, "Études Safavides I," *JESHO* 2 (1959): 77.

⁴⁴ The term *shahiseven* or *shahiseveni* signifies the ruler's appeal for loyalty due to the Sufi master (which I shall treat elsewhere). The word can be found as part of the name used for still existing tribal groups: Richard Tapper, "Black Sheep, White Sheep, and Red Heads: A Historical Sketch of the Shahsavan of Azarbaijan," *Iran* 4 (1966): 61–84, and "Shahsevan in Safavid Persia," *BSOAS* 37 (1974): 321–54, and Günther Schweizer, "Nordwest-Azerbaidschan und Shah-Sevan-Nomaden. Strukturwandel einer nordwestiranischen Landschaft und ihrer Bevölkerung," in E. Meynen and E. Plewe, eds., *Erdkundliches Wissen*, Heft 26 (Wiesbaden, 1970), 81–148.

⁴⁵ Hans Müller, *Die Chronik Hulasat at-tawarih des Qazi Ahmad Qumi (Veröffentlichungen der Orientalischen Kommission* 14), (Wiesbaden, 1964), 14 ff., trans., 73–81.

⁴⁶ Laurence Lockhart, "The Persian Army in the Safavi Period," *Der Islam* 34 (1959): 89–98, and R. M. Savory, "The Sherley Myth," *Iran* 5 (1967): 73–81.

⁴⁷ Klaus Röhrborn, "Regierung und Verwaltung Irans unter den Safawiden," HdO, 1. Abt., VI, 5. Abschn., Teil 1 (Leiden, 1979), 38. The title cited herein, "Sufiyan-i qadim-i Gilani" according to *Takmilat al-akhbar*, seems to be significant.

⁴⁸ The famous Shiᶜi theologian Mulla Muhammad Baqir Majlisi is considered as "the persecutor of sufis and heretics" (Browne, *LHP* 4 [1959]: 120).

⁴⁹ Minorsky, *Tadhkirat al-muluk*, 13 ff. and 126, and Röhrborn, *Provinzen und Zentralgewalt Persiens*, 37 (according to *Tarikh-i Ṭamasiya*).

⁵⁰ Of course, this does not justify the conclusion that they were of no importance in the later history of Iran: there are post-Safavid dynasties originating from Qizilbash tribes (e.g., the Afshar and the Qajar).

Addendum: After finishing the present paper I received the Teheran review *Ayanda*, vol. 9/2–3 (1362) with the following note (300): *Tarikh-i Qizilbashan*, ed. by Mir Hashim Muhaddith according to a unique manuscript of Kitabkhana-yi Milli-yi Malik, written between 1007 and 1013.

2

VERA BASCH MOREEN

Annenberg Research Institute
Philadelphia, Pennsylvania

The *Kitab-i Anusi* of Babai ibn Lutf (Seventeenth Century) and the *Kitab-i Sar Guzasht* of Babai ibn Farhad (Eighteenth Century): A Comparison of Two Judaeo-Persian Chronicles

THERE EXIST only two Judaeo-Persian documents of direct historiographical interest to both Jewish and Iranian history. They are the *Kitab-i Anusi* (hereafter KA), "The Book of a Forced Convert," of Babai ibn Lutf and the *Kitab-i Sar Guzasht-i Kashan dar bab-i ᶜIbri va Guyimi-yi Sani* (hereafter KS), "The Book of Events in Kashan Concerning the Jews; Their Second Conversion," by Babai ibn Farhad, the grandson of Babai ibn Lutf. The KA deals primarily with the periodic persecution of Iranian Jews between 1617 and 1762 and refers to a few other events in the reigns of Shah ᶜAbbas I (1581–1629), Shah Safi I (1629–42), and Shah ᶜAbbas II (1642–66). The chronological span and the subject matter of the KS are more limited. It deals primarily with hardships endured by Iranian Jews, particularly those of Kashan, between 1721 and 1731.[1] The KS also refers to a number of other events belonging to the reign of Shah Sultan Husayn (1694–1722), the reigns of the two Afghan shahs, Mahmud (1722–25) and Ashraf (1725–30), and the latter's conflict with and defeat at the hands of Tahmasp Quli Khan, the future Nadir Shah (1736–47).[2]

Both chronicles were discovered early in this century and have been summarized by Wilhelm Bacher.[3] M. Seligsohn translated parts of the KA

---

* A shorter version of this paper was presented at the Fifteenth Annual Conference of the Association for Jewish Studies, Boston, Massachusetts, December 1983.

as early as 1902.[4] Despite some more recent investigations,[5] very little effort has been made until now to evaluate the historical merit of these documents from the point of view of their importance for Iranian history in general and the history of the Jews in Iran in particular. Since I have written book-length studies on both chronicles,[6] this article is limited to a brief comparison of their most important features. A comparison of their contents, style, and problems reveals a great deal about the authors and the manner in which the chronicles are related to one another beyond the kinship of the authors. Even a brief comparison will show, I believe, that both works are authentic reflections of the times in which they were written.

There can be little doubt that Babai ibn Lutf's KA deserves to be mentioned first not only because of its chronological precedence but also because the events it describes can be more fully corroborated by outside sources, thus making it a more reliable historical document. In addition, Babai ibn Farhad acknowledges the KA as the model and inspiration for his writing of the KS.[7]

Babai ibn Lutf provides very little autobiographical information in the KA. He acknowledges Kashan as his home and refers briefly to his impulse to flee at the start of the persecutions while giving at the same time his reasons for not doing so. In some later verses he seems to count himself among the *anusim*, the Jews forced to convert to Shiʿi Islam during the major outbreak of persecutions between 1656 and 1662, who recently adhered to Judaism. We remain in the dark about his official function, if any, within the Jewish community of Kashan. His chief reason for recording the persecutions is, in his own words, the desire to record God's miraculous deliverance of Iranian Jewry. He compares this deliverance in moving terms with the one commemorated in the Book of Esther.[8]

The KA is a chronicle in verse, a *masnavi* in the *hazaj mahzuf* meter containing, in its longest version, some 5,115 verses. The exact time of its writing cannot be ascertained although it seems plausible to assume that most of it was written after 1662. The language of the KA is classical Persian, but it is colored by linguistic peculiarities characteristic of the colloquial rather than the written language. Babai ibn Lutf resorts to using occasional Hebrew words, especially when referring to Jewish religious terms. The structure of the extant manuscripts shows some important problems, but these do not seriously hinder the unraveling of the content of the chronicle.[9]

Most of the KA describes the persecution of Iranian Jews during the reign of Shah ʿAbbas II (1656–62) with special emphasis on events in Kashan, the author's home town. These persecutions spread in various degrees to other Iranian towns, and Babai ibn Lutf tries to describe how each Jewish community dealt with the emergency. In order to provide a better perspective for the persecutions during the reign of Shah ᶜAbbas II, Babai ibn Lutf refers to a number of anti-Jewish incidents that occurred during the reign of Shah ᶜAbbas I. Chief among these, and fully corroborated by a Western source, is the shah's reaction to accusations of magic against his person made by two squabbling factions of the Jewish community of Isfahan. Shah ᶜAbbas I punished the community by presenting it with the choice of being devoured by ferocious hounds or converting to Islam. A few preferred martyrdom but many more converted temporarily. According to Babai ibn Lutf, Shah ᶜAbbas I also fell easy prey to the arguments of the Jewish apostate Abu'l-Hasan Lari who tried to enforce a demeaning headgear on all his former coreligionists. But the shah eventually reversed his decision after experiencing a "miracle" at the tomb of the Jewish "saint" Serah bath Asher.[10]

These tendencies in Shah ᶜAbbas's character are fully in accord with descriptions of him in contemporary Iranian sources such as the *Tarikh-i ᶜAlam-ara-yi ᶜAbbasi* of Iskandar Beg Munshi, the major chronicler of his reign. Babai ibn Lutf is to be counted among the shah's admirers despite the events mentioned above. He describes in moving and largely accurate terms the circumstances surrounding the death of Shah ᶜAbbas.[11] His expression of sorrow rings genuine, reflecting, perhaps, the feelings of most of the shah's ordinary subjects.

The KA is never quite clear about how many Jews converted during the reign of Shah ᶜAbbas I. In any case, these conversions seem to have been confined to Isfahan. But Babai ibn Lutf states explicitly that full religious liberty returned to the Jews, including to the recent converts, upon accession of Shah Safi I, the grandson of Shah ᶜAbbas I.[12] This freedom seems to have continued throughout most of the reign of his successor, Shah ᶜAbbas II. But between 1656 and 1662 there was an outburst of persecutions against, it would seem, all non-Shiᶜis in Iran. The first victims were the Armenians, but soon after the Jews and, no doubt, the Zoroastrians were affected as well.[13] The actual cause(s) of these persecutions remains difficult to ascertain. Whereas in the case of the Armenians it can be argued persuasively that their wealth was coveted (by this time they held in their hands most of the lucrative commerce of the kingdom), this argument does not explain the persecution of the Jews. By all accounts, Iranian Jews were mostly artisans and petty merchants occupying, together with the farming Zoroastrians, the lower rungs of Iranian society. The instigator of the persecutions was not Shah ᶜAbbas II but his Grand Vizier, Muhammad Beg.[14] Most of the major Jewish communities of Iran were forced to convert and remained *anusim*—a Hebrew term synonymous with the Shiᶜi state of *taqiyya* that denotes outward compliance with the dominant faith and secret practice of one's true faith—for approximately six years.

Religious zeal on the part of Muhammad Beg seems to have been the most important reason for the forced conversions. Extortion, a common cause for persecutions in history, seems not to have been Muhammad Beg's original goal. In fact, at the outset of the persecutions the new converts were rewarded monetarily and became exempt from the *jizya*. The most important Iranian chronicle of the period, the *ᶜAbbasnama* of Muhammad Tahir Wahid Qazvini, mentions the conversion of the Jews as a wondrous event not in the least because the Shah was willing to forgo a reliable source of revenue. But when the tide turned and the Jews regained freedom of worship, extortion did come into play as most of the communities had to return the "reward" money and even more than that sum. In some cases the *jizya* was demanded retroactively.[15] Eventually, the more tolerant frame of mind of Shah ᶜAbbas II prevailed over that of his vizier whose machinations at the court brought about his downfall.[16] But, although Shah ᶜAbbas II reversed his oppressive policies, it is clear from the KA and the KS that this period of *anusut* left the Jewish communities of Iran greatly impoverished materially as well as spiritually.

The KS of Babai ibn Farhad is shorter, numbering only 1,309 verses. It is also written in *hazaj mahzuf*. Babai ibn Farhad acknowledges openly his conscious imitation of his grandfather's chronicle.[17] No doubt Babai ibn Farhad perceived the events of his generation to be comparable to those of his grandfather's time but, as we shall see, this perception is highly questionable.

Babai ibn Farhad lived in an even more turbulent period in Iranian history than Babai ibn Lutf. The reign of Shah ᶜAbbas II was generally peaceful. Such aggression as occurred was initiated mostly by the Safavids themselves.[18] But Babai ibn Farhad witnessed the downfall of the Safavid dynasty, the Afghan invasion of Iran (1722), the brief and unsettling rule of two Afghan monarchs, Mahmud (1722–25) and Ashraf (1725–30), the invasion of northwest Iran by the Russians (1722–25) and by the Ottomans (1726–30), and the rise to power of Tahmasp Quli Beg, (Nadir Shah, 1736–47).[19] Although the KS states repeatedly that Iranian Jews suffered greatly as a result of the numerous battles, sieges, and plunders of the various armies, it does not single them out. The entire population of Iran suffered greatly. In fact, the KS claims that the Jews suffered less during the Afghan conquest and occupation than did the Shiᶜi majority.[20]

During the reign of Shah ᶜAbbas II, Babai ibn Lutf's generation witnessed the deliberate persecution of all major Iranian Jewish communities. Babai ibn Farhad and his coreligionists experienced no such concerted effort. Only the Jewish community of Kashan, Babai ibn Farhad's home town, converted to Islam. This occurred not as a result of coercion but as a quasi-voluntary act initiated by the leaders of the community who believed that they were thereby saving the Jewish community from financial ruin. The largest part of the KS concentrates on these events, describing what led up to the brief apostasy of Kashan's Jews between 1729 and 1730 and the circumstances that led to their open return to Judaism. This incident, tragic as it was in its own way, fails to have the same impact as the persecutions described in the KA. They were more restricted geographically, and the Jews of Babai ibn Farhad's home town had the choice of saving their faith by paying a certain sum demanded of them; they chose to convert in order to avoid making the payment.[21]

Although this option was probably far from favorable (it is not clear whether it would have caused the financial ruin of the community), the Jews of Babai ibn Lutf's day were faced with a much more drastic choice: conversion to Islam or death or, in some instances, exile to uninhabitable places.[22] By comparing the situation in his day to that of his grandfather's day, Babai ibn Farhad is actually trying to justify them in a rather unconvincing manner. His comparison does not stand up to historical scrutiny and, at one level, Babai ibn Farhad himself is aware of the incongruity. He presents two versions concerning the return to Judaism of the Jews of Kashan. In the first, the original *nasi* or head of the Jewish community responsible for enforcing the conversions to Islam, although not completely exonerated, is credited with sparing no effort to regain freedom of worship for the Jews. In a second version, in a chapter actually written by one Mashiah ben Raphael but included in the KS, another individual is given credit for this deliverance. After this chapter Babai ibn Farhad picks up the narrative again and gives ambiguous credit to both communal leaders. The truth of the matter cannot be determined without further evidence, but the ambivalence reflects the community's own division into factions, a division apparent throughout the Kashan episodes. While attempting to highlight the similarities between the predicament of his own generation and that of his grandfather, Babai ibn Farhad stresses the fact that the former were *anusim* for seven months while the latter endured this condition for seven years.[23] Such a facile comparison, far from highlighting a real similarity serves, in my opinion, only to underscore the differences between the two works.

The KA and the KS differ substantially on stylistic grounds as well. The most pronounced difference is in their language. Although they are both more colloquial than classical in their rhetoric and vocabulary, the KS is the more colloquial of the two. Both the language and the rhetoric of the KA seem to be a more conscious imitation of Iranian epics. While we cannot identify these epics with any certainty, it is safe to assume that they were the great popular epics of classical Persian literature to which everyone had access in an oral form. Babai ibn Lutf betrays an attempt, however awkward, to follow the sonorous poetry and rich, heroic imagery of these models.[24] From the Jewish side he was undoubtedly influenced by biblical narratives, especially by the Book of Esther.

No such literary influences, however remote, can be detected in the KS. The only obvious influence on it is the KA. Whereas the KA is hardly original in its language and imagery, the KS is even less imaginative in both respects. Its vocabulary is more limited and its Hebrew vocabulary much larger. This last phenomenon raises an interesting issue, for it is unlikely that Babai ibn Farhad was more learned in Jewish matters than his more articulate grandfather. In Babai ibn Farhad's frequent resort to Hebrew, and even Aramaic, words, one suspects his lack of knowledge of appropriate rhyming Persian synonyms. When added to the evidence presented by the content of the chronicle itself this phenomenon is yet another indication that the Jewish community of Kashan in Babai ibn Farhad's day was more closed off to outside, non-Jewish, influences than in Babai ibn Lutf's time. This was probably as much a result of the earlier persecutions as of the turbulent times surrounding the downfall of the Safavids.

Despite its colloquial garb, Babai ibn Lutf's chronicle attains occasional moments of poetic eloquence. On the other hand, Babai ibn Farhad's work has nothing in common with poetry beyond its versified appearance. Even this is deceptive, because very few of his lines live up to the elementary requirements of traditional verse, that is, of possessing meter and rhyme. Almost none of the lines of the KS scan properly and many have faulty rhymes.[25] The KA, although not free of these deficiencies, is closer to the classical historical *masnavi* genre it tries to emulate.

Both works have structural and chronological problems that require careful scrutiny. At times there is a close connection between these two problems. The KA has a group of chapters out of place, belonging to a different chronological unit.[26] As indicated above, the narrative of the KS is interrupted by a chapter written by another author presenting a different point of view. This chapter is followed by two *ruba'iyat* and one *ghazal*, also the work of Mashiah ben Raphael, praising the communal leader of his choice. The reason for the inclusion of Mashiah ben Raphael's work in the KS is never made clear.

The chronological sequence of events in both works is not readily apparent. It has to be disentangled from a mass of references to internal Jewish communal events and external events referring to contemporary Iranian history. Relevant Iranian chronicles are helpful in the latter task, but our Judaeo-Persian chroniclers' references to larger events of Iranian history have to be used with caution. A close examination of these references reveals not only inaccuracies but also the narrow and highly selective nature of these two works. They concentrate, primarily, on tales of persecutions; they tell us very little about the communal and economic structure of Iranian Jewry or about sociopolitical currents in contemporary Iranian history in general.

There seem to exist fewer manuscripts of the KS than of the KA attesting, perhaps, to an awareness among Iranian Jews themselves of the greater importance of the latter.[27] Nevertheless, despite the important differences in content and style between the two works, they are both unique and valuable historical documents that contain largely accurate information about little known Jewish communities. A careful study of the KA and the KS leads to the conclusion that they are serious popular reflections of the times in which they were written. They thus provide an interesting and much needed balance to views of Iranian history obtained primarily from official royal chronicles. Furthermore, they are testimonies for the history and culture of Jews in Iran, both of which need much more investigation. Specifically, they provide proof of the spiritual decline of Iranian Jewry, a decline clearly discernible as one goes from the KA to the KS. Some scholars have felt that this decline was pervasive in the environment of the late Safavid state; our evidence would certainly indicate this to be so.[28] The "blame" for this decline does not rest solely, if at all, on the Iranian Jews but should be seen as the inevitable reaction to the increasing political and religious turbulence that accompanied the unraveling of the Safavid state.

Notes

[1] There is one incident in the KS which can be placed sometime in 1694, soon after the ascension of Shah Sultan Husayn (August 6, 1694). It is described in chapter 4 of the KS. For the reasons behind the dating, see my "The Kitab-i Sar Guzasht-i Kashan of Babai ibn Farhad," *PAAJR* 52 (1985): 141–42.

[2] See the introduction to my *Iranian Jewry during the Afghan Invasion: The Kitab-i Sar Guzasht-i Kashan of Babai ibn Farhad* (Wiesbaden: Franz Steiner Verlag, 1990).

[3] "Les juifs de Perse au XVIIe et au XVIIIe siècle d'après les chroniques poètiques de Babai b. Loutf et de Babai b. Farhad," *REJ* 51–53 (1906–7).

[4] "Quatre poèsies Judeo-Persanes," *REJ* 44 (1902): 87–103, 244–59.

[5] Walter J. Fischel, "Toldoth Yehudei Paras bi-mei shosheleth ha-Sefevidim," *Zion* 2 (1937): 273–93; Habib Lavi, *Tarikh-i Yahudan-i Iran* 3 (Tehran, 1956–60); Hanina Mizrachi's selected Hebrew translations in *Toldoth Paras u Meshorereihem* (Jerusalem, 1966); a fragment transcribed in Persian script in Amnon Netzer's *Muntakhab-i ash^{c}ar-i farisi* (Tehran, 1971); Ezra Spicehandler, "The Persecution of the Jews of Isfahan under Shah ^{c}Abbas II (1642–1666)," *HUCA* 46 (1975):

331–56; and Amnon Netzer's "Redifot u-shemidot be toldoth yehudei Iran bi-me'ah ha-17," *Pe'amim* 6 (1980): 35–56.

⁶ *Iranian Jewry's Hour of Peril and Heroism* (New York and Jerusalem, 1987) and note 2 above.

⁷ *Iranian Jewry*, chap. 4, note 7.

⁸ *Iranian Jewry's Hour*, 28–31.

⁹ Ibid., 31, 37–39, 44–45.

¹⁰ Ibid., 56–58, 80ff., 115–16, Appendix A, Appendix C, note 12.

¹¹ Ibid., 59–61, Appendix B.

¹² Ibid., 93–94.

¹³ On the persecution of the Armenians, see the chronicle of Arakel of Tabriz, *Livre d'Histoires*, translated by M. I. Brosset in *Collection d'Historiens Armeniens* 1 (St. Petersburg, 1874–76). As for the persecution of Zoroastrians at this time, we lack direct evidence. However, their lowly condition always made them primary targets of persecutions. See Moreen, "The Status of Religious Minorities in Safavid Iran Between 1617 and 1661," *JNES* 40 (1981): 119–34.

¹⁴ *Iranian Jewry's Hour*, 62ff., 149–52.

¹⁵ Ibid., 60–66, 102.

¹⁶ Vera B. Moreen, "The Downfall of Muhammad [ᶜAli] Beg, Grand Vizier of Shah ᶜAbbas II (reigned 1642–1666)," *JQR* 72 (1981): 81–99.

¹⁷ See note 7 above.

¹⁸ *Iranian Jewry's Hour*, 23–25.

¹⁹ See the introduction of *Iranian Jewry*.

²⁰ Moreen, "The Kitab-i Sar Guzasht-i Kashan," 145–46.

²¹ *Iranian Jewry*, chaps. 7–9.

²² *Iranian Jewry's Hour*, 60 ff., Appendix C.

²³ *Iranian Jewry*, chaps. 11, 12, 14, and 14, verse 970.

²⁴ *Iranian Jewry's Hour*, Appendix E.

²⁵ Professor Herbert Paper suggested to me in a conversation at the AJS conference that it is inappropriate, perhaps even unfair, to compare the style and rhetoric of these two chronicles to those of classical Persian poetry. Babai ibn Lutf and Babai ibn Farhad certainly did not have the education of traditional classical poets, nor were they, in all likelihood, living among Jews more educated than themselves. Viewed in this light, their literary efforts are nothing short of miraculous, and they are humble testimonies of the authors' love for and acquaintance with Persian literature. Nevertheless, insofar as these two chronicles are written works in Persian, they belong to the corpus of Persian literature, albeit to its folk expressions. It therefore seems appropriate to me to point out, certainly not in order to condemn, the basic differences between these two works and the models by which they were influenced however indirectly.

²⁶ *Iranian Jewry's Hour*, 37–39.

²⁷ Ibid., 34–37.

²⁸ See the discussion of this view in Roger Savory, *Iran under the Safavids* (Cambridge, 1980), chap. 9.

3

MICHEL M. MAZZAOUI

Department of History, University of Utah
Salt Lake City, Utah

The Religious Policy of Safavid Shah Isma^cil II

THE MAIN FEATURES of Iran's Safavid history may be recognized as, first: the revolutionary period of the founder of the dynasty, Shah Isma^cil I; second, the period of consolidation during the long reign of Shah Tahmasb; and third: the golden age of Shah ^cAbbas. Before the establishment of the dynasty in 1501, there was a long period of gestation which some historians take as far back as Shaykh Safi al-Din Ishaq Ardabili, the Sufi ancestor of the family (*dudman*), in the mid-thirteenth century. And after Shah ^cAbbas, there was another long period of a century or so characterized by weakness and decline ending in 1722 with Shah Sultan Husayn.

Under the Safavids, Iran became a centrally united entity stronger than it had ever been since the Muslim conquest in the first half of the seventh century. Some writers have sensed a revival of pre-Islamic Sasanid times, expressing this phenomenon in such terms as *vahdat-i milli* (national unity) or "Aufstieg zum Nationalstaat" in the words of Walther Hinz writing in Germany in the 1930s, discredited by Vladimir Minorsky and more recently by Alessandro Bausani.[1] The concept of "national awakening" is best reserved for the Iran of the Pahlavis.

Aside from the Safavids, this idea of a "united entity" could be seen taking shape at the same time in other parts of the central Muslim lands: in the Ottoman Empire, in the Mamluk system of Egypt, Syria, and the Holy Cities of Arabia, in the Uzbek region of Central Asia, and under the Mughals in India. The system of government, administration, and culture in these four entities, as well as in Iran of the Safavids, show striking similarities: Turkic ruling dynasts and military establishments, Persian bureaucratic administration, and Arabic foundations of religion and Shariᶜah law. This post-Caliphal, post-Mongol, post-Timurid settlement of the Middle East question[2] breaks down under the painful pressure of an alien culture brought about by the colonial experience from 1800 on. Then comes Westernization, modernization, secularization, and the so-called passing of traditional society, which a large contingent of indefatigable political and social scientists (and not a few modern Middle East historians) have since been trying to analyze, interpret, and describe. They seem to have left very little room for the current and curious phenomenon of Islamic resurgence.

One major difference, perhaps the only one, between Iran and the other four states of the Ottomans, Mamluks, Uzbeks, and Mughals was the decision on the part of the founder of the Safavid system to opt for Shiᶜism. As soon as he came to power, Shah Ismaᶜil ordered that henceforth the Shiᶜi-ithnaᶜashari *madh'hab* would be the only one officially recognized, and the Jaᶜfari legal system would be applied. Many theories have been advanced to explain this surprising turn of events, none of which is completely satisfactory.[3] We are told that excessive force was used to implement the shah's order, and that Shiᶜi scholars from other parts of the Muslim world (from Jabal ᶜAmil in south Lebanon, and from Bahrayn, Qatif, and al-Hasa in the Persian Gulf region) flocked to Iran to participate in the new Shiᶜi renaissance.

The conversion to Shiᶜism (if such an expression can indeed be used within an Islamic context) was slow. In fact, it is said that Iran did not become predominantly Shiᶜi until the high Qajar period in the nineteenth century.[4] Attempts were made to spread Shiᶜism in Anatolia in the west and in Mavara'annahr in the east, but the Safavids failed in both endeavors. And in any case, the religious factor did not play such a dominant role in the continuous struggle between the Shiᶜi Safavids and their Sunni neighbors, the Ottomans in the west and the Uzbeks in the east.[5]

Internally, however, it appears that Shiᶜism was gaining ground during the reign of Shah Ismaᶜil and more so during that of his successor Shah Tahmasb. The transfer of the capital by Tahmasb from Tabriz, the city of the revolutionaries, to Qazvin, the city of the Ulama, is said to have been undertaken in part to consolidate Shiᶜi gains. There were other reasons for the move.[6] However, there are signs that during the short reign of the next shah, Ismaᶜil II, a policy was started to arrest the trend toward Shiᶜism and perhaps even to return Iran to the Sunni fold. The extremely short reign of this shah, as well as the opposition his policy encountered at the hands of already entrenched Shiᶜi interests, offered very little chance for the experiment to succeed. Ismaᶜil II's abortive attempt may at best be considered one more move toward Shi^ci-Sunni reconciliation—a recurring theme throughout Islamic history.[7]

The first Isma^cil died in 1524 after a reign of twenty-three years. His successor Tahmasb ruled over half a century, dying on May 14, 1576. A struggle for the succession immediately broke out among the shah's older sons. A faction of Qizilbash amirs (the traditional power behind the throne until Shah ^cAbbas put an end to their meddling in the affairs of state) put the shah's fifth son, Haydar Mirza, on the throne, soon to be assassinated by members of another faction. The confusion lasted several weeks during which time a powerful and ambitious daughter of the dead shah, Pari Khan Khanum, played a major, albeit not very clear, role. It was finally decided to pass over the shah's first son, a half-blind weakling (who later, nevertheless, became Shah Muhammad Khudabandah), and invite the second son who ascended the throne on August 22, 1576, as Shah Isma^cil II, already more than forty years old.

As a young man, Isma^cil demonstrated his capabilities in various positions to which his father had appointed him. He might even have been too ambitious for his own good. Thus Tahmasb saw fit to lock him up in a fortress prison away from the capital where he spent twenty years writing poetry and becoming expert in astrology among other things. It was to this prison that a Qizilbash delegation came and escorted him to the capital Qazvin where he was crowned. He ruled for only fifteen months and died mysteriously on November 24, 1577.

One of the few things secondary historians tell us about Isma^cil II is that, when he assumed power, he ordered the execution of all the male members of the family. One of his nephews, the future Shah ^cAbbas, miraculously survived, we are told. Almost nothing else is mentioned about this man and his short reign.

E. G. Browne calls him "the blood-thirsty Isma^cil," and describes his reign as "short but sanguinary." "He rivalled the most ruthless of the Ottoman Sultans."[8] John Malcolm, in an earlier age, says, "The short reign of this unworthy prince was marked by debauchery and crime."[9] An ambassador of Shah ^cAbbas, Uruch Beg Bayat, who turned Shi^cah Catholic and became better known as Don Juan of Persia, told his Spanish readers around the year 1600 of "a certain marked disquietude of disposition, and a tendency towards rebellion, attributable to the overweening ambition of the arrogant youth."[10] Roger Savory, who certainly had more to say about Isma^cil II than all the others, also stated that he "early served notice that his mind had been affected by his long imprisonment."[11] Only Marshall Hodgson, who probably never had time to read the sources, had something good to say about the man: "He evidently had some talent and a free-ranging curiosity."[12]

Therefore, to give this man his due in an attempt to rehabilitate him, it is best to have a closer look at the sources. Two of them deal in some detail with Isma^cil II's short reign: Hasan-i Rumlu's *Ahsan at-Tavarikh*, and Iskandar Munshi, *Tarikh-i Alam-Ara-yi Abbasi*. Both works are considered among the best and most authentic and authoritative of Safavid chronicles.[13] The account in both sources is factual, and in no way does it justify the negative value judgments in the secondary historians just quoted.

Rumlu, according to the Abd al-Husayn Nava'i text published in 1979, ended his chronicle with the Hijrah year 980, but then decided to extend it to 985, thus covering the death of Shah Tahmasb, the short reign of Isma^cil II, and the accession of Muhammad Khudabandah. In fact, he dedicated his chronicle, or rather this volume of it, to Isma^cil Mirza.[14] Munshi, on the other hand, was writing this part of his *Tarikh* in 1025/1616, about forty years or so after these events.[15] Rumlu's account is sketchy and hesitant, while Munshi's is "official" and full of details and rumors—sufficient to draw a more or less full picture of the life and times of the short reign of Shah Isma^cil II.

Both accounts try to make sense of the utterly confused and confusing three-month stretch from Tahmasb's death on May 14, 1576, until Isma^cil's enthronement on August 22. The attempt by Haydar Mirza, Tahmasb's fifth son, to seize power, and his almost immediate assassination in the palace, is described by Munshi in graphic and gruesome detail. It is basically a succession struggle between various contenders to the vacant throne. The role of Pari Khan Khanom requires a special treatment which should add considerably to our knowledge about the influence of ambitious women at the Safavid court.

Aside from this rather sad and hopeless episode was Isma^cil's slow, careful, but calculated march from the Qahqahah prison fort to the capital Qazvin, a distance of about 150 miles. After spending twenty years in jail (19 years, 6 months, and 21 days, according to Munshi), the forty-year-old prince was not apt to trust anyone. For weeks he stayed at a mansion outside the city until he was sure the situation in the capital was under control. The order to execute all possible contenders to the throne was done with deliberation—and in many cases for good reason. Several of the brothers, cousins, and nephews had either acquiesced to Haydar's accession or were plotting with other Qizilbash amirs to promote their own cause. (And by the way, lest we forget, the great Shah ^cAbbas himself had one of his sons executed and another one blinded.) Pari Khan Khanom, who at this point seems to have been on Isma^cil's side, survived the massacre of the princes only to lose her head during the next reign. Savory, in another of his works on the Safavids, significantly quotes the shah as saying, "The royal tents cannot be held up by old ropes."[16]

And then comes the most important development during Isma^cil's short reign, the one to which Hodgson refers when he says the shah had "a free-ranging religious curiosity." Already Rumlu was saying (this in the Nur Osmaniya manuscript used by Nava'i and not found in the Charles N. Seddon edition and translation of *Ahsan al-Tavarikh*, 2 vols. [Baroda, 1931–34]):

> Isma^cil cut off the land grants (*suyurghals*) to the *sadat* and ulama, and wanted the people to follow the Shafi^ci *madh'hab*. This caused the Qizilbash to be displeased with him.[17]

No further details are given in Rumlu's account.

Munshi, however, reserves a whole section on this religious issue, to which he attaches a related matter having to do with the specific Shi^ci words to be used in striking the new coinage.

About this time (*dar in asna*),[18] says Munshi, there was much debate among the people concerning sectarian differences. On the basis of the shah's conduct and various remarks he had made in private regarding Shi^cite beliefs, people generally regarded him as being weak in his attachment to Shi^cism and suspected him of being a Sunni.[19]

Isma^cil objected to the Shi^ci custom of speaking ill (*ta^cn*) of the Prophet Muhammad's favorite wife ^cA'ishah, whom even ^cAli had treated well.[20] He argued this matter with the resident theologian at court, Khajah Afzal Tarkah. "To abuse ^cA'ishah, therefore, is to abuse the Prophet; and the Shi^cite theologians have exceeded all reasonable bounds in this respect." Some of the ulama, especially Mir Makhdum Sharifi, sided with the shah in these debates. The shah also wanted to abolish "the ritual cursing of the three Caliphs: Abu Bakr, Omar, and Osman." "For their part, the Ulama in the main gave oblique replies, and tried to avoid a confrontation."[21]

At one time, the shah asked Bulghar Khalifah (the head of the Sufi establishment, *Khalifat al-Khulafa*): "O Khalifeh, if someone should speak ill of your wife in a public place and revile her, would you be annoyed or not?" "I would," said Bulghar Khalifah, and then went on to give an evasive explanation. "You are indeed a simple-minded Turk!" the shah exploded in anger, and gave a sign to his Sufi guards (*qurchis*) who beat Bulghar half to death. The shah appointed a member of the Ustajlu Qizilbash tribe in his place in an attempt to win back this group after decimating them for their role in elevating Haydar Mirza to the throne.

Mir Makhdum Sharifi appears to have assumed the position of implementing the shah's new policy in the mosque. "The people's suspicion of the Shah increased, and there was much talk. People censured the Shah for his action in private, and the loyalty of the Qizilbash toward him began to wear thin, but no one dared to breathe a word in public. Relations between the Shah and the Ulama in general deteriorated." At one point, Khajah Afzal Tarkah, according to Munshi, "made some excellent remarks to the effect that the Ithna-ᶜashari rite was the true religion and the beliefs of the Sunnis false, but he remained silent on the question of the ritual cursing and of hostility toward the Companions of the Prophet,"[22] which is probably how the entire issue would have ended.

The majority of the Qizilbash amirs, according to Munshi's account, tried to remain neutral in the controversy. Their position was that they would not dare question the sincerity of the shah as their *murshid-i kamil*. Ismaᶜil on his part cleverly used the occasion to test their allegiance by broadly hinting that they should help him get rid of Sultan Hasan Mirza (son of Khudabandah) who he feared was plotting against him. They did. Forty Qizilbash, two from each tribe, were dispatched to perform the cruel act. "At the same time," Munshi concludes his account of the religious issue, "in order to remove the suspicions of the people that his faith had been corrupted, the Shah turned on Mirza Makhdum Sharifi and placed him under arrest . . . and there was no further talk of religion in the Shah's assemblies."[23]

As regards the related question of the new coinage that was to be minted marking the beginning of the new reign, the shah objected to having the coins carry the formula: "There is no god but Allah; Muhammad is the messenger of Allah; and ᶜAli is the *vali* of Allah." He claimed that the name of God should not appear on the coins which are sometimes handled by non-Muslims. He suggested a line of poetry:

Zi-mashriq ta bi-maghrib gar imam ast,
ᶜAli-o-Al-i u ma-ra tamam ast;

which in Savory's translation reads:

Though there be Imams from East to West,
Ali and his family are all-in-all to us.[24]

This line of poetry did actually appear on Ismaᶜil's coinage with the shah's name and place of mint appearing on the obverse.[25]

Ruling only for fifteen months, Shah Ismaᶜil II does not allow the historian to pass final judgment on him and his short reign. Judging by the historical record, however, especially the detailed account in Munshi's *Tarikh-i Alam-Ara-yi Abbasi*, there appears to be hardly any justification to describe him simply as a "blood-thirsty" tyrant and dismiss his reign as "short but sanguinary"—in the words of the great E. G. Browne. Ordering the execution of the royal princes to guarantee the security of his reign, Shah Ismaᶜil II was following a practice long condoned by the rulers of the time. However, his reservations about certain Shi^ci practices, expressed so soon after he assumed power, were ill-conceived. It is possible that, having spent such a long time in confinement away from the capital Qazvin, he may have been completely out of touch with religious developments in the country. Ithna-^cashari Shi^cism in Iran was already three-quarters of a century old since his grandfather, Isma^cil I, established it in the land. The chances of reversing the trend were minimal.

However, the battle with the entrenched Shi^ci establishment was not yet over when the shah was found suddenly and mysteriously dead. Had he lived longer he might have found other ways to implement his religious policy, and the entire course of Persian history would, in all probability, have taken a totally different turn.

Notes

[1] Walther Hinz, *Irans Aufstieg zum Nationalstaat im 15. Jahrhundert* (Berlin and Leipzig, 1936). A Persian translation of this work, using the words *"vahdat-i milli"* in the title, appeared in Iran during the height of Pahlavi nationalism. For a criticism of Hinz's approach see a review of his work by Vladimir Minorsky in *BSOAS* 9 (1937–39): 239–43. Alessandro Bausani, *The Persians* (London: Elek Books, 1971), takes a totally antinationalistic approach.

[2] This is covered imaginatively by Marshall G. S. Hodgson in volume 3 of his *The Venture of Islam* (Chicago: University of Chicago Press, 1974), under the rubric "The Gunpowder Empires."

[3] For an introductory treatment see Michel M. Mazzaoui, *The Origins of the Safawids: Šī^cism, Sufism, and the Ġulat* (Wiesbaden: Franz Steiner Verlag, 1972).

[4] Bausani stresses this several times in *The Persians*, e.g., "The effective conversion of the mass of the Persian people to Shi^cism . . . probably occurred in the eighteenth century," 139.

[5] Adel Allouche discusses this point with relation to the Ottomans in his *The Origins and Development of the Ottoman-Safavid Conflict (906–962/1500–1555)* (Berlin: Klaus Schwarz, 1983).

[6] See Michel M. Mazzaoui, "From Tabriz to Qazvin to Isfahan: Three Phases of Safavid History," in *Zeitschrift der Deutschen Morgenlandischen Gesellschaft*, Supplement III, 1 (1977): 514–22.

[7] An early attempt at Shi^ci-Sunni reconciliation is reported during the Buyid period. It involved the well-known Shi^ci scholar al-Sharif al-Murtada of Baghdad. A more famous one occurred during the period of Nadir Shah Afshar. In contemporary Muslim Middle East history it is a recurring theme.

[8] *A Literary History of Persia*, 4 vols. (Cambridge: Cambridge University Press, 1902–24), 4:98–99.

[9] *The History of Persia*, 2 vols. (London, 1815), 1:515.

[10] G. Le Strange, trans., *Don Juan of Persia* (London, 1926), 129.

[11] *Iran Under the Safavids* (Cambridge: Cambridge University Press, 1980), 69.

[12] Hodgson, *Venture of Islam*, 3:38.

¹³ For other primary sources see the critical apparatus in Walther Hinz, "Schah Esma^cil II. Ein Beitrag zur Geschichte der Safaviden" in *Mitteilungen des Seminars für Orientalische Sprachen* 36 (1933): 19–99; and Hans R. Roemer, *Der Niedergang Irans nach dem Tode Isma^cils des Grausamen, 1577–1581* (Würzburg, 1939). Roemer's reference to Isma^cil II in the title of his book is in conformity with other writers mentioned earlier in this discussion. More so is Hinz's final judgment (p. 98): "Voll Misstrauen und Grausamkeit, Hass und Mordlust, Goldgier und Rauschsucht, Geiz und Geilheit und Heuchelei und erbarmungslose Harte: ein Spielball wuster Leidenschaften, so erscheint uns der Mensch Esma^cil."

¹⁴ Hasan-i Rumlu, *Ahsan al-Tavarikh*, ed. ^cAbd al-Husayn Nava'i (Tehran: Intisharat-i Babak, 1357/1979). The relevant sections are pp. 598–658.

¹⁵ Eskander Beg Monshi [Iskandar Munshi], *History of Shah ^cAbbas the Great* (*Tarik-e ^cAlamara-ye ^cAbbasi*), trans. Roger M. Savory, 2 vols. (Persian Heritage Series, 28) (Boulder, Colo.: Westview Press, 1979). A third volume, an index to Savory's translation, compiled by Renée Bernhard, has also been published (New York: Bibliotheca Persica, 1986). Savory's translation, used throughout in this paper, has been closely compared with the original text, edited by Iraj Afshar (Tehran: Intisharat-i Amir Kabir, 2 vols., 1350/1972). The relevant sections on Isma^cil II are: Savory, 1:283–330; Afshar, 1:192–221. (See also my review of Savory's translation in *JAOS* 102 [1982]: 382–86.)

¹⁶ Roger M. Savory, "Safavid Persia" in *Cambridge History of Islam* (Cambridge: Cambridge University Press, 1970), 1:410. No reference to the original source is given here.

¹⁷ Rumlu, *Ahsan al-Tavarikh*, 647.

¹⁸ No specific date is given.

¹⁹ Savory's translation, 317; Afshar's text, 213.

²⁰ The reference is to the event when ^cAli defeated ^cA'ishah at the Battle of the Camel, and sent her respectfully back to Medina.

²¹ Savory's translation, 318.

²² Ibid., 319–21.

²³ Ibid., 323–24.

²⁴ Ibid., 324.

²⁵ For a reproduction of the coinage struck during Shah Isma^cil II's reign, with the suggested line of poetry, see Hinz, "Schah Isma^cil II," 82.

4
ROBERT D. McCHESNEY

Department of Near Eastern Languages and Literatures
New York University, New York

The Anthology of Poets: *Muzakkir al-Ashab* As a Source for the History of Seventeenth-Century Central Asia

TAZKIRAH WORKS (and here I specifically have in mind biographies/anthologies of poets, although the term *tazkirah* may be applied to the biographies of other professions as well) offer a rich source for historians of the Islamicate regions. In these works is found the very stuff of social history, the fabric of life, the warp and weft of everyday existence, and sometimes the ragged edges as well. Here one reads of the hopes and disappointments, accomplishments and failures, and sometimes even tragedies of individuals whose common characteristic is an innate or developed talent for literary composition. These are men (and in this case they are all men) whose social standing may be that of a wealthy amir or *khwajah* or, equally, that of a drifter, living on others' generosity and his own talents. Many of the people whose biographies appear in the *Muzakkir* are men of humble origins and modest means, men of an urban middle class.

Besides the characterization of individuals, such works often contain digressions on events in contemporary society which bore on the poet's work or significantly affected his life.

The history of seventeenth-century Central Asia, or that part of it familiarly known as Mawarannahr, the region embracing the urban centers of Bukhara, Samarqand, Tashkent, and Balkh, remains largely unknown except to the Soviet scholars who have dealt with it in broad strokes or in detailed studies of aspects of its economic history.[1] But even in these works, the human side of history still remains obscured behind the study of institutions or the examination of economic relations and agrarian conditions. We have very little feel for the quality of the individual's life, his dreams, the horizons of his physical and intellectual world, and his experiences. It is here that the *tazkirah* literature assumes considerable, if not a unique, importance. These works were sociological studies of their times. Although their object was to explain in a formal and conventional way individual creativity rather than the social relations of individuals and groups, in fact, in the attempt to convey the creative factors and impulses in the individual's life, his relations with others and the part he may have played in society had necessarily to be accounted for.

One such work, which is very familiar to scholars of Central Asia,[2] is the anthology *Muzakkir al-ashab* by Muhammad Badi[c] Samarqandi.[3] Muhammad Badi[c]'s nome de plume was "Malih," or, in the preferred dramatic form, "Maliha."[4] Although his work has long been recognized as an important source for the intellectual and social history of late seventeenth-century Central Asia, it remains unpublished.

The Author and His Times

Muhammad Badi[c] Samarqandi was born in Samarqand in 1060 (1650). His father, Muhammad Sharif, was a mufti in the Dar al-Fatwa (Legal Decisions Office) in Samarqand. Muhammad Sharif was the major, if not the sole, influence on his son's intellectual development during his first thirty years. Through his references to his father, Muhammad Badi[c] hints at a psychological relationship in which the father was dominant, perhaps even overbearing. It is clear that he had decided on a career in judicial administration for his son and that Muhammad Badi[c] had not resisted. Muhammad Sharif was forty-two years old when his son was born. As far as we know he was the only son. Until Muhammad Sharif's death in 1080/1669 he kept his son at his side and under his thumb. He was the boy's only teacher, tutoring him in the standard subjects of logic, theology, astronomy, and Greek philosophy (*hikmat*). As the boy grew into a man, he also trained him in the techniques of fatwa preparation. However, it is curious that he provided no training in fiqh, a subject Muhammad Badi[c] would turn to only after his father's death.

About Muhammad Badi[c]'s childhood and young adulthood we are told almost nothing aside from his studies, a fact one may ascribe to the conventions of biography. But while his father was still alive, he became interested in and began writing poetry. Composing poetry offered both a social and literary outlet. It brought Muhammad Badi[c] into contact with other writers at the meetings or majlises which poets attended, often at the house of a well-to-do patron of the arts. His father apparently encouraged him or at least did not discourage him except for an admonition against writing the flattering and often calculatedly obsequious verse by which poets sought monetary compensation. Whether Muhammad Badiᶜ's recording his father's advice represents a kind of literary convention (like the saying frequently attributed to scholars who either refused or were refused patronage—"the scholar who consorts with princes is corrupted") or whether it indeed was given, he himself writes, "I followed his advice with only one exception."[5] That exception was a piece of verse written on behalf of ᶜAbd al-Karim Bi Nayman, governor of Samarqand in the 1080s and 1090s (1670s and 1680s),[6] a man whom Muhammad Badiᶜ frequently refers to as a great patron of the arts and a lover of culture, a fact all the more remarkable when viewed against the backdrop of Samarqand's failing economy and political troubles during this time.

When Muhammad Sharif died at age seventy-two, it was almost as if the son were released from a kind of intellectual bondage. He first attended to the funeral and burial of his father and tells us he read the service over his father's body and buried him in the "mufti's enclosure" (*muhawatah'yi muftiyan*)[7] of the Samarqand cemetery, on the former estate (*chahar bagh*) of the tenth-century theologian, al-Maturidi, who was also buried there. The muftis' enclosure was the final resting place of "four hundred and forty four" other muftis, according to Muhammad Badiᶜ.[8] It was an exclusive part of the cemetery, which besides being restricted to muftis, was only open to them with the permission of the leaders (*akabir*) of Samarqand.

Muhammad Badiᶜ immediately went to Bukhara and petitioned the khan for his father's office and salary, a request which was granted, he says, in toto. The khan of Bukhara (and Samarqand) at the time was Sayyid ᶜAbd al-ᶜAziz Khan, posthumously called the "Pilgrim Khan" for his *hajj* at the end of his life. He was the sixth Chingizid ruler of Mawarannahr of the Tughay-Timurid (Ashtarkhanid, Janid) line, established in Samarqand and Bukhara in 1599.[9] (ᶜAbd al-ᶜAziz Khan traced his sayyidship through his paternal grandmother, a descendant of the Eighth Imam, Muhammad Riza. She had lived in Mashhad with her father, Abu Talib Mirza, superintendent of the Razavi shrine until her marriage in 997 or 998/1589 or 1590 to ᶜAbd al-ᶜAziz's grandfather, Din Muhammad, during the Shibanid/Uzbek occupation of Mashhad.[10])

Having obtained his father's posts and income, Muhammad Badiᶜ then left Mawarannahr. On the reasons for his leaving, the contemporary Iranian anthologist, Muhammad Tahir of Nasrabad, writes, "Mawlana Badiᶜ Samarqandi . . . is highly regarded and has good relations with His Highness ᶜAbd al-ᶜAziz Khan and as a result was named to accompany the ambassador, Khwajah Niyaz, to Isfahan."[11]

Muhammad Badi^c himself gives no official explanation for the trip. In his autobiographical entry he writes, "That year [i.e., the year of his father's death, 1080][12] I resolved not to remain in Mawarannahr, especially Samarqand but to head for ^{c}Iraq and the Hijaz. I got as far as Isfahan."

He left Mawarannahr in the company of Hajji Faridun Beg (Sadiq) a.k.a. Hajji Baqa and Mirza-yi Mas^{c}ud (Mas^{c}uda) the son of Zamana-yi Zarkash (see below ff. 152a, 312b). Both were poets and the latter seems to have been a native Isfahani (f. 202a). Exactly when the party left Mawarannahr remains an open question. Muhammad Badi^c himself does not help resolve the matter despite his frequent use of dates. His own arithmetic either suffers from copyists' mistakes or was simply wrong at times. For instance, he says that he spent the first thirty years of his life under his father's tutelage and that his father died at the age seventy-two in 1080. This would mean he was born in 1050. But at the end of his own entry in *Muzakkir*, one page after the above date in the same manuscript, which is supposed to be the autograph, he writes, "This is 1100 and I am forty years old."[13] However, if we figure backward from the apparently indisputable fact that he wrote the main part of his work in 1100 (mentioned no fewer than seven times) one arrives at 1090 as the year in which he went to Iran, for he says he spent three years in Iran and then seven more years in Samarqand and Bukhara (by implication) before finishing the book.[14] In addition, he frequently refers to meeting new poets in Iran in 1090[15] while en route to Isfahan. Mirzoev, as cited by Gulchin-i Ma^{c}ani,[16] and perhaps relying on Nasrabadi, says Muhammad Badi^c left Mawarannahr as a member of the embassy in 1088/1677. The only reference in my notes to that date refers to a poet who left Mashhad for Hebron and Jerusalem in 1088 and met the author at Nishapur (f. 139b). It is conceivable that the poet, who happened to be Shah Shawkat, who would abandon his original plans and join Muhammad Badi^c, spent two years in Nishapur (i.e., until 1090.)

If 1090 is the correct date (and that would perhaps accord a little better with the circumstances of Muhammad Tahir Nasrabadi's life, especially his withdrawal from the coffeehouse scene to the Lunban Mosque where Muhammad Badi^c met him), then one has to account for the decade that elapsed between Muhammad Sharif's death and the trip to Iran. This I cannot do and there is nothing in his work to suggest that he returned to Samarqand for ten years to work before leaving for Isfahan. To the contrary, his own words (see above) state that he left Mawarannahr the same year his father died. Perhaps then the date given for his father's death is incorrect and should be 1090 rather than 1080. If so one could then place

Muhammad Badi^c's birth in 1060 which would conform to the age he gives himself in 1100. Muhammad Badi^c's three years in Iran (provisionally 1090–1093) left a very great impression on him and were, as he says, "the reason for this book."[17] He traveled to Isfahan by way of Mashhad, Nishapur, Bastam, Samnan, and Kashan, or perhaps one should more accurately say by way of the coffeehouses of those cities. In seventeenth-century Iran, the coffeehouses were the gathering places of the literati. Muhammad Badi^c, whose main interest in the trip from the outset, whatever his official duties may have been, was to learn about the literary life of Iran, made it a point to visit these hotbeds of cultural life. In Mashhad, he mentions poets he met in two different coffeehouses, both near the Razavi shrine.[18] And it was probably in a coffeehouse in Nishapur that he first made the acquaintance of Shah Shawkat of Bukhara, whom he characterizes as a "qalandar"[19] and whom others tended to think of as "eccentric" or even perhaps demented. E. G. Browne, citing the *Riyaz al-^{c}Arifin*, says that Shaykh Muhammad ^{c}Ali Lahiji "Hazin" recalls once seeing Shawkat wandering in the snow, with bared head and feet, and wrapped in a felt cloak.[20] One of Shah Shawkat's friends was Darvish Khalil, also a Bukharan. The two were inseparable, says Badi^c, and both wore the qalandar's felt cloak (*qaba-yi namad*). But the darvish was not simply eccentric. He showed a number of signs of mental instability (*majnun sifat*).[21] These men must have been a new experience for Muhammad Badi^c, and a marked contrast to the circle of acquaintances his father probably had. The attraction still must have been strong, for Shah Shawkat joined up with Muhammad Badi^c at Nishapur and traveled with him all the way to Isfahan. It may well have been he who led him to the coffeehouses in Nishapur, Samnan, and Kashan and introduced him to the regulars.

When the party finally reached Isfahan, Muhammad Badi^c took lodgings "outside the Jubarah (Chubarah) Gate near the qushkhanah (falconry)."[22] In the capital, the man from Samarqand gathered information on Iranian poets during frequent visits to the coffeehouses of the Maydan-i Shah district, especially the Agha Qiyas coffeehouse, the one he calls "the seventh coffeehouse at the Qaysariyayh end of the square (maydan)" (f. 65a). He also mentions a group of coffeehouses clustered near the Jubarah Gate (f. 268a). Another gathering place for poets was the "new madrasah of Shah ^{c}Abbas" (f. 233a). (I assume here he is referring to the Shaykh Lutf Allah mosque-*madrasah* on the eastern side of the Maydan-i Shah, although it was some seventy years old by this time.) There poets met to read and criticize their own compositions, and to discuss others' works (Muhammad Badi^c tells of hearing of other poets whom he never met at these salons) and to discuss other topics of interest including politics and religion. At

Kashan, Muhammad Badi^c tells us he had a good-natured argument with Baqiya (Baqi) of Kashan, a professional panegyrist and a disciple of Kalim, over the latter's Shi^{c}i beliefs (f. 47a). Elsewhere he tells of discussing the subject of "the madhhabs" (beliefs) and "mu^{c}taqadat" (doctrines) of "Uzbeks and Qizilbash" (f. 112b).

But the greatest influence on him during his stay in Isfahan was meeting the great Muhammad Tahir Nasrabadi whose famous *tazkirah* was one of the models for Muhammad Badi^c's own work. Nasrabadi was in his sixties and had long since established his position as the preeminent poet in Isfahan's literary circles. In Muhammad Badi^c's eyes, Nasrabadi was "the finest of the time, the most perfect of the age and the most eloquently gifted of all" (*afdal al-zaman, akmal al-aqran, ablagh al-bulagha, afsah al-fusaha*), attributes which he accorded no one else. As befitted the relative stature of the two men, Nasrabadi mentions briefly (in fairness, it should be said all his notices are brief) that Muhammad Badi^c "came one day to the mosque at Lunban and we conversed."[23] The Samarqandi, on the other hand, says he stayed in Isfahan "seven" months during which time he repeatedly visited Nasrabadi at the Lunban mosque. It was there that the latter had been conducting his salons ever since withdrawing from the coffeehouse circuit about a decade earlier.

Whoever's memory was the more accurate, the condescending Nasrabadi's or the courting Samarqandi's, evidence suggests that the two met more than once and that Nasrabadi was taken with the visitor from Samarqand, a region of the Persian-speaking world that must have seemed culturally rather remote at that time. Muhammad Badi^c writes that it was at Nasrabadi's salons that he met a number of Isfahan's leading poets, including Mir Ilahi and Qadi Mir Isfahani, and that he attended these gatherings with his road companions, the bohemian Shah Shawkat, Hajji Faridun Beg "Sadiq" (to whose poetry he devotes thirteen pages), and Mirza-yi Mas^{c}ud" (ff. 151b–152a). Nasrabadi in a noble gesture gave Muhammad Badi^c a copy of his complete divan which the latter unfortunately dropped by accident into the Oxus River during his return trip home.[24]

From Isfahan, Muhammad Badi^c retraced his route, having bid farewell to his "wild and crazy" acquaintance, Shah Shawkat, and his other offbeat friends. He arrived back in Samarqand three years after he left and began, in effect, a new career, combining his legal studies and practice with writing poetry, attending literary salons, and preparing the materials for his book. For seven years, beginning in 1093/1682, he tells us, he worked and studied in both Samarqand and Bukhara. For some time his place of work was in the Dar al-Fatwa, as an apprentice mufti apparently (he describes himself as one of the *talamidh al-fatawa*). It may have been in Bukhara that he studied Arabic, *fiqh*, *hadith*, and *tafsir*—subjects he tells us he now pursued (f. 221b). These all would have been to further his career in the judicial administration of the khanate of Mawarannahr. By 1100/1689, he had gained sufficient experience and qualifications to be transferred, presumably as a promotion, into the Dar al-Qada, the center of Samarqand's judicial administration and the location of the Shar^ci court. His patron there and the man who brought about his transfer was Qadi Mirakshah, a man of his father's generation and one of the leading officials and worthies of the city.²⁵

In addition to his appointment to the Dar al-Qada (apparently as a mufti if his training is any indication), Muhammad Badi^c sought and received a professorship at the Shibani Khan Madrasah²⁶ which was given him after his name was put forward by Amir Ibrahim Makhdumzadah.²⁷ My notes contain a copy of the passage which reads *"Amir Ibrahim . . . tadris-i madrasah-i maghfarat nishan Shibani Khan keh khud mansub budand bi-da^ci shafaqat kardand mansub gardidam"*—"Amir Ibrahim . . . who himself held the position of professor at the madrasah of the late Shibani Khan, offered it to the petitioner and I was appointed" (f. 221b).

We assume that the posts and the salaries that went with them allowed Muhammad Badi^c to pursue his first love—documenting the literary scene in Samarqand. His work in the judicial administration was not sufficiently remarkable to generate notice in the lists of outstanding jurists or scholars of that period.²⁸ But whatever recognition he failed to gain from his legal work is more than made up for by what he achieved through writing the *Muzakkir al-ashab.*

Muhammad Badi^c began work on his anthology after returning from Iran in 1093/1682. It was his experience in Isfahan that was the main impetus to his work, although the very fact of his trip and what he tells us of his itinerary strongly suggest that literature and literary experiences were what he sought from the outset.

Mirza Muhammad Tahir Nasrabadi, doyen of poets in Iran's capital, seems to have been the catalytic element in Muhammad Badi^c's decision to be compiling his material into a book. He would expand on Nasrabadi's own *tazkirah* which, as it was known to Muhammad Badi^c, contained "sections (*firqah-ha*) on ^cIraqi, Khurasani, Badakhshani, Hindustani, and Turkistani poets" (f. 152a).

Besides the inspiration of Nasrabadi's work, Badi^c consciously took as models Dawlatshah's *tazkirah* (*Tazkirat al-shu^cara*), the works of Jami, Asafi, and "other people who wrote about contemporary poets." He also looked to the work of a near contemporary, Muhammad Baltu (a.k.a. Mulla Sami) of Samarqand who had anthologized the poets of Mawarannahr from the beginning of the regime of ^cUbayd Allah Khan Shibani (r. as khan

1533–40) until the forced abdication of the khanate by Nadr Muhammad
Khan Tughay-Timuri in 1055/1645 (f. 8b).[29]

Work on the book went on for about ten years beginning in 1094 (f.
124a), but the bulk of the writing seems to have been done in 1100. The
author frequently refers to that year as "now" (ff. 33b, 36a, 37b, 56a, 218a,
221a, 238a). Apparently little if any writing was done in 1101, and then
between 1102 and 1104 (ff. 303a, 293b, 300b, 305b, 315a, and ms. 58,
ff. 245a, 248b) an annex to the book was composed. (The date of 1093
given by Gulchin-i Ma^cani in *Tarikh-i tazkirah-ha-yi farsi* for the work
is the numerical value of the book's title and corresponds with the in-
ception of writing.)

Whatever his acknowledgments of obligation to other anthologies, Muhammad Badi^c produced a work uniquely his own in format and narrative
idiosyncracies. Its general shape is that of a biographical dictionary with
a table of contents (ff. 13a-15a) followed by the entries themselves arranged
alphabetically by *takhallus* (pen name). In general, the author held to the
order and contents set out at the beginning, although one or two changes
do appear.

Each entry provides some information, more or less detailed depending on the author's knowledge or discretion about the life of the poet
and includes lines, sometimes pages, of the poet's work. This order is followed until the author reaches the end of the entry for Muhammad Baqa
Khwaja *ra 'is* Nasafi ("Samandar"). Then on f. 90a, ms. 4270, begins "The
Second Discourse," *Maqalah-yi Duwwum*. (There is no preceding section
called "The First Discourse" nor any other section with a similar heading.)
The subtitle of this *maqalah* is "The Events of 1097," i.e., November 28,
1685, to November 16, 1686. For the next ten folios (through f. 99b) a
detailed account is given of the struggle for Mawarannahr waged by the
khans of Bukhara and Khwarazm. At the top of f. 100a the anthology
resumes with the entry for "Sami^c" of Samarqand. According to my notes,
"The Second Discourse" appears in the same hand as the rest of the copy,
in this case ms. 4270 which is reported to be the author's autograph. The
table of contents does not include the interpolated "Second Discourse,"
however. From the standpoint of the work this section is not as out of
place as it first appears. Samandar, whose entry precedes, is none other
than Khwajah Samandar Tirmidhi, the author of *Dastur al-muluk* (ed. M.
A. Salakhedinova, Moscow, 1971), a work in the *furstenspiegel* tradition
of the *Qabus-namah*. The book's editor states that the section incorpo-
rated in the entry for Samandar in *Muzakkir al-ashab* is more or less identical with the twenty-first *bab* of the *Dastur al-muluk*. In the *Dastur* the
contents and style of the twenty-first *bab* appear even more out of place
than in *Muzakkir*. The section on the events of 1686 is rather clumsily

appended to a book whose chapters are otherwise devoted to ethical counsel for kings and include the subjects of justice, courage, a monarch's duties, ministers, love, and diplomacy. In the *Muzakkir* the "Second Discourse" interrupts at some length the biographies and verses, but is at least relevant to the entry under which it appears. The same cannot be said for the *Dastur*. One assumes that Muhammad Badi^c included the account not simply as an example of Samandar's creativity but perhaps more because it provided important information about Samarqand and the social and economic conditions of the city contemporary with his writing the *Muzakkir*.

The "Second Discourse" is not the only such digression interrupting the flow of the biographies. Further on, when he reaches the entry for Mulla Sharaf al-Din A^{c}lam b. Akhund Mulla Farhad b. Mawlana Nur al-Din, author (Sharaf al-Din, that is) of *Tarikh-i Raqimi*, a late seventeenth-century work of chronograms and historical data, Muhammad Badi^c provides his own addendum. His aim, he says, is to fill in missing dates and correct inaccurate ones. To the work which he describes as "beginning with the Imam-i A^{c}zam Zayn al-^{c}Abidin and continuing down to 1094," he adds seven folios (ff. 129a-135b) of "corrected" information from Ubayd Khan's conquest of Herat on 18 Safar 936 (which Sharaf al-Din dates to 18 Safar 934[30]) to the death of the Samarqand governor, an Uzbek amir and patron of the arts, Khushikah Bi, on 29 Jumada II 1102. (One gets the distinct impression that Muhammad Badi^c was a closet *mu'arrikh* and took delight in showing off his historiographical talents.)

He then returns to the original format, continuing on with Khwajah Shihab al-Din "Shihabi" of Miyankal and working his way to the end of the alphabet and "Yakta-yi Samarqandi" (Muhammad Baqi) (entry ending on f. 287a). The author then concludes with a "khatimah," ff. 287a-b. This appears to have been the completed work as it stood in 1100/1688–89. Up to this point 1100 is consistently referred to in the text as "now" or "this year." Indeed, in the entry for "Yakta-yi Samarqandi," the last entry alphabetically, he writes, "Now, which is 1100, I hear that he is wearing the clothes of a *qalandar*."

The remaining thirty-three folios of ms. 4270 are entitled "mulhaqat" (appendices). According to internal evidence, they were added between 1102 and 1104 and include discussions of unusual events and of poets who had come to the author's attention after he finished his work. The former include: (1) a case of litigation over control of the extensive Ahrari properties in Samarqand; (2) the economic hard times that had come to the cities of Mawarannahr, especially Samarqand, the author's home, since the voluntary abdication of the "pilgrim khan," ^{c}Abd al-^{c}Aziz Khan in 1082/1671; and (3) the mismanagement and embezzlement connected with the efforts of the Mughal ruler, Awrangzib, to renovate the Timurid necropolis of Gur-i Amir in Samarqand. (The Indian Mughals were descendants of the Timurids.) The latter includes the biographies of twenty-four new poets before it breaks off at f. 320b.

In working on the *Muzakkir*, I used three manuscripts from the collection of the Institute of Orientalism in Tashkent—nos. 4270, 2727, and 58. Besides being defective at the end, ms. 4270 is also missing an interior folio. Although the leaves are consecutively paginated, there is a one-folio lacuna between ff. 232 and 233. Missing is the conclusion of the entry for Mir Nur al-Din "Nakhat" and the beginning of Najat-i Sabzawari's biography. In the appendices, ms. 4270 ends with the entry for Mirza ᶜAbd al-Rahim b. Mirza ᶜIzzat Juybari. In ms. 58 (ms. 2727 is also defective at the end), the Juybari poet's entry is followed by eighteen more biographies arranged in no apparent order and interrupted four times by short digressions entitled respectively "min al-nawadir" (a rarity); "min al-ghara'ib" (an oddity); "min al-badihiyat" (an extemporaneity), and "min al-diqqah" (a nicety). These segments contain individual anecdotes about various people and things that happened to them.

Muhammad Badiᶜ used a variety of sources for the information in his work including Nasrabadi's *Tazkirah* (f. 199a, ms. 4270), the Persian translation of Abu Saᶜid ᶜAbd al-Rahman b. Muhammad al-Idrisi (d. 1015 C.E.) *al-Qand fi tarikh Samarqand* (more familiarly known as *Qandiyah*) with its twelfth-century continuation by Nasafi (d. 1142 C.E.) (f. 24a), and a certain *Riyaz al-shuᶜara* (f. 57b), (not the well-known work by ᶜAli Quli Khan "Walih," see Storey, 830–32). Muhammad Badiᶜ's principal research was not done in libraries, however, but in the field, and most of his sources were oral. He listened to poets tell their stories and recite their poems and he listened to them talk about others. He himself met most of the poets whose entries are included in his work. In all he gave listings to 204 poets. (This count is based on the three manuscripts used here. Gulchin-Maᶜani, perhaps just as a round number, says the Afghan manuscript he heard about had 250 poets, see 2:237).

Thanks to these personal contacts and, perhaps more so, to his willingness to go beyond the strict conventions of seventeenth-century *tazkirah* writing (using Nasrabadi's work as representative of the genre), his book contains a good deal of intimate information about his subjects, their careers, their families, their aspirations, and their idiosyncrasies. He did not set out, as far as we know, to produce a sociological study of the poets of his era. But his interests coincide in many respects with those of a latter-day social scientist and so, over and above his aim of memorializing for posterity the artistic achievements of his subjects, he also provides unusual insights into the social life of his time. One senses that beneath the exterior of the careful anthologist beats the heart of a gossip-monger or at least a good storyteller. Crime, sexual peccadillos, drug overuse, and common everyday venality and malice are all such a visible part of the record he keeps that it is easy at times to think of him as eavesdropper and voyeur, at least in comparison with the distant impersonal objectivity displayed by Nasrabadi in his work. Muhammad Badi[c] clearly loved a good tale, and in Samarqand in the 1680s there was no shortage of good tales to tell.

Composing poetry was not an art limited to the upper classes in Samarqand. Poetry was a pastime for all levels of society. Among the city's preeminent poets were members of such leading shaykhly families as the Ahrari, the Mirak Shahi, and Dahpidi as well as men who earned their livings as blacksmiths and grocers. What one does not find in the work, however, is much information on those whose poetic medium was Turkish. From what one can gather in the way of a fleeting impression here and there, Persian, at this time at least, was the predominant if not exclusive vehicle for poetic creativity in Samarqand. For example, one poet, a *qadi*-judge from Afarinkent, was described as a good speaker of Turkish (f. 46b) as if this was a somewhat unusual phenomenon. Two other poets, "Masrur" (Mulla [c]Iwad Beg Nayman) (f. 197a) and "[c]Unwan" ([c]Ibad Allah, a Khalaj Turk) (f. 154b) were of Turkish origin, but nothing is said of their proficiency in Turkish or whether they did any composition in the language. Although others may also have been equally fluent in both Persian and Uzbek Turkish, there is hardly a trace of a Turkish element in either the names or the careers (the military being a predominantly Turkish profession at this time) of his subjects.[31] Where the Turkish element does appear is in the form of the patrons who sponsored and encouraged the Persian literary tradition, men like [c]Abd al-Karim Nayman and Khushikah Bi *ataliq*.

In the *Muzakkir al-ashab*, the 150-odd Mawarannahrid poets (mostly from Samarqand but representing Bukhara, Balkh, Tashkent, Nasaf, Shahr-i Sabz, and Hisar as well) worked at some thirty-eight different professions. This excludes the professionally unemployed—the qalandars and dervishes. It is difficult to estimate the number of poets who could actually support themselves through poetry. Only one, Nu'ayma of Bukhara, appears to have been a professional panegyrist (f. 230a). He worked at [c]Abd al-[c]Aziz Khan's court, although it is not known how long he held the position. On the other hand, we do have some idea of the number of poets who may have been appointed to government jobs because of their accomplishments in literature. Certainly jobs requiring appointment or confirmation by the khan are prominent among the careers followed by our poets. About one third of the careers mentioned by Muhammad

Badi^c are either in government service or, as in the case of a madrasah lecturer or waqf administrator, required khanly appointment.

In a forthcoming study, I will examine the careers and professions of Samarqand and Bukharan poets of the late seventeenth century and here would only note that employment in government or government-related work (such as education) was an important tool of patronage. However, it was by no means considered crucial to one's recognition as a poet to receive official patronage. Two thirds of the 204 poets anthologized in *Muzakkir* (both Iranian and Mawarannahrid) supported themselves without government help.

To conclude this article, I will focus not on the professions followed by poets but rather on the more general picture of society given by Muhammad Badi^c with special reference to three of the most visible aspects of the literary life of the time as depicted in the pages of *Muzakkir*. These comprise the style of popular religious expression, the structure of patronage, and the victimization of intellectuals by violence and drugs.

The Style of Religion

One of the areas of cultural life for which the *Muzakkir* is especially informative is that of sectarian relations and the content of popular religious practice. Conventional wisdom, drawing its conclusions from the portrayal of sectarian relations in the eastern Iranian regions found in politically motivated written sources, characterizes the formation of the Ithna ^{c}Ashari Shi^{c}ite state of the Safavids in the early sixteenth century as the critical moment in inter-Muslim relations in the region. From about 1500 on, this view would have it, the religious history of the Persian-speaking world was marked by a deep animosity between the adherents of Shi^{c}ism in the region, more or less that of modern-day Iran, and the devotees of Jama^{c}i-Sunnism in Mawarannahr, Afghanistan, and Hindustan.[32]

Without pursuing all the assumptions and implications in this construct, let us simply review the information that *Muzakkir* gives us about Shi^{c}i/Jama^{c}i-Sunni interplay in the region.

First, it is important to distinguish religion as an aspect of state policy, in which adherence to a specific doctrine is a test of political loyalty, from religion as a set of personal beliefs and practices within a family or community context. Muhammad Badi^c suggests such a distinction when he tells of meeting Mirza Sa^{c}id, a *munshi* from Kashan who worked for Shah Sulayman (the Safavid sovereign from 1667 to 1694). They met in the *munshi's* hometown and later at a coffeehouse in Isfahan. During their conversations, the two men discussed the "doctrines of the Uzbeks and Qizilbash" (f. 112b). The "doctrine (*mu^{c}taqad*) of the Uzbeks" is of course Jama^{c}i-Sunnism and that of the "Qizilbash" Ithna ^{c}Ashari Shi^{c}ism. "Uzbek" and "Qizilbash" are political code words signifying the two opponents in the long struggle for preeminence in the eastern Persophone regions (excluding Hindustan). In times of war or tension, the doctrine of the enemy was of course execrated and became a pretext for the atrocities each side visited on the other.

But this doctrinal polarization had little to do with the way in which people got along in everyday life, the level of personal tolerance or intolerance, or with the style of religious practice. For that Muhammad Badi[c] provides several invaluable insights, especially in how the Sunni-Shi[c]i polarity was perceived and acted upon in daily affairs.

Personal beliefs and the way in which they guide public practice or display are as variegated as human society. Badi[c], like any good observer, is interested in the apparent anomalies, the oddments that stand out and attract notice. His keen eye helps us understand the norms of his time and the limits of tolerance.

For example, there was a tendency, especially among the young, to question one's beliefs and to look for fulfillment through ways either neglected or, better yet, rejected, by one's parents' generation. The great Iranian poet and anthologist, Mirza Muhammad Tahir Nasrabadi, had a grown son, Mirza Badi[c] (pen name Hayat) whom Muhammad Badi[c] met while in Isfahan. During the Samarqandi's stay at the capital, Nasrabadi senior offered him hospitality and then asked his son to accompany the visitor from Mawarannahr when he left Isfahan for home. The two traveled together to Mashhad and during the trip discussed the Isfahani's religious ideas. According to Muhammad Badi[c], Nasrabadi junior held to "a kind of unitarianism" (*naw[c]i ittihad*) which "the Shi[c]is call Sunnism and the Sunnis call Shi[c]ism" (f. 58b). Unfortunately, we are not told what the principles of this "unitarianism" consisted of. A similar instance is recorded in a slightly different way in the course of the biography of the Mawarannahrid poet, "Mufid" of Balkh. Mufid's career took him from Balkh to Samarqand where he worked a while as a panegyrist (*wassaf wa maddah*) for the Dahpidi family. But his acerbic wit got him into trouble with his patrons and other Samarqandis and he was publicly denounced in the courtyard of the Yalangtush Bi Madrasah (perhaps the Tilla Kar Madrasah) on Rigistan Square about 1660 (f. 194b). He left Samarqand and returned to Balkh, but finding employment there either difficult or unfulfilling continued on to Hindustan in hopes of an appointment from the Moghul sovereign, Awrangzib. His wish was never realized, though, and he eventually wound up in Mashhad. There, the story goes, he grew his mustaches "longer than the limit," at which point he was asked "If you are a Sunni, why such mustaches and if you are a Shi[c]i why such a beard?" He responded, "I want to follow both sects" (f. 195a).

Tonsorial affectation is not, of course, uncommon as a device for communicating one's philosophic principles. What is interesting here is what the episode tells us about the convention—the somewhat unorthodox combination of conventions in this particular case—and the apparent tolerance, if not amusement, with which it was received.

In the regional context there were many popular beliefs, practices, and displays which bridged the apparent doctrinal gulf between Ithna ᶜAshari Shiᶜism and Jamaᶜi-Sunnism. These included the cult of ᶜAli and the cult of the *ahl al-bayt* (the famous "five" including the Prophet Muhammad, his daughter Fatimah, her husband ᶜAli, and their two sons, Hasan and Husayn); the celebration of the Passion of Karbala (f. 17b), and the special reverence for the tomb of the Eighth Imam, Imam Riza, in Mashhad. Although this site is often formally considered as quintessentially "Shiᶜite," it was a pilgrimage object of both Shiᶜites and Jamaᶜi-Sunnis.

Then, as if to underscore the complexities and anomalies that circumstances could give rise to, we have the case of "Darvish Adam Mashhadi," a man who was a puzzle even to Muhammad Badiᶜ. The darvish, "tall with blond hair and a ruddy complexion" (f. 24b), used to sit on a raised platform or bench (*suffah*) just inside the shrine of the Eighth Imam off the Khiyaban-i Payan Pay (near the Madrasah-i Pa'in Pa) "with his back towards the Divanah-i Taq and facing the back of the Takht-i Abdali" (f. 24b). He earned his living by casting lots for people in need of advice. What struck the visitor from Samarqand was that the (diminutive) length of his mustaches immediately proclaimed he was not a Shiᶜite. Muhammad Badiᶜ writes, "What I noticed about him was that like his mustaches his religion is not well defined. Nonetheless, he is a good conversationalist and a goodnatured man." The writer, perhaps to provoke a response he could use in his book, quoted a somewhat leading verse to the dervish:

With the infidel, Muslim (i.e., Sunni),
Zoroastrian and Shiᶜite we are one
From God's Paradise our doctrine comes

There is a play here on the word "mashrab" (doctrine) which has the meaning "mustaches" as well.

If he had hoped for some kind of ecumenical declaration he was disappointed, for the dervish reportedly replied, "Away with you, oh Sunni, all the people of the world have lost right religion and abandoned proper behavior."

Throughout his travels in Iran, Muhammad Badiᶜ had contacts with many Twelver Shiᶜis but never does any sectarian antagonism show through in his work. He speaks only of discussions and debates about doctrinal differences and makes it clear that the basic distinctions separating

Sunni from Shi^ci were well understood. Only where an individual's behavior blurred the distinctions or appeared as anomalous (as in Mirza Badi^c Hayat's and Dervish Adam's cases) does he show a need to amplify and explain.

Politically, the distinctions were more sharply drawn and the official stance less ambiguous. As an aside it is worth mentioning again that the Tughay-Timurids (or Ashtarkhanids), the sovereign family of Mawarannahr and Balkh throughout the seventeenth century, laid claim to sayyidship (descent from the Prophet Muhammad) as part of their official titulature and regalia. What is interesting is that the line of descent through which the claim to sayyidship was made joined the Tughay-Timurid genealogy only at the end of the sixteenth century when Din Muhammad (d. 1598) married one of the daughters of the administrator of the shrine of the Eighth Imam in 1590 or 1591. The administrator was a Razavi *sayyid*, a descendant of the Eighth Imam. Moreover, the first child of this marriage was born at Mashhad and named Imam Quli (Servant of the Imam). The second son, Nadr Muhammad, was the father of ^cAbd al-^cAziz Khan and Subhan Quli Khan, who were contemporaries of Muhammad Badi^c. This apparent contradiction, that the upholders of the Hanafi Jama^ci-Sunni tradition in Central Asia claimed sayyidship through the Eighth Imam of the Twelver Shi^cites, troubled neither the khans nor their supporters. What it seems to have done was enhance the status of the Mashhad shrine in the eyes of Mawarannahrid Sunnis, at least from a political perspective. (It was already deeply revered by the common man.)

On the other hand Jama^ci-Sunni politicians must have been sensitive to any charge of appearing to show favoritism to Shi^cites as a group. Although it antedates our period of interest, there is a telling anecdote in *Muzakkir* from the period of the Uzbek occupation of Herat at the end of the sixteenth century. In this anecdote a zealous Jama^ci-Sunni *qadi*-judge from Bukhara was shocked to see Shi^cites "dressed like Sunnis" enjoying the confidence of the Uzbek governor, Qul Baba Kukaltash. At first the *qadi*'s accusation of consorting with the enemy was laughed off but he eventually succeeded in forcing the governor to purge the Shi^cites (f. 52a-b). Here too the question of mustache length enters the discussion.

The interaction of Shi^cites and Jama^ci-Sunnis is only one aspect of religious life as portrayed in *Muzakkir*. The two related phenomena of asceticism and dervishism particularly fascinated Muhammad Badi^c. His middle-class upbringing and preparation for a conventional bureaucratic career probably heightened his interest in the unconventional ways of the dervishes. While traveling through Iran with the qalandar, Shah Shawkat, he had direct and intense exposure to the attitudes, behavior, and lifestyle of a *qalandar* who was thought fairly outrageous by his contemporaries. When Muhammad Badi^c writes about another poet, Mulla Baqa-yi Samarqandi, whom he describes as disposed toward dervishism and always looking for the "corner-sitters" and "niche-choosers" (neutral epithets for dervishes and *qalandars*) with whom he likes to make friends, the writer is also writing about himself. He too was fascinated by the nonconformist and, if his anthology is any indication, was constantly seeking out the dervish hangouts wherever he happened to be—in Mashhad, Kashan, Isfahan, Samarqand, or Bukhara.

His epitome of an ascetic, the Samarqandi poet Afkar (who at various times also used the pen names Imtiyaz, Ra^{c}na, and Afarin under each of which he claimed to have composed a divan), was called "the Ascetic" (Zahid) because of his outward display of "zuhd," ascetic piety. Muhammad Badi^c provides a reverential and very lengthy description of Zahid (ff. 15b-23a). (In a manuscript of 320 folios covering 161 poets, this is four times the average amount of space devoted to each poet.) The account concludes, incongruously and rather shatteringly considering the subject, with a matter-of-fact statement that Zahid-i Afkar was murdered in his sleep, his house burglarized, and his killer never found.

Muhammad Badi^c tells us that during Zahid's lifetime he used to be overcome by "God-agony" (*dard-i khudavandi*) which would so overwhelm him that he would sob and weep through the night. During the day, he practiced extreme self-discipline and abstention and shunned contact with worldly people, passing his time instead in solitary *dhikr*. He refused to sleep on a bed and was famous for having performed forty "forties" (i.e., forty days of seclusion, fasting, and bodily mortification). His favorite retreat was a cave outside Samarqand called the Cave of Ecstasy (*Ghar-i ʿAshiqanah*). According to the anthologist, it was from these experiences that his best poetry came. Although this pattern of devotion is a familiar one and replicates a pattern ascribed to the Prophet Muhammad himself, among the poets anthologized by Muhammad Badi^c it was very unusual and considered quite radical.

It was not the kind of practice necessarily associated with the *qalandar*/dervishes. Many of the people labeled "dervish" or "qalandar" by the author are not particularly ascetic. They are often unemployed or work at one of the street professions like fortune-telling in all its varied guises. Many lived by begging or off the food and lodging provided by the ubiquitous *khanagahs* which were founded and endowed to support such devotional practice.

Muhammad Badi^c also gives some valuable information, although slight, of the existence and activities of non-Muslims in the literary life of Mawarannahr. One poet, "Tibb-i Haziq ["The Good Doctor"], one of the Jews of Balkh," worked as a silk maker and also prepared tonics (*shurbat*) for illnesses. By the time the author added his addenda to *Muzakkir* (i.e., before 1104), Tibb-i Haziq had died of poisoning, whether self-administered is not said. Muhammad Badi[c] acclaims him as one of the outstanding poets of Balkh (f. 315b).

Another poet, also apparently Jewish for he lived in the Jewish Quarter of Samarqand, was Fattah (f. 178a-b). He is portrayed as a man with a broad knowledge of and respect for the Torah, the Gospels, and the Qur'an. He was well versed, according to our author, in the "abrogating religion of Moses" as well as that of "Ahmad" (i.e., Muhammad). He was a musician who sang the Psalms while accompanying himself on the [c]*ud*. He knew something of divination by geomancy and had a close relationship to the ill-fated ascetic, Zahid-i Afkar. In poetry he was a disciple of his own father. He had lived in Samarqand and Bukhara but was residing in Balkh when Muhammad Badi[c] wrote his work.

From the *Muzakkir*, a picture of the complexities and variations of religious affiliation and devotional styles emerges. It is a picture full of human touches and almost devoid of the doctrinal inflexibility which the more politically sensitive chronicles reflect.

The Structure of Patronage

Another aspect of the social life of poets on which Muhammad Badi[c] sheds much light are the demands and expectations of patronage. For the artist, getting a government job or patronage assignment usually required considerable mobility. The *Muzakkir* provides a general idea of the horizons of the world of patronage within which artists were likely to expect some compensation for their talent, whether in the form of a gift, a subsidy, or a job.

For the subjects of this anthology, the geographic horizons of the patronage world comprised the cities of Samarqand and Bukhara, the two most desirable places to be both from the standpoint of money and artistic stimulation. The city of Balkh was a close third and Tashkent a distant fourth. One must always keep in mind, of course, Muhammad Badi[c]'s loyalty to Samarqand, his hometown. In Mahmud b. Amir Wali's *Bahr al-asrar* written a half century earlier for the sovereign at Balkh, that city, not surprisingly, appears as the center of intellectual and artistic life. One undoubtedly would find similar examples for Bukhara.

For artists, their personal achievements, or often their failures, combined with the economic climate in a particular city, encouraged or required moving from one place to another. For some of our subjects, staying in one place overruled other considerations and they would accept unsatisfying positions in order not to move. One such case was Mulla Rahmat (pen name Rahma), a *divan* clerk in Samarqand. His father had clerked for three of the leading Nayman amirs of the mid-seventeenth century, Farhad Bi, Khusraw Bi, and Nazar Bi. Rahma himself was hired by the prominent Nayman amir and one of the great patrons of the latter part of the century, ᶜAbd al-Karim Bi the son of Khusraw Bi, when ᶜAbd al-Karim became governor of Samarqand. But the latter was assassinated (in 1084—see f. 251b, ms. 58) and Rahma lost his position. He drifted from job to job in Samarqand without finding employment to his liking. Eventually, he went to work for another amirid patron, Khushikah Bi, but had to move to Bukhara, much against his will, according to Badiᶜ. Most literary figures took mobility for granted and indeed hoped for it when it meant leaving a rural area for the city. The poet and chronogramist, Mawlana Sharaf al-Din, author of the *Tarikh-i Raqimi*, left his hometown of Andijan in the Farghana Valley to get an education in Samarqand. He stayed and was named to the post of *aᶜlami* (chief mufti[33]) of the army in Samarqand. Later, after the death of Mulla Baqi Jan Bukhari, he became *Aᶜlam-i Kalan* (grand mufti) in Bukhara (f. 123a). Although he remained loyal to Andijan and built and maintained a *masjid* there, he never went back.

A more peripatetic poet-scholar was Mawlawi Ibrahim, whose pen name was Ghubar. He studied at Balkh and then went to work for ᶜAbd al-ᶜAziz either in Maymanah or Samarqand before the latter became khan in 1055. On ᶜAbd al-ᶜAziz's accession, Ghubar departed for Hindustan. His leaving the khan's employ just at the moment of the enthronement strongly suggests some kind of conflict. Ghubar's literary talents also appear to have been less than outstanding, for he was unable to find work in India. He returned to Mawarannahr and was appointed by the khan to a lectureship (*tadris-i farjah*) at the Yalangtush Bi Madrasah in Samarqand. (The phrase Yalangtush Bi probably refers to the complex of two *madrasahs* on the Rigistan, the Shir Dar and Tilla Kar, both under one administration. Yalangtush Bi had commissioned and endowed both structures.) Later, "when hardship and famine beset Samarqand" (probably circa 1077–78/1666–68), he was transferred to Bukhara at his own request and was named to a lectureship at the Juybari Madrasah. He died there in 1092 (ff. 157a-b).

Mufid of Balkh was one of the most restless of the poets anthologized in *Muzakkir*. Having established his reputation at Balkh, he came to Samarqand to work for the Dahpidi family/Sufi order as their *maddah* or resident eulogist. He left Samarqand, after offending some of its more influential citizens by some verses that he wrote, and returned to Balkh. There he presented Subhan Quli, Balkh's sovereign, with a panegyric *qasidah* in the hope of thus securing a job. But as the poem did not interest Subhan Quli, Mufid kept moving, eventually reaching India, the land of promise for struggling writers and intellectuals. He made no more of an impression on the Mughal court than he had on the Balkh royal house and so drifted first to Kashmir and then to Mashhad. He was living there when Muhammad Badi^c was writing the *Muzakkir* (ff. 194b-195a).

Many of the biographical sketches tell of the poets' often frustrating and frustrated efforts to secure recognition and some kind of living allowance. The Mughal court was a kind of intellectual's America, a place where one's talent would be recognized and rewarded. In fact, from the evidence of the poets' lives, it proved very difficult to break into the circle of artistic patronage in Delhi. Mulla ^cIwad Beg Nayman, whose pen name was Masrur, received stipends from "amirs and padshahs" in Mawarannahr, according to Muhammad Badi^c, but he abandoned it all to go to Hindustan. There, unfortunately, he received no recognition whatsoever and left in disappointment for Mecca. En route, he died (ff. 197a-198a). Another figure who was unable to get employment under Awrangzib was Amir Jalal "Kitabdar" ("the Librarian" after the post he held under ^cAbd al-^cAziz in Bukhara) (f. 57a). In another case, two close friends, Khwajah ^cAbd al-Rahim, pen name Mun^cim, who had worked as *ra'is* (market inspector) in Bukhara, and Mulla Mani^c of Samarqand, a student at the Ghaziyan Madrasah in Bukhara, set off together to seek their fame and fortune in India. The former was appointed to a qadiship by Awrangzib, for which his stint as *ra'is* was good training. But his companion, Mani^c, never did manage to secure a position and was supported by Mun^cim until the latter's death (ff. 196a, 210b-211a).

The successful emigres, the ones who were able to get what were considered suitable positions, tended to be men like Khwajah ^cAbd al-Rahim whose training and experience were in the fields of law and the religious sciences, both in considerable demand. The cachet attached to a Bukharan education appears also to have been important, although other factors must have counterbalanced the *madrasah* background of Mulla Mani^c, for example. (See ff. 37a, 237a-b for similar cases).

Employment for literary figures, whether in Mawarannahr or India, was wholly dependent on the interests and needs of the prospective patron. In the *Muzakkir* we notice that Samarqand, Bukhara, and Balkh wax and wane as attractive destinations for poets as patrons emerge and disappear in those places. Although the great families—the Juybari in Bukhara, the Ahraris and Dahpidis in Samarqand, and the Parsa'is in Balkh—promoted and supported the arts throughout the seventeenth century, the figures who appear as great patrons are as often not from these families. Patronage appears to have depended more on individual interest and willingness to spend than on a sense of collective responsibility to support culture in one's home city. In Samarqand, in the latter half of the seventeenth century, such individuals included ^cAbd al-Karim Nayman and Khushhal Bi *ataliq*, both Uzbek amirs, and (Muhammad) Baqir Khwajah Juybari.

Besides employment in government and education which these patrons, especially the politicians, could provide, other means of rewarding talent were also used. One of the most common was the literary salon (called variously *majlis*, *mahfal*, or *ma^crikab*) over which the patron presided and during the sessions of which participants recited their new compositions, discussed and criticized others' works, and engaged in literary games and contests. (For similar assemblies attended by the author in Bukhara and Nishapur, see ff. 20a, 30a.)

One of the most popular tests of a poet's skill was the extemporaneous completion of a *ghazal*. Often the presider would recite a *matla^c* (the first distich or *bayt*) of his own composition and then give a prize to the poet who could compose the best lines completing the ghazal. The ghazal form required a single rhyme and the introduction of the poet's pen name into the *maqta^c* (the last distich). At one such contest, Baqir Khwajah Juybari is said to have distributed 270,000 tangas in prizes (f. 58a).

Muhammad Badi^c tells of a salon he himself attended presided over by ^cAbd al-Karim Nayman. It was a beautiful spring day and the session was held out of doors in the courtyard of the *dawlat-khanah* (palace) built by Baqi Muhammad Khan (d. 1014/1602) in Samarqand. In honor of that spring, which had been given the name "banafsh" (the spring of the violets), ^cAbd al-Karim asked all those present to compose a *qasidah* in praise of the violet. Badi^c says he composed one but does not tell us whether prizes were given out (f. 22a). The celebration of Nawruz, the vernal equinox, was a regular time for public performances of poetry recitation. Khwajah Muhammad Yusuf Ahrari (d. 1063/1653) always held a majlis on Nawruz at which poets unveiled their latest creations.

^cAbd al-Karim Bi Nayman chaired a weekly *majlis* at Samarqand for *madrasah* students. At these salons he would have scholars propose a subject on which the students would speak extemporaneously. The student who did the best was given an unspecified reward and honored as "scholar of the week." These sessions were obviously important to the morale of a city in dire economic and political difficulties. Muhammad Badi^c adds to his description of these weekly sessions for students the postscript that although Samarqand was "outwardly in ruins" at this time, as the result of the Khwarazmian and associated nomadic depredations, "inwardly, thanks to [^cAbd al-Karim's] bounty and justice it seemed like Paradise" (ms. 58, f. 252a).

One of the indirect rewards which these salons could produce was salaried employment. The salons offered scholars and would-be litterateurs a regular opportunity to make an impression on a person with the power to recommend for appointment if not actually appoint. In Bukhara, ᶜAbd al-ᶜAziz Khan was in the habit of spending Friday afternoons at gatherings of poets and scholars (ms. 58, f. 241a), and it is probably safe to assume that these contacts provided him with a pool of talent for government appointments. There is no indication, as far as I have found, that these salons, even those attended by the most prominent and powerful figures in a city, were deliberately exclusive. Intellectuals sometimes stayed away from them for philosophic and moral reasons (to avoid the taint of consorting with amirs and the like), but admission seems to have been given to any who wanted to attend.

Distaste for contact with politicians seems to have been a sentiment rare among the poets Muhammad Badiᶜ includes in his work. For the most part, as far as one can tell, talent was what counted and what motivated a patron. Of course, as in any community, politics, professional jealousies, and irrational likes and dislikes no doubt influenced who did or did not receive patronage in individual cases. Since wealth was in the hands of a relatively small number of individuals—the members of the royal family, the Tughay-Timurids, the great Uzbek amirs, and the leading Tajik (Persophone) families—rather than under corporate management, the level of irrationality in the system was probably lessened.

There is one instance recorded in which urban chauvinism deprived a talented poet of employment, but this appears to be an isolated case. According to Muhammad Badiᶜ, a young man ("possessor of a mustache") named Muhammad Samiᶜ "Afsar" came to Samarqand. His family was originally from Andijan in the Farghanah Valley but had moved to Balkh where he was born and brought up. In Samarqand he tried to get the attention of the critics and taste makers (*ashab-i mawzun wa ashab-i mazmun*). But his efforts to gain recognition (and some kind of position) were obstructed, according to Muhammad Badiᶜ, by people who felt that one had to be born and raised in Samarqand to be considered a poet. In the face of this reaction, he ceased trying to make his mark and withdrew from the salons. If Muhammad Badiᶜ does not say he personally intervened on behalf of Afsar, he does suggest it. "When the writer of this book happened to meet him and when the matter became known to him, moreover since it was impossible to hide the fact that his poems were intricately wrought and witty, he came into the public eye" (ff. 33a-b). Implicit in this is the message that someone with literary ambitions probably had an easier time in his native town than did an outsider, but this is hardly a surprising finding.

What is of interest here are the mechanisms by which talent could emerge, achieve recognition, and obtain reward. While in many cases informal and subject to the level of interest of the wealthy at any given time, still the structure for promoting and supporting the arts remained fairly stable even in the face of extreme political and economic disturbances.

The Poet as Victim: Crime and Drugs

The seamier side of life in urban Mawarannahr is also depicted by Muhammad Badi[c]. Violent crime existed, and as it touched the lives of the relatively privileged who are described in *Muzakkir*, one must assume that it was endemic and widespread.

Mulla Ni[c]mat b. Mirza Atash was a murder victim. He was a well-educated bureaucrat and a *hafiz* who not only could recite the entire Qur'an from memory but knew all seven canonical readings besides. He had had a classical theological training in Arabic grammar and syntax, logic, theology, philosophy (*hikmat*), astronomy, hadith-reports, qur'anic exegesis, and jurisprudence. His special expertise, though, was "insha'," the polished literary style of the government clerk, in the study and practice of which he was especially diligent. When Beg Oghlu Khurd held the governorship of Samarqand, Mulla Ni[c]mat was appointed *ra'is*, market inspector. When the governor died, the mulla moved to Bukhara and worked as a *munshi* at the court of [c]Abd al-[c]Aziz Khan until the accession of Subhan Quli to the throne in 1092/1680. At that time, along with many other high-level bureaucrats he retired, or was dismissed, from government service. He moved into the Nadr Divanbegi Arlat Madrasah which stands on the east side of the complex called "Lab-i Hawz" (Reservoir's Edge) in Bukhara. There he returned to the study of the [c]ulum for about a year after which he withdrew into complete seclusion in his *hujrah,* cell, at the *madrasah*. One day, in 1093/1681, someone came to his room and found the door closed. When they opened it, Mulla Ni[c]mat's body was discovered, apparently murdered, though his room had not been ransacked nor any of his belongings taken. Muhammad Badi[c] suggests no motive for the killing nor does he indicate that anyone was apprehended (ff. 230b-231b).

Another victim of murder, the ascetic poet Zahid-i Afkar, was killed "on a Saturday in 1083/1672–73" at his home in the "Guzar-i Digrizan" (Foundrymen's Quarter) in Samarqand. In his case, the motive appeared to have been robbery. All his books, furniture, and some of his household utensils were stolen. Beneath his pillow, a ghazal written in his own hand and with allusions to murder in it was found. It proved of no value, however, in the hunt for the criminal, and no one was ever caught (f. 22a-b).

Criminal investigations appear to have been the jurisdiction of the *shahnah*, a police function first associated with Mongol rule over the

Iranian lands. The office is known to have existed in late seventeenth-century Bukhara. One poet, Nasha (Muhammad Salah), told Muhammad Badi^c, "Once in Bukhara I was arrested by the *shahnah* on a charge and brought before the khan. He ordered me executed" (f. 180b). Fortunately for Nasha, another writer, Mulla Qatli, intervened and the poet was set free. From this as well as references to the office of *ra'is*, it appears that the policing of markets and public morals fell within the latter's jurisdiction, while the office of *shahnah* (perhaps generally equivalent with *darughah*, *kutwal*, and *mir shab*) handled criminal and political cases and was subject to the khan's direct review rather than to the Shar^ci court to which the *ra'is* was subordinate.

Two of the 204 anthologized poets thus met with violent ends. It is necessary, however, to keep the issue of violent crime as a socially disruptive force in its proper context. Muhammad Badi^c lived in Samarqand, and if we assume that public fears and uncertainties are accurately reflected in the way in which he portrays dangerous or threatening phenomena, then murder was not a great worry. Or perhaps we should say random and inexplicable murder was not a great worry. Far more disturbing to the public safety and its sense of security and recurring throughout the *Muzakkir* as a kind of leitmotif was the unrestrained violence brought by the bandit Uzbek groups which periodically brought immense suffering and devastation to Samarqand. They too threatened murder, but for them there was not investigation or accountability.

Drug addiction and abuse is another social problem that affected the poets of the *Muzakkir*. Four of the poets anthologized by Muhammad Badi^c—Mulla Muhammad ^cAbid Samarqandi (Fida'), Hajji ^cArab Shah Balkhi (Agah), Khwajah Abu'l-Qasim (^cIzzat) from one of the oldest and richest families of Bukhara, and Khwajah ^cAbd Allah (Nadim) of Hisar-i Shadman, also from a respected family—had such severe drug habits that their behavior elicited comment (and depiction) in the *Muzakkir*. Three of these poets died of overdoses while the fourth, Khwajah Abu'l-Qasim, was still alive in 1100. From this, one assumes that moderate drug use was probably widespread.

Such an assumption is reinforced by another item of information from the anthology. Perhaps to control the sale and use of drugs for reasons of health and safety or simply as a revenue source, official drug centers called (euphemistically?) "Dar al-Bazm" ("the Banquet Hall") were found in every major city. These were places where opium and the condiments with which it was consumed were dispensed. (In one place, f. 228b, the Dar al-Bazm is also called *kuknar-khanah*, opium den.) In all the cases, the poets either lived at the Dar al-Bazm or spent a great deal of their time there. As each large city had such an establishment, one concludes that a sizeable constituency for drugs must have existed. In Bukhara, the Dar al-Bazm was located in the Labb-i Hawz district near the *madrasah*-mosque complex built in the late sixteenth and early seventeenth century by Qul Baba Kukaltash (d. 1598) and Nadr Divanbegi Arlat (f. 59b). In Samarqand there were at least two such establishments. One was at the Rigistan, the central square flanked by the three *madrasah*s built by Ulugh Beg in the fifteenth and Yalangtush Bi in the seventeenth centuries. It was from this Dar al-Bazm that Hajji ʿArab Shah's body was removed after an overdose (f. 32b). There was another near the "Timchah-yi Ab" (River Warehouse?). This one is alternately called "Dar al-Kayf" (after the drug bhang).

We have no information on how or whether such establishments were regulated. One assumes that the *ra'is* would have had an interest in such places. They appear to have been quite public and thus subject to official scrutiny. Their existence was tolerated but does not seem to generate much enthusiasm from Muhammad Badiʿ. The physical and mental damage caused by addiction and the financial cost of supporting a habit are underscored by the anthologist who still describes the plight of the victims with considerable compassion.

One, Khwajah ʿAbd Allah Hisari ("Nadim") who was familiarly known as "Dopehead" (Kuknari) came from a well-to-do family in Hisar-i Shadman whose antecedents were Dahpidi, the Samarqandi family of Naqshbandi shaykhs. He had traveled widely in India and "experienced its luxuries and wonders" (f. 228a). Muhammad Badiʿ tells us that he mixed there with all levels of society "high-born or low, rich or poor, healthy or sick, evil or good." Eventually he returned to Samarqand with a group of *qalandars* or "jaridahs" (from the word "tajrid" meaning solitude or celibacy). While begging in the streets of Samarqand, Nadim was picked up by some dandies (*zurafa*) who thought they detected a poet behind the beggar's chantings. They had him attend their salon at which his skill at poetry was revealed. At what point his problems with opium began is not said, but when he was not attending the literary salons he seems to have lived at the Dar al-Bazm.

Samarqand was the center of the Dahpidi family, and when the shaykhs learned that this poet and addict was a relative they took him under their wings. They made sure that he was supplied with food and clothing to which otherwise he seems to have been indifferent. They also tried to persuade him to move out of the Dar al-Bazm, going so far as to promise him all the opium he needed as well as as much *gazak* as he wanted. (*Gazak* appears to have been some sort of paste or condiment with which the opium was consumed.) They told him he could have his "kuk" and eat it too and so he accepted a *hujrah* room, perhaps at one of the *madrasah*s or *khanagah*s. But he was unable to break his dependence on the Dar al-Bazm and would frequently return there. As Muhammad Badi[c] puts it, "when he was not in his room, they knew where to find him" (f. 228b). The anthologist adds that the good clothes and the money given him not only by the Dahpidis but by others who recognized his literary talents were in turn given by him "to beggars and to the opium-dealers (*kuknar-dar*), the opium preparers or blenders (*kuknar-mal*), and others at the Dar al-Bazm" (f. 228b).

Despite his inability to break his dependence on the Dar al-Bazm, the Dahpidis looked after him to the bitter end. He died at the Dar al-Bazm and, after going for the body, Khwajah Awliya Dahpidi, in a show of familial respect, personally performed the ritual funeral washing of the corpse and its preparation for interment as well as the burial services at the Khwajah Abu Yusuf Hamdani khanagah outside the Chahar Rahah Gate.

Muhammad [c]Abid Samarqandi was another tragic case. His abuse of opium led to the deterioration of his mental faculties and ultimately to his death. He spent all the money he had inherited from his father on drugs. But, notes Badi[c], he was still a good poet (f. 177a).

Another poet and addict who squandered an inheritance was Khwajah Abu'l-Qasim. His father, Qadi Khwajah Shah, was a prominent judge in Bukhara, and his grandfather, Mirza Sharif, had been a leading scholar (*a[c]lam al-[c]ulama*) and one of the top specialists in legal theory in his own day. Among muftis, according to Muhammad Badi[c], who was himself something of an expert in this regard, "his [Mirza Sharif's] *riwayat* is a *sanad*," that is, his authority on a given matter is sufficient proof without reference elsewhere, "and they accept no other authority than his" (f. 59a).

The grandson made his mark as a poet receiving recognition (i.e., patronage) from "padshahs and amirs" while writing under three different pen names (Mukarram, Hatim, and lastly, [c]Izzat), the second of which (meaning "generous") he may have used while still having money to spend. Badi[c], however, remembers him for his extravagant style of living and his drug addiction. While his father was still alive he lived the life of a playboy and after his death squandered the sum of 120,000 tangas in a short time on high living and drugs. Still alive at the time the author was writing, he had been reduced to a pathetic and forgotten figure (f. 59b).

Muhammad Badi[c] depicts many other aspects of life in late seventeenth-century Mawarannahr. Here I have attempted to draw together some of the main issues in the lives of the poets he includes in his work. The reader can see from this selection the range of subjects and the kind of detail available in the *tazkirah* genre, always bearing in mind the differences of emphasis and observation that will distinguish one *tazkirah* from another. The historian interested in the social and economic history of the Islamicate regions has in the *tazkirah* a rich and little-used source of information.

82 / ROBERT D. MCCHESNEY

Notes

¹ For some general surveys see S. F. Tolstov et al., eds., *Istoriia Uzbekskoi SSR* (Tashkent, 1955), 1:391–446; R. Kh. Aminova et al., *Istoriia Uzbekskoi SSR* (Tashkent, 1967), 1:550–89; I. M. Muminov et al., *Istoriia Samarkanda* (Tashkent, 1969), 1:255–302; I. I. Muminov, ed., *Istoriia Bukhary* (Tashkent, 1976), 109–19. On specific economic aspects see M. A. Abduraimov, *Ocherki agrarnykh otnoshenii*, 2 vols. (Bukhara, 1970); also the numerous works of Ol'ga Chekhovich and Elena A. Davidovich. A good brief survey in English of the central concerns of Soviet orientalism vis-à-vis the social and economic history of Mawarannahr is Elena A. Davidovich, "Some Economic and Social Aspects of 16th Century Central Asia," *Central Asian Review* 12 (1964): 265–70.

² For example, in *Istoriia Samarkanda*, the work is cited three times. Also A. M. Mirzow, "Novy Istochnik po Literati Irana Sefevidskog Perioda," *Trudy Mezh Kongressa Vostokovsov* (Moscow, 1960), 2:269–93 for a general appreciation of the anthology.

³ For a description and references to other manuscripts than those used here see Ahmad Gulchin-i Maᶜani, *Tarikh-i Tazkirah-ha-yi Farsi* (Teheran, 1971/1350), 2:236–41; also C. A. Storey, *Persian Literature* (London, 1927–29), 1:825 under the title *Tadhkirah al-Shuᶜara-yi Subhan Quli Khan*; A. Semenov, ed., *Sobranie yostochnykh rukopisei AN Uz. SSR* (Tashkent, 1957), 1:320.

⁴ Muhammad Tahir Nasrabadi, *Tazkirah-i Nasrabadi* (Tehran, 1317), 443, gives the form "Malih." The "a" ending is the vocative form, i.e., "Oh Malih!" and was apparently the fashion in Mawarannahr at the time. Muhammad Badiᶜ uses the form frequently when giving the pen names of his entries. For example Sa'ib is Sa'iba, Qatiᶜ, Qatiᶜa, etc.

⁵ *Muzakkir al-ashab* (henceforth *MA*) f. 221b (ms. 4270).

⁶ *MA*, f. 222a. The beginning of his term as governor is uncertain. Muhammad Badiᶜ tells us he eventually fell from favor and, with his son, was executed. He then gives a chronogram which yields the date 1096 (*MA*, ms. 58, f. 252a-b).

⁷ The author writes, "They had walled in an area of the cemetery, making it an enclosure (muhawatah)" (f. 221b).

⁸ Ibid.

⁹ This sovereign clan is better, though less appropriately known by the names "Janid" and "Ashtarkhanid." For the reasons why "Tughay-Timurid" is more correct see my article, "The 'Reforms' of Baqi Muhammad Khan," *Central Asiatic Journal* 24 (1980): 76–77.

¹⁰ Hajji Mir Muhammad Salim, (*Silsilat al-salatin*), Bodleian Library ms., ff. 137a-b; Mahmud b. Amir Wali, *Bahr al-asrar fi manaqib al-akhyar*, India Office Library ms. 575, fourth *rukn* ff. 203b-204b. On Shahr Banu Begum's life, see ibid., ff. 205a-206b. She died in 1040/1630–31.

¹¹ Nasrabadi, 443.

¹² See discussion below.

¹³ *MA*, f. 221b.

¹⁴ For the entire context see ibid.

[15] See, for example, f. 66b where the author says he was at Bastam "during the holiday (Ascension) in Rajab 1089." Also f. 152b (author meets Aga Mansur cAshiq in Simnan in 1090) and f. 312b (the year 1090 when the author begins his travels "in the company of Hajji Baqa Bukhari and MasCuda son of Zamana.") Mirzoev's departure date of 1088 is possible but seems somewhat early. Perhaps 1089 would be better.

[16] Gulchin-i MaCani, 2:238.

[17] MA, f. 221b.

[18] MA, f. 25b (a coffeehouse opposite the lattice-work enclosure [shabakah] of the imam's tomb) and f. 181a (a coffeehouse near the "Payan Pay" section of the shrine area).

[19] MA, f. 139a-b.

[20] Cited by E. G. Browne, A Literary History of Persia (Cambridge, 1969 reprint), 4:265.

[21] MA, f. 277a.

[22] In the northeastern part of the city (see L. Golombek, "Urban Patterns in Pre-Safavid Isfahan," in R. Holod, ed., Iranian Studies 7 (1974): Studies on Isfahan, 1:43, fig. 3. V. M. Minorsky, ed. and trans., Tadhkirat al-muluk (London, 1943), 95, provides a line in the Safavid budget for the qushkhanah.

[23] Nasrabadi, 443.

[24] MA, f. 152a.

[25] MA, f. 254b.

[26] On the building of this madrasah and its endowment see R. G. Mukminova, K Istorii Agrarnykh Otnoshenii v Uzbekistane XVI v (Tashkent, 1966).

[27] The title "Makhdumzadah" at this time meant a descendant of the "Makhdum-i ACzam," Khwajah Kasani (d. 21 Muharram 949/May 7, 1542, according to the Tarikh-i Raqimi, Royal Asiatic Society, ms. 166, f. 129b). He was founder of the Dahpidi-Naqshbandi order and the leading spiritual figure of the first half of the sixteenth century in Mawarannahr. Amir Ibrahim may perhaps be identified with the Mir Ibrahim from Samarqand, the eldest son of Qadi Mirakshah. He is mentioned in Muhit al-tawarikh, (Paris, Bibliothèque Nationale, Blochet i., no. 472), f. 174b. He had been in Samarqand until 1105/1693–94 when he was transferred to Bukhara and appointed sadr.

[28] See, e.g., Muhit al-tawarikh, ff. 161b-168b; Mir Muhammad Amin-i Bukhari, Ubaydallah-namah, ed. and trans. A. A. Semenov (Tashkent, 1957), 289ff.

[29] I have yet to find reference elsewhere to this work (the title of which does not appear in my notes—except as "tadhkirah" which is implied in the context). I have also found no reference to another tazkirah of Mawarannahrid origin. Mulla Sadiq Samarqandi's Riyad al-shuCara, cited by the author on f. 51b, except in Istoriia Samarkanda, 291, where the source appears to be Muzakkir al-ashab. This work too is apparently a contemporary one. Both would be sources of major importance to the intellectual and social history of Mawarannahr in the seventeenth century.

[30] Tarikh-i Raqimi, RAS ms. Morley, 166, f. 117b.

[31] H. F. Hofman, Turkish Literature (Utrecht, 1969), sect. 3, vols. 1–6 is the most comprehensive survey of persons writing in Turkish in Mawarannahr. I have

scanned the work and find very little for the latter part of the seventeenth century. Random cross-checking of the poets in *MA* turned up no references in Hofman.

[32] Browne, *Literary History*, 4:24, speaks of "a barrier of heterodoxy . . . erected between the Turks, Egyptians and other Sunnis to the West and their fellow-believers to the East in Transoxiana, Afghanistan, Baluchistan, and India." A recent version of this view is given by C. E. Bosworth, "Ma Wara al-Nahr," *Encyclopaedia of Islam* (London: E. J. Brill, 1983) 5:859. "The long-term result of this warfare [between Safavids and Uzbeks] was the virtual sealing-off of Transoxiana from the rest of the Islamic world through the erection by the Safavids of this bulwark on their northeastern frontier."

[33] B. A. Akhmedov, *Istoriia Balkha* (Tashkent, 1982), 153, for a discussion of the office.

5
JOHN E. WOODS

Departments of History and Near Eastern
Languages and Civilizations, University of Chicago
Chicago, Illinois

Timur's Genealogy

THE ALLEGED ORIGINS and descent
of the Central Asian warlord conqueror Timur Barlas or Tamerlane
(1336–1405/736–807) are preserved in two Arabic genealogical inscriptions
in Gur-i Amir, the Timurid family mausoleum in Samarqand. The first is
carved on his nephrite cenotaph standing on the ground floor of the
building; the second, on his marble tombstone lying in the crypt below.[1]
Neither inscription is dated, but the former cannot have been executed
before 1425/828—twenty years after Timur's death—when the nephrite
block or blocks on which it was cut were brought to Samarqand by his
grandson Ulugh Beg (1394–1449/796–853).[2] Both attribute to Timur a
common ancestry with Chingiz Khan.

Virtually identical versions of this genealogy are also found in three
literary sources produced before 1428/831. The earliest of these is a short,
untitled, illustrated family tree of the Mongol and Barlas houses written
by a certain Husayn b. ᶜAli Shah, using both the Arabic and Uyghur
scripts.[3] The precise date of the work's composition is unknown, but
recent scholarship suggests that Husayn might have completed his
genealogy under the patronage of another of Timur's grandsons, Khalil-
Sultan (1384–1411/786–814) and perhaps even earlier.[4] In the year
1426–27/830, an anonymous author presented Timur's son Shahrukh with
another work, the *Muᶜizz al-Ansab*, a Persian continuation and adaptation
of the Chingizid section of the fourteenth/eighth-century Mongol historian
Rashid al-Din Fazl Allah's genealogical work, the *Shuᶜab-i Panjgane*,

greatly expanded to include the Barlas tribe, the clan of Qarachar, and the house of Timur.[5] Shihab al-Din ʿAbd Allah Bihdadini, better known as Hafiz Abru, also interpolated a section on the Barlas into the third and final recension of his history of the Timurids, the *Majmaʿ/Zubdat al-Tavarikh-i Baysunghuri*, written between 1427/830 and 1430/833. Although he refers to a "genealogical tree of imperial offspring" (*shajare-yi nasab-i awlad-i humayun*), he evidently consulted a number of texts (*nusakh*) in the preparation of this section which is nevertheless practically the same as the Barlas genealogy in the *Muʿizz al-Ansab*.[6] Finally, the collection of more extensive and varied information on Timur's putative ancestors was begun in 1419–20/822 by Sharaf al-Din ʿAli Yazdi for the Prologue (*Muqaddime*) to his official biography of Timur in Persian, the celebrated *Zafar-name*.[7] Completed in 1427–28/831, the seemingly legendary elements in Yazdi's Prologue are not substantiated by earlier writings, yet they merit careful scrutiny in studying the family traditions of the Timurid dynasty and the political ideology of the Timurid state.

In connection with the question of Yazdi's sources for the Prologue, it should be noted that several sections of it closely resemble or are identical with the corresponding parts of the anonymous *Shajarat al-Atrak*, said to be an abridgment of the lost *Tarikh-i Ulus-i Arbaʿe-yi Chingizi*, a history of the Mongol world empire composed by or for Ulugh Beg.[8] It is therefore possible that the Prologue of the *Zafar-name* and the *Tarikh-i Ulus-i Arbaʿe-yi Chingizi* derive from a common source, perhaps the lost *Tarikh-i Khani*, an anonymous Mongol history written in Turkish with Uyghur characters.[9] Whatever the provenance of the *Shajarat al-Atrak*, the relevant passages from it will be cited along with references to Yazdi's Prologue.

The genealogical data from the tomb inscriptions, Husayn's illustrated Chingizid-Timurid family tree, the *Muʿizz al-Ansab*, and Yazdi's Prologue are presented in table 1. The standard Arabo-Persian romanization of some of the names in the genealogy has been modified in order to reflect Turkish and Mongol usage where it can be ascertained. Italicized forms represent the namesakes of Timurid princes born between 1394/796 and 1426/830 (see table 3), and the names enclosed in square brackets do not appear in the epitaphs. After describing this genealogy and the legends associated with it, this essay will focus on the controversy surrounding their authenticity and significance in the secondary literature. Finally, the interpretations of these materials by three modern scholars will be reviewed in the light of additional evidence from the early Timurid period.

Like the Chingizids, the Timurids claimed aristocratic Mongol origins from Buzunchar or Bodonchar Khan Mungqaq ("the Fool"),[10] one of the three offspring of the miraculous union of the widow Alan-Qoʾa and the

TABLE 1
The Chingizid-Timurid Genealogy

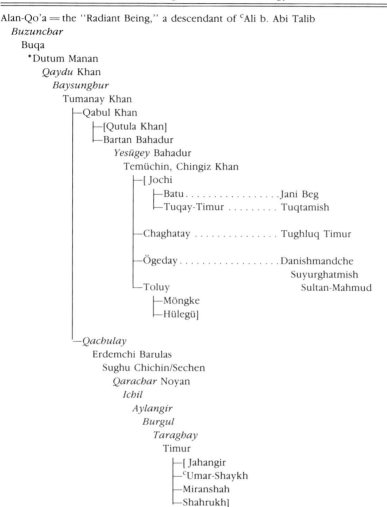

Alan-Qo'a = the "Radiant Being," a descendant of ^cAli b. Abi Talib
 Buzunchar
  Buqa
   *Dutum Manan
    Qaydu Khan
     Baysunghur
      Tumanay Khan
      ├─Qabul Khan
      │ ├─[Qutula Khan]
      │ └─Bartan Bahadur
      │   *Yesügey* Bahadur
      │   Temüchin, Chingiz Khan
      │   ├─[Jochi
      │   │   ├─Batu . . . . Jani Beg
      │   │   └─Tuqay-Timur . . . . Tuqtamish
      │   │
      │   ├─Chaghatay . . . . Tughluq Timur
      │   │
      │   ├─Ögeday . . . . Danishmandche
      │   │   Suyurghatmish
      │   └─Toluy   Sultan-Mahmud
      │   ├─Möngke
      │   └─Hülegü]
      │
      └─*Qachulay*
         Erdemchi Barulas
         Sughu Chichin/Sechen
         Qarachar Noyan
          Ichil
           Aylangir
            Burgul
             Taraghay
              Timur
              ├─[Jahangir
              ├─^cUmar-Shaykh
              ├─Miranshah
              └─Shahrukh]

"Radiant Being" of Mongol mythology. The Timurid versions of the stem
from Alan-Qo'a to Tumanay Khan common to both houses agree in most
respects with earlier Mongol sources such as the anonymous *Secret History
of the Mongols*, composed in the Year of the Rat (1228/625–26) in the
Mongol language, and the Persian historical and genealogical works of
Rashid al-Din Fazl Allah (d. 1318/718), *Jami^c al-Tavarikh* and *Shu^cab-i
Panjgane*. A striking exception to this statement occurs in Timur's tomb

inscription which associates Alan-Qo'a with the Virgin Mary by implicitly identifying her supernatural consort, who "appeared to her as a perfect man," with the Abrahamic Holy Spirit mentioned in the Qur'an (19:17), while openly declaring him a descendant of ᶜAli—cousin, foster brother, and son-in-law of the Prophet Muhammad. Fantastic when considered solely from the point of view of its historicity, this association nevertheless manifests a kind of spiritual reality when seen in the context of similar efforts throughout the central Islamic lands to reconcile Mongol and Semitic traditions after the definitive conversion of the Mongol conquerors to Islam in the second half of the fourteenth/eighth century. Moreover, it is worth noting that in so linking the houses of ᶜAli and Chingiz Khan, this claim combines the two most powerful notions of dynastic legitimacy current in post-ᶜAbbasid, late Mongol Iran and Central Asia.[11]

The Mongol sources themselves, however, are not unanimous in their presentation of the Alan-Qo'a-Tumanay Khan stem. For example, Buzunchar's son Buqa in Rashid al-Din is replaced by Barim Shi'iratu Qabichi in *The Secret History*, while, according to Rashid al-Din, Qabichi was the second son of Tumanay.[12] In addition, Rashid al-Din reports but then discredits another tradition that omits the Buqa/Qabichi generation entirely, claiming that Dutum Manan or Menen Tudun was descended directly from Buzunchar.[13]

They differ even more fundamentally in the question of Dutum Manan's progeny as table 2 shows. *The Secret History* inserts an additional generation, represented by Qachi Külüg, between Menen Tudun and Qaidu, making Qaidu the grandson rather than the son of the former as in Rashid al-Din. Timur's clan, the Barlas or Barulas, are then associated with two of Menen Tudun's seven sons, Qachi'u and Qachula, the latter evidently congruent to Rashid al-Din's Qachulay, the third son of Tumanay. According to *The Secret History*:

> The son of Qachi'u was named Barulatai. He had a big body and was ravenous at food. He became [the ancestor of] those which have the clan name Barulas. Because the sons of Qachula were ravenous at food, one named them the Yeke Barula and the Üchügen Barula and made [of them] those which have the clan name Barulas. The Barulas such as the Erdemtü Barula and the Tödö'en Barula were those.[14]

Thus, the traditions preserved in *The Secret History* establish a complex double origin for the Barulas or Barlas: the descendants of Qachi'u through Barulatai and the descendants of Qachula, subdivided into "greater" (*yeke*) and "lesser" (*üchügen*) branches. The Erdemtü and the Tödö'en are then considered septs of these two subdivisions. Both the Qachi'u and Qachula

TABLE 2
The Chingizid Genealogy in *The Secret History* and Rashid al-Din

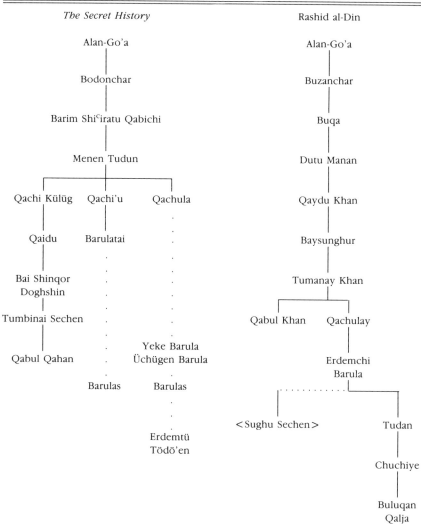

| The Secret History | Rashid al-Din |

Alan-Go'a — Alan-Go'a

Bodonchar — Buzanchar

Barim Shi'iratu Qabichi — Buqa

Menen Tudun — Dutu Manan

Qachi Külüg   Qachi'u   Qachula — Qaydu Khan

Qaidu   Barulatai — Baysunghur

Bai Shinqor Doghshin — Tumanay Khan

Tumbinai Sechen — Qabul Khan   Qachulay

Yeke Barula
Qabul Qahan   Üchügen Barula — Erdemchi Barula

Barulas   Barulas

<Sughu Sechen>   Tudan

Erdemtü Tödö'en

Chuchiye

Buluqan Qalja

lines parallel the imperial Chingizid house issuing from Qachi Külüg who is not mentioned at all in the works of Rashid al-Din.

For Rashid al-Din, the Barlas were uniquely descended from Qachulay, and he traces them through the following four generations: Qachulay— Erdemchi Barule—Tudan— Chuchiye (JWJYH)—Buluqan Qalja (QLJ).[15] While Rashid al-Din's Erdemchi and Tudan are clearly identical to the

Erdemtü[16] and Tödö'en mentioned above, Chuchiye (transcription uncertain) is not found in *The Secret History*. Buluqan Qalja and his son Erke, however, are attested in both works: according to *The Secret History*, Buluqan Qalja was appointed chiliarch by Chingiz Khan in 1206/602–603, and Rashid al-Din places Erke Barulas in the service of Chingiz Khan's grandson Qubilai at the time of Möngke's death in 1259/659.[17]

In the Mongol sources, Timur's ancestor Sughu Chichin or Sechen ("the Sage") is mentioned only by *The Secret History* as heading, along with his son Qarachar, one of the two delegations of Barulas attending the tribal assembly that first proclaimed Temüchin—the future Chingiz Khan—ruler of the Mongols around 1190/586.[18] Unfortunately, the work supplies no further information about which of the various Barulas groups he and Qarachar might have represented. Absent from Rashid al-Din's *Jami^c al-Tavarikh* and *Shu^cab-i Panjgane*, the name of Sughu Sechen has been attached by the unknown Timurid author of the *Mu^cizz al-Ansab* to the line of Qachulay as the son of Erdemchi Barule and brother of Tudan.[19] This affiliation is also found in Husayn's untitled Chingizid-Timurid genealogy, the Timurid tomb inscriptions, and the Prologue of Yazdi's *Zafar-name*.[20] Thus, except for the inclusion of Sughu Sechen, this part of the Timurid genealogical materials follows most closely and is corroborated by the writings of Rashid al-Din. Moreover, the fact that Sughu Sechen appears in both *The Secret History* and the traditions of the Timurid family suggests that the framers of Timur's genealogy were thoroughly familiar with the sources of Chingizid history in the Mongol language as well as those in Persian.

Sughu Sechen's son Qarachar Barulas appears in two other places in *The Secret History*: in 1206/602–603 he—along with his kinsmen Buluqan Qalja, Qudus, and Qubilai—received the command of a thousand, and, at the time of the Partition (*qismat*) before 1227/624, he was assigned to the four-thousand-man retinue of Chingiz Khan's second son Chaghatay.[21] Although the transfer of Qarachar's chiliad (*hazare*) to Chaghatay is confirmed in both of Rashid al-Din's works,[22] the information contained in the *Shu^cab-i Panjgane* is more detailed; it is also more confusing, since two men named Qarachar are included in the list of the Chingizid prince's major military personnel. The first is called Barulatay Qarachar of the Barulas people (*az qawm-i Barulas*), and the second is referred to as Qarachar Noyan of the Barulas people and the stirps of Buzunchar Khan, "The Fool" (*az urugh-i Buzanchar Khan Mungqaq*). It is unfortunately impossible to determine whether these names designate two distinct Barlas chieftains or whether they in fact refer to the same person, but the correspondence between Rashid al-Din's Barulatay Qarachar Barulas and Barulatai, the son of Qachi'u, in *The Secret History* should be noted. At any rate, in the parallel entry of the *Mu^cizz al-Ansab*, both are conflated into a single individual, "Qarachar Noyan of the Barlas people."[23]

In addition to the Barlas under Qarachar, Rashid al-Din also specified leaders and units of the Jalayir, Sulduz, and Sunit tribes in Chaghatay's suite. Furthermore, he believed that the formidable Chaghatayid legions of his own day were composed primarily of the natural descendants of this original corps, though he conceded that their ranks might have been swollen by other peoples as well. With one rather doubtful exception to be discussed later, however, neither he nor his successors furnish any further information on the ethnographic and social history of the Chaghatayid appanage khanate generally or the fortunes of the Barlas in it specifically.[24] As a result, these Timurid sources mentioned at the beginning of this essay must now be examined.

Sharaf al-Din ^cAli Yazdi begins the history of the Barlas in the Prologue to his *Zafar-name* with the account of Tumanay Khan's twin sons, Qabul and Qachulay, and the "vision" of the latter. One night, Qachulay dreamed that he saw four stars ascend successively from the breast (*jayb*) of his brother Qabul. The last of these filled the entire world with its brilliance, diffusing light to other bodies which sprang from the fourth star and continued to glow even after it had set. He then saw seven stars rise one after another from his own breast followed by an eighth, a great star which cast its light everywhere and from which emanated lesser bodies, each illuminating a different region. The next morning, he recounted this occurrence to his father Tumanay Khan who interpreted the first dream as portending the initial paramountcy of the issue of Qabul—presumably his sons Qutula Khan and Bartan Bahadur, his grandson Yesügey Bahadur, and finally his great-grandson Temüchin who, as Chingiz Khan, would subjugate the whole world and divide it among his sons. The second dream augured accordingly that Qachulay's descendant in the eighth generation would also be a great conqueror whose sons would share in his victories. Tumanay Khan then called on both his sons to swear solemn oaths in his presence, and he had it set down in Uyghur script that henceforth the sovereignty (*takht-i khani*) would reside with Qabul while Qachulay was to hold the military and administrative authority (*shamshir va hukm-rani*). This document, a covenant of dual kingship, was then stamped with the imperial seal and deposited in the khan's treasury for safekeeping.[25]

Yazdi is silent on Qabul Khan's fifth son Qutula Khan who actually succeeded his father and whose heroic reign as reported by Rashid al-Din must be symbolized by the first star issuing from Qabul's breast in Qachulay's vision.[26] Rather, he continues his narrative with the account of the sons of Qabul and Qachulay, Bartan Bahadur and Erdemchi, who reconfirmed the covenant of Tumanay Khan upon assuming their fathers' positions. In view of his command of the army (*sardari va lashkarkashi*), Erdemchi was given the honorific "Barlasi" and became known as Erdemchi Barlas.[27] The earliest attempt to explain the meaning of the Barlas tribal eponym in the Timurid sources, Yazdi's interpretation was repeated as late as the seventeenth/eleventh century by the ruler of Khiva and historian Abu al-Ghazi Bahadur Khan, who further glossed the term in Eastern Turkish or Chaghatay as "the person who marches at the head of the army."[28] Though the actual significance of the name of the Barlas tribe in Turkish or Mongol remains unknown, its constant association with military leadership in Timurid tradition is significant.

According to Yazdi, Erdemchi Barlas had twenty-nine sons of whom the most outstanding was Sughu "the Sage." Along with Sughu Sechen, however, the *Mu'izz al-Ansab* only mentions three others: Tudan, Yüge, and Bakalkay (?). The progeny of the latter two in the Timurid genealogical work spans seven generations and numbers nearly one hundred fifty individuals, many contemporary with Timur and his offspring.[29] A trusted advisor of Yesügey, Sughu Sechen was present at the birth of Temüchin and foretold his future greatness as Chingiz Khan just as had been prefigured in his grandfather's vision.

Yazdi's account of Sughu Sechen's death, following shortly that of Yesügey "in the Year of the Boar, 560," raises both chronological and evidential questions. First of all, in addition to the continuing uncertainty in dating many events in the early years of Chingiz Khan including his birth and the death of his father, is the fact that 560 (November 18, 1164–November 6, 1165) overlaps the years of the Ape and the Cock in the twelve-year Turko-Mongol cycle and that the nearest year of the Boar began in March 1167/Jumada I 562.[30] Secondly, as indicated above, according to *The Secret History*, Sughu Sechen must have survived Yesügey by at least fifteen years if he had in fact been present at Temüchin's first election in 1190/586. Yazdi also adds that Sughu Sechen left a number of minor orphans, but mentions only the names of Qarachar Noyan and a younger brother Tughachar.[31]

Yazdi's Qarachar Noyan was one of the first tribal leaders to declare loyalty to Temüchin and frequently advised him as Chingiz Khan on matters of state throughout his career of world conquest. When Chingiz Khan sensed the onset of his final illness, he summoned his sons and brothers along with Qarachar Noyan. After receiving the obeisance of Chaghatay, Ögeday, and Toluy—no representative of the house of Jochi was present—he praised the sagacity of the Barlas chieftain and enjoined his sons to follow his counsel and command. Chingiz Khan then sent for the original covenant of Tumanay Khan preserved in the treasury to which he appended a codicil investing Ögeday and his house with the supreme imperial office and bestowing Transoxiana and the lands adjacent to it (*va digar vilayat kih muttasil bi an'ast*) on Chaghatay. Chaghatay was commended to the care of Qarachar Noyan who was also made responsible for control of the affairs of the administration and the army (*zabt-i umur-i mamlakat va sipah*) for the rest of Chingiz Khan's life. To assure compliance with these stipulations after his death, Chingiz Khan had Qarachar Noyan legally adopt Chaghatay. Finally, Chingiz Khan ordered all present to ratify a second instrument recognizing these arrangements. This document was given to Ögeday, while the custody of the venerable covenant of Tumanay Khan was entrusted to Chaghatay.[32]

Yazdi accords Qarachar Noyan an important role in the Chaghatayid appanage khanate where he busied himself with regulating the important matters of authority and rule (*tadbir-i muhimmat-i saltanat va jahandari*) while Chaghatay Khan spent his time reveling and hunting.[33] To a certain extent, this view of Qarachar Noyan's position as guardian, intimate, and chief executive officer is borne out by remarks in other Timurid chronicles independent of Yazdi and his sources such as Mucin al-Din Natanzi's *Muntakhab al-Tavarikh-i Mucini* (completed in 1414/817) and Hafiz Abru's *Zubdat al-Tavarikh-i Baysunghuri*. In the first, Qarachar Noyan is said to have been given the command of the khan's household (*imarat dar khane*), while the fiscal administration (*vizarat*) was left in the hands of the Muslim bureaucrat Mascud Beg Yalavach in the time of Chaghatay's grandson Qara Hülegü. In the second, as generalissimo (*amir al-umara*), he is said to have undertaken the direction of matters of rule, law, and custom (*zabt-i umur-i mulk va yasa va yusun*) under Chaghatay Khan himself.[34] The *Mucizz al-Ansab* adds on the authority of "the historians of the Turks and Mongols" that he also carried out legal decisions in accordance with the code of Chingiz Khan (*vazic-i muchalga dar Ture-yi Chingizkhani*).[35]

Chaghatay's death in 1241/639 was followed by that of Qarachar Noyan the following year, although Yazdi maintains that he survived the khan by thirteen years, dying at the advanced age of eighty-nine in "the Year of the Hare, 652."[36] He left a number of sons of which Yazdi's Prologue and the *Shajarat al-Atrak* list Shirgha, Yesunte Mongke, Lala, Ildar (spelled Yilduz in both texts), and Ichil ('JYL, 'YJYL).[37] The *Mucizz al-Ansab* and Hafiz Abru name sixteen and nineteen of Qarachar Noyan's male offspring respectively, and then trace in detail the progeny of seven including Il, Qul, and the five previously mentioned.[38] It was therefore these seven clans along with the issue of Yüge and Bakalkay that made up the Barlas tribe in Turkistan and Transoxiana in the middle of the fourteenth/seventh century. Hafiz Abru further indicates that it was during the time of troubles that befell the appanage khanate after Chaghatay's death as a result of the wars of succession among the khan's sons and grandsons that the Barlas established hereditary domination in the region of Shahr-i Sabz or Kish south of Samarqand.³⁹ In addition to the house of Ichil, the *Muᶜizz al-Ansab* records more than seven hundred descendants of Qarachar's other sons.

The position of Chaghatayid generalissimo devolved upon Qarachar's son Ichil Noyan in the time of the khans Alghu and Mubarakshah.⁴⁰ After participating in the enthronement ceremonies for Baraq Khan in 1266/664, this Barlas chieftain left the Chaghatayid appanage khanate for Azarbayjan, seat of the Toluyid Ilkhan Abaqa (1265–82/663–80), in the suite of Prince Tegüder, another grandson of Chaghatay.⁴¹ In an article published in 1955, the Turkish scholar Ahmet Zeki Velidi Togan cited independent evidence for Ichil Noyan's move to the Ilkhanate from two passages in a very early manuscript of Rashid al-Din's *Jamiᶜ al-Tavarikh* copied at Baghdad in 1317/717.⁴² According to the first, "two trusty amirs of [the Barlas] came to [the Ilkhanate] with Tegüder; their names are [Ichil Noyan and] Kökechü Bahadur," and the second states in connection with Barulatay Qarachar Barlas, "one of his sons, a great amir, was in the service of Abaqa Khan who held him in great honor; he migrated⁴³ with Prince Tegüder [and his name was Ichil Noyan]." In other manuscripts of Rashid al-Din's work and in printed editions based upon them, the words in brackets have been omitted, while in the Baghdad manuscript, it appears that these lacunae could have been filled in by a second hand (see figure 1). As a result, it is difficult to know whether Togan's discoveries should be considered authentic corroboration of Ichil Noyan's career in Iran or whether they are to be accounted mere forgeries. In the latter case, the identity of the perpetrator of this hoax and his failure to adulterate other manuscripts of Rashid al-Din's *Jamiᶜ al-Tavarikh* as well would make a fascinating study in its own right.

According to the *Muᶜizz al-Ansab* and Hafiz Abru, Ichil Noyan had two sons, Qutlugh Qiya and Aylangir ('YLNKYR).⁴⁴ Hafiz Abru asserts, moreover, that it was Qutlugh Qiya and not his father Ichil who emigrated to the Ilkhanate and that many of his descendants remained in Ilkhanid service. Aylangir Noyan, on the other hand, is said to have stayed behind in Transoxiana where he honored the covenant of Tumanay Khan by swearing allegiance to the Chaghatayid khan Duva (1282–1306/681–706), succeeded to the post of his forefathers (*mansab-i imarat va madar-i mulki*), and inaugurated a thirty-year period of prosperity.⁴⁵ Neither Yazdi nor the *Shajarat al-Atrak*, however, supplies any information about the incumbent in this office during the hiatus of more than a decade between

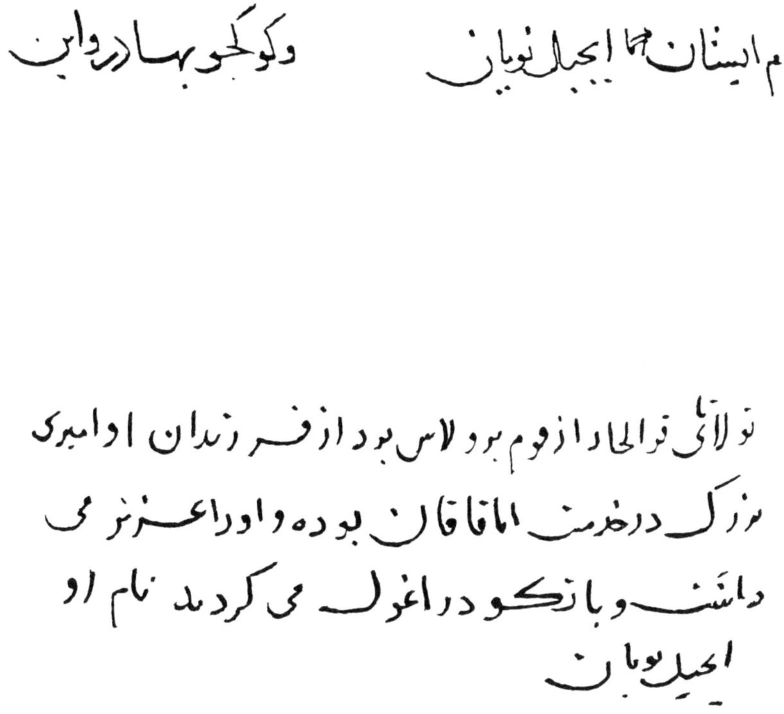

نام ایستان ۲۶ اچل نویان   دکوکجو بهـادردواب

نو لاأی نوالجاد ازموم برد لاس برد ازفـر زندان ادامیرک
مزرک درظمت الماقان بود ه واردا عـنز می
داشنـ و بانکو دراغول ـ می کردمد نام او
اچلدبان

FIGURE 1. Rashid al-Din. *Jamiᶜ al-Tavarikh* (Revan Köşkü, 1518, fols, 41b and 131a). Courtesy Topkapi Saray Museum.

Ichil Noyan's alleged departure for the Ilkhanate and the accession of his son. The account of Aylangir Noyan's tenure thus appears to have a very important literary function to insure the structural continuity of Yazdi's narrative on the Barlas in the Chaghatayid khanate and the claims of Timur that flow from it. Yet, without providing any further details about Aylangir Noyan, both texts proceed directly to the "usurpation" of the Ögedayid ᶜAli-Sultan, who raided the imperial treasury and destroyed the covenant of Tumanay Khan around 1340/740.[46]

Yazdi's Prologue concludes with a brief section on Timur's grandfather and father Burgul and Taraghay.[47] Aylangir Noyan had only one son named Burgul (BRKL, BWRKL) who in turn had two sons, Amir Balte and Amir Taraghay. The *Muᶜizz al-Ansab*, however, indicates that Burgul also had a brother, Chamish, some of whose descendants, such as Taghaybugha

and his family, would figure prominently in later periods.[48] Yazdi lauds
Taraghay's personal piety and comments on his association with his
spiritual guide, Shaykh Shams al-Din Kular or Kulal, an initiate in the
Suhravardiye religious brotherhood. Finally, he gives Taraghay's death date
as "the Year of the Rat, 762" (March 12, 1360–March 12, 1361/11 Rabi[c]
II 761–4 Jumada I 762).

In comparison to the material in the Prologue just examined, the body
of Yazdi's *Zafar-name* minimizes Timur's descent from Qarachar Noyan,
his blood ties with the Chingizids, and the part played by the Barlas in
the politics of the Chaghatayid khanate, raising questions about the ideological compatibility of the two parts of the work.[49] For example,
Qachulay's vision and Tumanay Khan's interpretation of it are mentioned
without allusion to the covenant between the founders of the houses of
Chingiz Khan and Timur. Later, Yazdi speaks of "The Ten Thousand of
Amir Qarachar" (*tuman-i Amir Qarachar*)—which he calls elsewhere "The
Grand Ten Thousand" (*tuman-i kalan*)—presumably a reference to
Chingiz Khan's original assignment of Barlas troops under Qarachar Noyan
to Chaghatay; in the *Mu[c]izz al-Ansab* and Hafiz Abru's *Zubdat al-
Tavarikh-i Baysunghuri*, this unit, headquartered in Shahr-i Sabz, is designated variously "The Great Chiliad" (*ulugh ming*), "The Great Ten
Thousand" (*ulugh tuman*), and "The Thousand of the Great Chiliad"
(*hazare-yi ulugh ming*).[50] Near the end of the *Zafar-name*, Yazdi recalls
simply that Timur was a ninth-generation descendant of Tumanay Khan
who traced his lineage through Buzunchar Khan back to Turk, the son
of Japheth. He adds that Timur's grandfather Burgul and his father Taraghay
had abandoned the exercise of political power, leaving it to their paternal
cousins (*abna-yi a[c]mam*) instead—in the middle of the fourteenth/eighth
century, Haji of the line of Yesünte Möngke was the Barlas tribal elder
(*agha* [sic]) in Transoxiana and the great commander (*ulugh nuyan*) of
the ten thousand of Shahr-i Sabz.[51]

Yazdi's major source, the *Zafar-name* of Nizam al-Din [c]Ali Shami
(completed in 1404/806), is even more reticent on these matters. After
recapitulating Chingiz Khan's division of personnel and territory, Shami's
official biography mentions Qarachar Barlas—competent, courageous, and
trustworthy—as commander of Chaghatay's choice military retinue and
as the noble ancestor of Timur. In turn, Timur's decision to "revive the
house of Chaghatay" in 1370/771 by enthroning the Ögedayid Suyurghatmish Khan is portrayed as the vindication of Chingiz Khan's farsight-
edness in commending his second son to Qarachar Barlas in the first
place.[52]

Other contemporary and near-contemporary sources lying outside the
early Timurid historiographical tradition serve up a potpourri of conflicting

information on Timur's paternal descent and socioeconomic status. Composed during the first decade of the fifteenth/ninth century, the travelogue of the Castillian envoy Clavijo and the political pamphlet of Archbishop Jean of Sultaniye concur that Taraghay and his son Timur were of noble birth, yet of modest means.[53] The North African scholar-statesman Ibn Khaldun (d. 1406/808), who interviewed Timur at Damascus in 1401/803, affirms that he was related to the Chaghatayids on his father's side.[54] Moreover, according to the Damascene polemicist Ibn ᶜArabshah writing twenty-five years later, it was said on the one hand that they lived as vulgar herdsmen lacking both reason and religion (*min al-faddadin wa ta'ifa awshab la ᶜaql lahum wa la din*) and on the other that Taraghay had labored as an impoverished shoemaker (*iskafan faqiran jiddan*). He subsequently concedes, however, that it was more likely (*asahh*) that Taraghay had in fact been a centurion (*amir mi'a*) in the army of the warlord of Transoxiana and one of the pillars of his government (*ahad min arkan dawlat al-sultan*).[55] Clavijo, Jean of Sultaniye, and Ibn ᶜArabshah all agree that, irrespective of his origins and standing, Timur had gained his early notoriety as a rustler and a brigand. The warlord conqueror himself is even alleged to have censored the accounts of some of his youthful exploits in the court chronicles ostensibly so as not to offend the credulity of their readers.[56]

Likewise, both official and unofficial works present a bewildering array of data about Timur's mother. Yazdi's *Zafar-name* only gives her name—Takine Khatun—and the *Muᶜizz al-Ansab* vaguely connects her with the Yasavuri tribal grouping settled in the hinterland of Samarqand.[57] Timur himself maintained that she was descended from the legendary Iranian monarch Manuchihr, and, while Ibn ᶜArabshah's research in Persian chronicles showed that she was a Chingizid princess, Jean of Sultaniye considered her of lowly origin (*de ville condicion*).[58] Thus, these sources contain little either to verify or refute the Timurid pretensions to aristocratic Mongol origins or sometime political prominence in the Chaghatayid khanate. Only a single anecdote related by Ibn ᶜArabshah resonates with the account of Qachulay's vision found in Yazdi's *Zafarname* and the *Shajarat al-Atrak*: Timur's grandmother (*jaddati fulana*), an accomplished soothsayer, had dreamed that one of her sons or grandsons—as Lord of the Fortunate Conjunction (*Sahib al-Qiran*)—was destined to conquer kings and kingdoms.[59]

Around the beginning of this century, the eminent Russian academician Vasili Vladimirovich Bartol'd became the first modern scholar to subject the Timurid genealogical traditions to scientific scrutiny. Though not questioning the authenticity of the genealogy itself, he focused his negative criticism of the traditions on the lack of credibility of two essential points:

the legend of Qachulay's vision and the covenant of Tumanay Khan, and the unsubstantiated claims advanced on behalf of Timur's ancestors under the Chaghatayid khans. The first Bartol'd dismissed outright as a fantastic and deliberate fabrication which he imputed to the untrustworthy "Uighur writers"—unable "to discriminate between the historical and the legendary"—who hoped to ingratiate themselves with Timur.[60] On the second, he wrote:

> Rashid al-Din refers to Qarachar only as one of Chaghatay's military chiefs but Timur's historians ascribe to him the role of an all-powerful ruler of the Chaghatay ulus. The same is said of Qarachar's son and grandson whom historians of pre-Timurid times do not even mention. It was evidently impossible to invent similar legends about members of the two following generations whose memory was still too fresh. Even in the official history Timur's father and grandfather are treated as private individuals. Nothing is said about when and how Hajji's ancestors came into power.[61]

It was thus Bartol'd's judgment that Timur was in reality nothing more than an opportunistic outlaw whose pretensions to aristocracy were utterly groundless.

In the 1955 article on Timur's genealogy previously mentioned, Togan took issue with some of his mentor Bartol'd's conclusions on the basis of a more thorough examination of the sources. Togan argued that evidence from the works of Rashid al-Din pointed to the genuineness of the Barlas tribal tree, but he declined to comment on the significance of the Qachulay-Tumanay Khan episode. In addition, he studied the marriage alliance patterns of Timur and his sisters before the death of Taraghay in 1360/762 to demonstrate that the family possessed a certain degree of respectability and influence in the Chaghatayid appanage khanate before the emergence of Timur a decade later. Finally, Togan tried to show with less success that Timur's family owned tax-free estates in Transoxiana outside their ancestral territories around Shahr-i Sabz and mentioned—without citing a source—possessions near Tashkent and in Khvarazm. The Timurid chronicles that Togan may have had in mind actually refer to the first group of holdings as Timur's privately purchased domains (*khasse-yi sharife, dihha-yi zar-kharide*), probably acquired after 1360/762.[62] The alleged Timurid lands in Khvarazm appear to have consisted in reality of Jochid territories over which Timur wished to assert Chaghatayid authority.[63] Nevertheless, despite the questionable aspects of Togan's scholarly judgment in this respect, his findings are generally confirmed by the appraisals of Clavijo and Jean of Sultaniye, and provide a useful balance to Bartol'd's uncompromising skepticism.

A major revision of the Bartol'd-Togan debate was contributed by the Japanese scholar Eiji Mano in a meticulously documented article published in 1976.[64] Mano inclined toward Bartol'd's position in characterizing Taraghay and Timur as minor personages in mid-fourteenth/eighth-century Transoxiana, while yielding to Togan's view that Timurids and Chingizids probably did in fact share a common ancestor in Tumanay Khan. Mano then went on to explain this anomaly by portraying Timur as a self-made man who was essentially indifferent toward his lineage, however lofty it may have been. For Timur, according to Mano, the true keystone of his power was his status as chief (*amir, beg*) of the nascent Chaghatayid-Timurid military elite along with his enthronement of Chingizid figurehead emperors and his marriages with Chingizid princesses, not in an inconsequential genealogy. In this connection, Mano emphasized the importance of Timur's use of the title *küragan* or *küregen*, "son-in-law [of the khan],"[65] throughout his career of world conquest. In contrast, his descendants, as Timurid sultans ruling a contracting empire, wanted and needed a splendid myth of origin to reflect properly the magnificence of the dynasty. Consequently, in the years following Timur's death, they ordered their court historians to dig out, dust off, and embellish the family tree and its associated legends.

The importance that Mano gives Timur's political marriages in legitimating the early stages of his rise to power is surely beyond question; however, a second look at some early Timurid materials casts some doubt upon his views that Timur lacked any interest in his family tree and that his genealogy and its traditions were solely the work of subsequent generations. For instance, as indicated previously, the similarity between the presentation of the legends in Yazdi's Prologue to the *Zafar-name* and the lost *Tarikh-i Ulus-i Arba^ce-yi Chingizi* logically implies a common source predating both. It was also well known that Timur was profoundly committed to the intellectual pursuit of the science of genealogy in general. Moreover, as the number of his progeny is said to have reached nearly one hundred, family record keeping acquired a real practicality for him,[66] and it appears certain that imperial birth registers were consulted in the compilation of later works such as the *Mu^cizz al-Ansab*.[67] Likewise, Husayn b. ^cAli Shah's illustrated Chingizid-Timurid tree also seems to have been produced either during Timur's lifetime or only very shortly after his death. In addition, following a pattern unique in Timurid history, thirteen of Timur's grandsons and great-grandsons born between the years 1394/796 and 1426/830 were given the same names as ten of their supposed ancestors in the Chingizid-Timurid genealogy (see table 1); they are listed along with their exact or approximate birth dates in table 3. Finally, Timur's diplomatic correspondence with his major rivals, a source as yet

TABLE 3
Timurid Princes with Turco-Mongol Ancestral Homonyms
1394–1426/796–830

[Muhammad] *Taraghay* (Ulugh Beg) b. Shahrukh, born 1394/796
Ichil b. Miranshah, born 1394/797
Qaydu b. Pir Muhammad b. Jahangir, born 1396/798
Aylangir b. Aba Bakr b. Miranshah, born ca. 1396/798
Baysunghur b. Shahrukh, born 1397/799
Burgul b. Khalil-Sultan b. Miranshah, born 1399/802
Buzunchar b. Pir Muhammad b. Jahangir, born before 1405/807
Qarachar b. Miranshah, born before 1405/807
Yesügey b. ᶜUmar b. Miranshah, born before 1407/809
Aylangir b. Pir Muhammad b. ᶜUmar-Shaykh, born before 1409/812
Buzunchar b. Pir Muhammad b. ᶜUmar-Shaykh, born before 1409/812
Qachulay b. Rustam b. ᶜUmar-Shaykh, born before 1425/829
Qarachar b. Suyurghatmish b. Shahrukh, born before 1426/830

not fully exploited, contains much valuable information on Timur's ideology of conquest that may be relevant to an understanding of his attitudes toward his origins as well as toward the Chingizid dispensation. To cite only one example here, he cryptically boasted in a letter to the Ottoman sultan Yildirim Bayazid, provisionally dated in 1400/803, that he, too, was "of the Ilkhanid dynasty."[68]

In order to arrive at this understanding, the reconsideration of these materials will be predicated upon two basic presuppositions. In the first place, it will be posited that the Timurid family traditions may be most productively viewed as normative and ideal, rather than narrative and factual. The legends of Qachulay's vision and Tumanay Khan's covenant are therefore to be taken allegorically as elements of a kind of Timurid constitution. In the second, it will be assumed that Timur's attitudes toward these traditions did not remain fixed, but rather shifted several times in the course of his forty-five-year career from 1360/761 to 1405/807. This period should be roughly divided in half: the first segment extending slightly more than two decades from 1360/761 to 1381/782; and the second, nearly twenty-five years from 1381/782 to 1405/807.

During the second decade of the first period, Timur basically imitated the Chingizid policies of his warlord predecessors and rivals in the devolutionary Chaghatayid appanage khanate. In this regard, Timur's conservative policies consisted of upholding Chingizid law, elevating Chingizid puppets, and wedding Chingizid princesses. Each of these policies will now be discussed in detail.

Both foreign and indigenous sources confirm Timur's staunch adherence to Chingiz Khan's codification of Mongol customary law—the

Yasa(q) or "Triumphant Ture" (*Ture-yi Qahire*)—as far as the administration of his empire was concerned.[69] This attitude was especially fitting
in view of the political setting of the Chaghatayid appanage khanate, a
bastion of Chingizid tradition whose founder had been reckoned the
foremost expert on the code.[70] The alleged role of Qarachar Barlas as a
Mongol legal executive has already been noted, and his descendant Timur
is reported to have publicly acknowledged his support of the Chingizid
law code at the very outset of his career. In 1360/761, he told a group
of Mongol officers from Mughulistan or eastern Turkistan in his act of submission to the Chaghatayid ruler Tughluq Timur Khan "obedience to and
compliance with the celestial edict and the Chingizkhanid Ture are ob-
ligatory and necessary."[71] He subsequently invoked the "Triumphant
Ture" in convening formal assemblies and in justifying campaigns against
recalcitrants who either failed to show proper respect toward or live in
accordance with this code.[72] Furthermore, rebels against Timur's authority
were also accused of having contravened the "Triumphant Ture" by their
treason, additional evidence of his efforts to buttress his authority with
Chingizid law.[73] The Timurid sources also attest to the persistence under
Timur and his successors of a separate system of tribunals (*yarghu*)
paralleling the Islamic Shariᶜa courts and staffed by a specialized personnel
to render decisions and administer justice in conformity with Mongol customary law.[74]

As a non-Chingizid commoner (*qarachu*), however, Timur himself
could not legitimately exercise direct sovereignty under the Chingizid dispensation. Consequently, he resorted to the same device employed by
other usurping warlords throughout the devolutionary Mongol world
empire, proclaiming in 1370/771 Suyurghatmish, the son of Danishmandche of the line of Ögeday, as figurehead khan. When Suyurghatmish
Khan died in 1388/790, Timur seated his son Sultan-Mahmud on the imperial throne in his stead.[75] As previously noted, Shami celebrated Timur's
conduct in this regard as springing from his desire to revive the house
of Chaghatay and thereby both to justify the trust that Chingiz Khan had
originally placed in his ancestor Qarachar and to demonstrate his gratitude
for Chingizid favors conferred upon his family. Later, in connection with
the warlord's seizure of Khvarazm in the name of Chaghatayid legitimacy,
Shami elaborated on this theme, quoting Qur'an 4:58: "God orders you
to restore deposits entrusted to you to their rightful owners." Indeed, the
unknown author of the *Muᶜizz al-Ansab* considered all Timur's far-flung
campaigns to have been waged under this banner.[76]

But Timur's figureheads were Ögedayids, an apparent contradiction
between his actions and his court chronicler's account of them. Moreover,
though Ögedayids had twice reigned in the Chaghatayid khanate before

1370/771, neither instance had been particularly auspicious. The first had been ᶜAli Sultan who rebelled against the Chaghatayid Esen Timur Khan around 1340/740, who "set foot upon the throne of the khanate in illegality and usurpation" in the words of Yazdi, and who is charged with having destroyed the covenant of Tumanay Khan.[77] Several years later in 1347/747, the Qaraunas warlord Qazaghan had enthroned Danishmandche, a descendant of Ögeday's sixth son Qadan Oghul and father of Suyurghatmish. However, he was deposed and executed after a reign of scarcely a year on the charge that he was not of the line of Chaghatay, and thus might have alienated the officers and men of the nomadic military elite of Transoxiana.[78] Timur's immediate reasons for resorting to a policy apparently fraught with such peril are far from clear, although its long-range implications were probably not lost on him.

In any event, content with the subordinate status of amir or beg, Timur observed this legal fiction in the protocols of edicts, in coin inscriptions, in the weekly congregational mosque sermons, and in statements of policy. Documents and dinars were issued by the command of Amir Timur, but on the authority of the khan, and his name was called out from the pulpits on Fridays after that of the nominal sovereign.[79] Indeed, the *Shajarat al-Atrak* insists that Timur always ruled in accordance with the covenant of Tumanay Khan.[80] Timur himself told Ibn Khaldun that he was nothing more than "one of the deputies" (*na'ib min al-nuwwab*) of Sultan-Mahmud Khan and that he acted only upon his orders. The sense of Ibn Khaldun's statement is echoed several times by Jean of Sultaniye[81] and by the Mamluk chronicler Ibn al-Furat (d. 1405/807), who characterized Timur's role as that of "guardian (*atabak*) of the king of the Tatars" and termed Sultan-Mahmud Khan Timur's "master" (*ustad*).[82] Finally, ᶜAziz Astarabadi whose history of Qazi Burhan al-Din, the ruler of Sivas, was completed in 1398/800, also recognized Timur's contentions, but remarked that Sultan-Mahmud Khan had in fact been turned out by Timur expressly to silence criticism of his own lowly origins and baseless claims.[83]

Cynical and sincere, these commitments were solemnized in a series of marriages between Timur and his descendants with Chaghatayid, Ögedayid, and Jochid princesses and were expressed in the title *küragan*. In 1370/771, immediately after the defeat and execution of Amir Husayn Qaraunas, Timur wed his rival's widow Saray Malik Khanum (the "Greater Lady"), daughter of the Chaghatayid Qazan Sultan Khan,[84] and in 1397/800, he married Tukal Khanum (the "Lesser Lady"), daughter of the Chaghatayid ruler of Mughulistan Khizr-Khvaje Khan, just before his invasion of northern India.[85] Moreover, during his lifetime, his sons ᶜUmar-Shaykh, Miranshah, and Shahrukh along with his grandsons Muhammad-Sultan and Ulugh Beg were also given Chingizid wives,[86] though before 1405/807,

Timurid archival, numismatic, and narrative sources attest the application of the title to Timur and Miranshah only.[87]

Thus, though Timur deviated neither in practice nor in spirit from the Chingizid policies and positions of the Chaghatayid amirs and warlords before him, his assumption of power was nevertheless portrayed by the Timurid chroniclers as more "legitimate" than theirs. Qazaghan Qaraunas, his son ᶜAbd Allah, and his grandson Amir-Husayn all had elevated Chingizid puppets and Kay Khusrau Apardi, Shams al-Din Dughlat, Bayazid Jalayir, and Amir-Husayn Qaraunas had likewise taken Chingizid wives, yet Natanzi, for instance, spoke of the ascendancy of the Qaraunas and Sulduz in the Chaghatayid khanate during the two decades before 1370/771 as a "rebellion" (*khuruj*) and a "usurpation" (*taghallub*).[88] Consequently, three fundamental aspects of the genealogical traditions appear much more suited to the later Chaghatayid phase of Timur's career than to the early period of his imperial successors at the beginning of the fifteenth/ninth century. First and foremost, they clearly define his position vis-à-vis the Chingizids. No less important is the fact that they also assert the historical primacy of the Barlas over their various non-Chingizid tribal rivals in the Chaghatayid khanate. Finally, they establish the political centrality of the descendants of Ichil and Aylangir among the other houses of the Barlas.

Some evidence of Timur's emergent ideology of conquest is found in Natanzi's accounts of his first campaigns mounted beyond the frontiers of Transoxiana in the two adjacent regions of Mughulistan and Khvarazm. In the first—legally a part of the Chaghatayid appanage khanate—the chiefs of the Turco-Mongol military elite of eastern Turkistan, like their counterparts in Transoxiana, had seized control of the government after the death of the Chaghatayid Tughluq Timur Khan in 1363–64/764, raising his son Ilyas Khvaje to the khanate in his place.[89] The latter was inexperienced in the affairs of state and, according to Natanzi, "in a short time, total deviation and adulteration appeared in the 'Triumphant Ture.' " Actual power was usurped by various Mughal tribal chieftains, but was rapidly monopolized by the Dughlat warlord Qamar al-Din, a non-Chingizid commoner like Timur, who murdered the young khan Ilyas Khvaje in 1364/765, massacred almost all of his brothers, and may have even taken the unprecedented step of arrogating the imperial title for himself (*ism-i khaniyat-ra bar khud itlaq farmud*).[90] Subsequently, Qamar al-Din had on several occasions between 1364/765 and 1370/771 attempted to extend his influence over Transoxiana threatening the positions Amir Husayn Qaraunas and Timur Barlas had there. It is no coincidence, therefore, that Timur conducted his first military operations outside Transoxiana against this illegitimate Dughlat upstart and dangerous rival in eastern Turkistan as early as 1371/773.[91]

Likewise, Natanzi and other early court chroniclers painted Timur's conflict with the non-Chingizid Qunqirat governors of Khvarazm with a similar but more dubious Chingizid legitimist coloring. In 1372/774, Timur sent envoys to Husayn Sufi Qunqirat accusing him of taking advantage of disturbances in Transoxiana to expropriate the revenues of the cities of Kat and Khiva, both of which had allegedly also fallen legally within the fiscal jurisdiction of the Chaghatayid appanage khanate "since the time of Chingiz Khan."[92] In this case, however, Timur's assertion of such rights over Khvarazm on behalf of the House of Chaghatay finds absolutely no corroboration in any classical Mongol source. For example, according to Juvayni's well-known version of the stipulations of the Partition composed about 1260/660, Chingiz Khan gave to Jochi and not Chaghatay, "the territory stretching from the regions of Qayaligh and Khvarazm to the remotest parts of Saqsin and Bulghar and as far in that direction as the hoof of Tatar horse had penetrated."[93]

Moreover, in the first half of the fourteenth/eighth century, Ibn Battuta situated Khvarazm within the domains of the Jochid Muhammad Özbek Khan (1312–41/712–42) while al-ʿUmari termed the entire Jochid appanage khanate "the kingdom of Khvarazm and Qipchaq."[94] This evident inconsistency in Timur's claims was also resolved by Natanzi in an ingenious rewriting of the terms of the Partition:

> When Chingiz Khan divided [the empire] among his four sons long ago, he assigned each one several enclaves in the territories of the others so that by this means envoys would continually pass among them. Thus he gave Chaghatay Kat and Khiva in Khvarazm, the appanage of Jochi, and from that time until the appearance of the fortunate estate of Sultan Ghazi [Timur], the revenues of those two cities have been remitted without deficiency."[95]

Such irredentist tamperings with the canons of Chingizid history to justify Timur's earliest campaigns in areas of the Mongol world empire lying outside the Transoxianan region of Chaghatayid appanage khanate were to acquire an even broader and bolder application the following decades. Finally, Natanzi suggests that Timur initially decided to extend aid to the fugitive Jochid prince Tuqtamish in 1376/778 because his principal Chingizid rival for control of the Golden Horde had given himself over to drink, abandoning his administrative duties and forsaking the precepts of the "Triumphant Türe."[96]

When Timur thrust his pontoon bridge across the Oxus River in preparation for the invasion of Khurasan in 1381/782, however, he trespassed from the traditional territories of the Chaghatayids into old Islamic lands formerly held by their Toluyid Ilkhan cousins. His often repeated rationale for this audacious move was the collapse of the Chingizid dispensation in Iran, Iraq, and Anatolia and the absence of a suitable candidate to exercise legitimate and independent sovereignty in those regions. In this connection, Hafiz Abru pointed out that the death of the last effective Ilkhan Abu Saᶜid and the birth of Timur both fell in the same Islamic lunar year 736 corresponding to 1335–36 of the common era.[97] Additionally, Timur's court chroniclers expressed the Islamic sanctioning of their patron's actions through his encounters with two religious figures in Khurasan, the ecstatic fool Baba Sangu,[98] who consecrated his conquest of the province, and the gnostic Zayn al-Din Abu Bakr Tayabadi Khvafi,[99] who designated him the divine scourge of the godless local rulers.

From 1381/782 until 1388/790, Timur successively raided Khurasan, the southern Caspian littoral, Sistan, Persian Iraq, Luristan, Azarbayjan, Eastern Anatolia, Georgia, and Fars. Except for Natanzi, the earliest chronicle literature and the surviving diplomatic sources suggest that he carried out these operations in the name of "the Emperor of Islam" (*padishah-i Islam*)—his puppet Suyurghatmish Khan—without reference to Chingizid history, traditions, or claims. His letter to Sayyid ᶜAli Kiya of Gilan is particularly instructive in this connection. In this document, Timur reminded Sayyid ᶜAli of the punishment meted out to those who disobeyed the edicts of the Emperor of Islam and the honors that accrued to those who submitted to him. Sayyid ᶜAli's response in turn upbraided Timur for despoiling and slaughtering Muslims in contravention of both the Sacred Law and traditional Muslim practice.[100]

At Shiraz at the beginning of 1388/late 789–early 790, Timur received the news from Transoxiana that the Jochid forces of his erstwhile protege Prince Tuqtamish, now Khan, had invaded the Timurid home territories from the north and were threatening his capital Samarqand. Leaving a makeshift vassal government in Fars, he hurriedly recrossed the Oxus to confront this danger—possibly the most serious he ever faced. Though Tuqtamish Khan withdrew without engaging Timur's main force, he left chaos in his wake, and Timur spent the next three years from 1388/790 to 1391/793 reorganizing the defenses of Transoxiana and reestablishing his authority in Khvarazm, Mughulistan, and Khurasan, while preparing his counterattack against the lord of the Qipchaq Steppe. Among the Khurasanian rebels he subdued was Haji Beg Ja'uni-Qurbani who had gone so far as to render formal obeisance to Tuqtamish Khan and to elevate to power none other than the son of Timur's archrival, the Mughul warlord Qamar al-Din Dughlat.[101] Moreover, Suyurghatmish Khan sickened and died during this period, but Timur did not replace him immediately, and the imperial throne remained vacant for six months before the installation of Sultan-Mahmud Khan.[102] Timur's hesitation in this respect reflects his uncertainty over the legal and political implications of directly opposing a powerful, independent Chingizid in his own domains. The ambiguity of the problem of Tuqtamish Khan in the context of Timur's activities between 1381/782 and 1388/790 is clear in Shami's statement that the expedition against the Jochid khan had in fact been ordered by the newly enthroned Emperor of Islam.[103]

The Qipchaq Steppe campaign of 1391/795 appears to mark a watershed in the development of Timur's ideology of conquest and consequently his attitude toward his genealogy and the traditions underlying it. For example, in the 1394/796 "submission order" sent to Qazi Burhan al-Din of Sivas, Timur stated: "Formerly this kingdom belonged to Chingiz Khan and it was then transferred to others, finally reaching Hülegü. Today, by right of inheritance, it belongs to Sultan-Mahmud."[104] He thus tersely asserted the rights of his Ögedeyid figurehead Sultan-Mahmud over an area that had been historically dominated by the Toluyid house of Hülegü. In a similar vein he wrote more specifically to the Ottoman sultan Yildirim Bayazid that same year:

> When the world emperor Chingiz Khan conquered Iran and Turan by divine order and the sun of fortune ascended to the zenith of sovereignty, he divided the expanse of the empire among his sons. He made over the entire kingdom of Iran to his son Chaghatay whose officers and agents were occupied for a while in administering those lands. When Möngke Khan sat upon the throne of sovereignty, consolidated his position thereon, and gained independence in the affairs of rule, he sent his brother Hülegü with an army from the frontiers of Iran, conferring that kingdom upon him. He and his descendants held these lands for an extended period of time and we have long trod the path of dispute and contention with them over that kingdom; this has resulted on several occasions in confrontation and combat. Now, in that land, the House of Chingiz Khan is empty and his line is exhausted. . . . Therefore the princes and generals suggested to His Majesty, the Emperor of Islam, champion of "Water and Earth," descendant of sovereigns, star of the constellation of empire, shadow of God's mercy, light of the Ilkhanid eye, lamp of Chingizkhanid vision, succor of the Truth, the earth, and the faith, Sultan-[Mahmud] Khan (may God perpetuate his kingdom and diffuse his virtue and benevolence throughout mankind) that since the kingdom of Iran was devoid of Chingizkhanids, he should set out for his hereditary lands and wrest them from the hands of the usurpers.[105]

The most significant and controversial of Timur's claims in this letter is that Chingiz Khan had made Iran an appanage of Chaghatay's at the time of the Partition. The legality of Chaghatay's position is contrasted with the hint of malfeasance on the part of the Toluyid brothers Möngke and Hülegü which in turn casts the historical conflict between the Chaghatayids and the other Chingizid houses in an extraordinary mold shaped by Timur to serve his own ends. Iran had fallen to Sultan-Mahmud Khan by default, and the unspecified "usurpers" mentioned at the end of the passage appear to represent the non-Chingizids who assumed political power in the Ilkhanate after the death of Abu Saᶜid in 1335/736.

It is in a letter provisionally dated 1393/795 or 1394/797 and addressed to the Mamluk sultan of Egypt and Syria al-Malik al-Zahir Barquq (1382–99/784–801) that Timur gives the most cogent exposition of his rectification of Chingizid history. After quoting the "sovereignty verse" of the Qur'an (4:59), he first emphasizes the basic obligation incumbent upon any Muslim ruler to enforce the commands and prohibitions of the Sacred Law. His focus then suddenly shifts from these generalities to the question of Chingiz Khan's division of the Mongol empire:

When the self-sufficient perfection of the Lord of Eternity had vouchsafed Chingiz Khan the kingdoms of Iran and Turan, he divided these regions among his sons. . . . To his middle son, the Emperor Chaghatay, he gave the area from the Altai Mountains and Kucha to the frontiers of India, Harat, Ray, Fars, Azarbayjan, and Baghdad, including Almaligh, Isfijab, Samarqand, Bukhara, and Ghazna along with all those flourishing regions as yet unconquered. Most of Chaghatay's appanage was "deferred" (*dar ḥayyiz-i taʾkhir amad*); that is, Baghdad and Tabriz had not been subjected, and it was his wish—with the aid of God Most High and the power of good fortune—to lead a world-conquering army to those places. At this moment, Chingiz Khan departed this ephemeral abode, and after his death, Ögeday Khan remained in his place and sat upon the throne of sovereignty. When he, too, passed away, Möngke Qa'an, though he was not in the line of succession, usurped the rule by force. As the Emperor Chaghatay had also answered God's summons, Möngke Qa'an sent one of his own brothers, Hülegü [Khan] to subjugate those lands that the Emperor Chaghatay had not conquered. Consequently, the descendants of the Emperor Chaghatay rose up in dispute and dissension, claiming that those territories had belonged to the Emperor Chaghatay by the order of Chingiz Khan and that Möngke Qa'an had given them to Hülegü illegally. For this reason, the sword of retaliation was drawn from the sheath of retribution among the sons of the Emperor Chaghatay and Hülegü Khan.

There follows a lengthy section on an alleged alliance between the Chaghatayids and the Mamluks, and a discourse on the justice of the Ilkhan warlord successor Shaykh-Uvays Jalayir. Timur concludes:

> Consultation and conference were then held with the princes who declared, "These lands originally belonged to the Emperor Chaghatay and his sons; Hülegü and his house have seized them illegitimately. Even though he, too, is of the house of our emperors, he has no right to them, and they must be liberated from the hands of the usurpers.[106]

The epithet "usurpers" is now specifically applied to Möngke and Hülegü; the rights usurped are clearly those of the House of Chaghatay. The earlier rationale of a dearth of Chingizid dynasts was thus all but forgotten.

Here Timur is certainly referring to the Chingizid political coup in 1251/648 engineered by the Toluyid Möngke with the collusion of the Jochid Batu. In that year, Möngke appropriated the position of Great Khan, the supreme office in the Chingizid empire, previously vested in the Ögedayids. To consolidate his coup, the new emperor either massacred or banished the majority of the dispossessed descendants of Ögeday as well as those of his brother Chaghatay. These two families had been closely linked historically and politically and most of the Chaghatayid appanage rulers of Transoxiana and Mughulistan were appointed by the Ögedayid great khans and anti-khans in Mongolia for more than fifty years after the death of Chaghatay in 1241/638. As a result of Möngke's ruthless actions, Mongol history in the second half of the thirteenth/seventh century was marked by sporadic warfare among princes representing the four Chingizid houses and the political dissolution of the universal imperium into congeries of independent, mutually hostile appanage states. An attempt at reconciliation of the parties to the dispute at the beginning of the fourteenth/eighth century was little more than a hollow gesture.

Peter Jackson has skillfully collated and analyzed the accounts of these disruptive events in the heart of the Chingizid empire and the circumstances surrounding them.[107] His comparison of sources produced outside Toluyid Iran and China with the official Mongol chronicles has demonstrated the ways in which the victors' version of history attempted to put Toluyid actions and claims in the best possible light, while obscuring those of their rivals. Particularly important in this connection is his reconstruction of the Jochid version of Chingizid history.

In the letters sent to Burhan al-Din, Bayazid, and Barquq quoted above, the Ögedayid-Chaghatayid view appears to be refracted through the prism of Timur's own ambitions. Timur definitively ranges himself on the side of the dispossessed in this bitter episode of Chingizid history—as defender of the rights of the House of Chaghatay, Timur might indeed justify his offensives to liberate their usurped lands in Iran, Iraq, and Azarbayjan; but, as champion of the Ögedayids as well, he could demand the allegiance of all regional rulers, Chingizid and non-Chingizid alike.[108]

There is thus a close theoretical correspondence between Yazdi's story of the covenant of Tumanay Khan and the content of Timur's political aims. From this congruity it can be inferred that at some point Timur may have considered himself or may have wished to be considered by his contemporaries as exercising his rights legitimately throughout the entire Chingizid dispensation under the terms of a Tumanayid condominium. According to the covenant, Timur as chief Qaracharid was bound by the terms of Chingiz Khan's will to safeguard and restore the patrimony of both Ögedayids and Chaghatayids. He was therefore acting not only as the reviver of the House of Chaghatay, as Shami had written, but also of the House of Chingiz Khan as it had been left by the conqueror in 1227/624. This is perhaps the import of Timur's assertion to Yildirim Bayazid that he was "of the Ilkhanid dynasty," that is, that by descent and by covenant, Timur was both lord protector and coruler of a reinvigorated Tumanayid-Chingizid double kingship.[109]

The practice of naming Timurid princes after their alleged Turco-Mongol ancestors previously alluded to also points to the last decade of the fourteenth/eighth century as the beginning of Timur's conscious exploitation of his family traditions. Although the Iranian and Islamic personal names of Timur's own sons reveal no particular pattern, the study of Timurid royal onomastics down to the end of the fifteenth/ninth century shows the overwhelming predominance of Islamic principles. By far, the most popular Timurid prince name overall was Muhammad or some compound of it, accounting for fully 25 percent of nearly three hundred cases examined in the *Mu^cizz al-Ansab*. The Turco-Mongol examples from the period 1394–1426/796–830 illustrated in tables 1 and 3 stand out all the more sharply against this background and suggest more than just a passing interest in the Timurid family legends.

There is also a strong possibility that the illustrated *Nasab-name* by Husayn b. ^cAli Shah derives from this period as well. Nothing concrete is known about the author other than that he might have been the son of the ^cAli Shah Bakhshi who copied a manuscript of Mir Haydar Majzub/Tilbe's *Makhzan al-Asrar*.[110] Husayn's work, consisting of thirteen folios, is bound in a collection of more than six hundred specimens of calligraphy, painting, and drawing in various stages of completion known as the *Jung-i Baysunghuri* ("The Miscellany of Baysunghur"). Although linked to Timur's grandson Baysunghur (d. 1434/837), many of the pieces are earlier or associated with other princes. For example, on folio 6a is an inscription by Baysunghur's half-brother Ibrahim-Sultan (d. 1435/838)

FIGURE 2. Seal of Husayn b. ^cAli Shah (*Jung-i Baysunghuri*, fol. 32a). Courtesy Topkapi Saray Museum.

dated 1420–21/823, on folio 16a is a poetic chronogram calligraphed by ^cAli Khvaje Tabrizi Khvarazmi on the beginning of the short independent rule of Khalil-Sultan, and on folio 59b is a large painting of Khalil-Sultan and his entourage watching an urban riot from the walls of a citadel. Husayn's genealogy is undated, however, and attempts to establish its chronological provenance have proved largely unconvincing. On the basis of the kneeling posture of Timur's portrait—possibly the earliest known representation of the conqueror (see figure 3), Osman Sertkaya argues that the work predates 1402/805 when he asserts that Timur proclaimed himself emperor.[111] Togan opts for the date 1423/826 by which time he calculates that the princes featured prominently in the genealogy would have attained majority.[112] Internal evidence leads to another interpretation to be proposed below.

The folios of Husayn's genealogy are out of order in Baysunghur's Miscellany, but Sertkaya has rearranged them correctly. He has also deciphered the Uyghur legends that label most of the more than fifty portraits, only two of which—the Jochid Jani Beg Khan and Timur—are in color. The ensemble is a Chingizid-Timurid family tree similar in many respects to those discussed earlier.

The Alan-Qo'a-Tumanay stem common to both houses follows the traditions of Rashid al-Din, and the Qachulay-Timur segment is identical to the genealogies of the *Mu^cizz al-Ansab*, Yazdi's *Zafar-name*, and the Timurid tomb inscriptions. The major difference lies not in Husayn's

FIGURE 3. Timur (*Jung-i Baysunghuri*, fol. 33b). Courtesy Topkapi Saray Museum.

treatment of the broad outlines of the Timurid lineage, but in his Chingizid focus, emphasizing the Toluyid and Jochid houses at the expense
of the middle two brothers—even though the portraits of Chaghatay and
Ögeday are included, none of their descendants is featured. In contrast,
both the Toluyid lines in China and Iran are depicted in relative detail,
while the Jochid house shows only the main male branch of Batu's family

down through Jani Beg Khan. The omission of the Tuqay-Timurid line to which Tuqtamish belonged is certainly significant.

The portrait of Jani Beg Khan is followed by those of his daughter Shakar Beg, and her daughter, Sevin Beg or Khanzade, by the Qunqirat governor of Khvarazm. Khanzade (d. 1411/814) was married to two of Timur's sons: Jahangir and Miranshah. A few months before he died, she bore her first husband a son, Muhammad-Sultan, and, after her marriage to Miranshah, she gave birth to a second Timurid prince, Khalil-Sultan, in 1384/786. The portrait of this prince, identified with a Uyghur rubric, is included after hers in the Jochid-Chingizid segment of Husayn's genealogy.

Husayn's genealogy also contains the portraits of five of Timur's sons—Jahanshah, Jahangir, ꜤUmar-Shaykh, Miranshah, and Shahrukh—and three of his grandsons—Muhammad-Sultan, Pir Muhammad, and an unnamed son of Miranshah, presumably Khalil-Sultan, shown this time as a Timurid. Here, as in the case of the Chingizids, his focus is noteworthy, stressing the families of Jahangir and Miranshah—especially Khalil-Sultan—while playing down those of ꜤUmar-Shaykh and Shahrukh.[113] Jahanshah and Jahangir were the sons of Turmish Agha Khatun, Timur's only free wife to bear him male heirs—his other sons were all mothered by slave concubines. Both predeceased Timur: Jahanshah died about 1372/773 at age five and Jahangir died in 1376/777 at age twenty-one. Husayn gives the boy Jahanshah major treatment, while the *MuꜤizz al-Ansab* relegates him to the same secondary rank as Ibrahim, another of Timur's sons who died in youth. The *MuꜤizz al-Ansab* also claims that Jahangir was Timur's eldest son, but evidence from the chronicles suggests that ꜤUmar-Shaykh was in fact older.[114] He, too, died before his father in 1394/796. Consequently, of his five sons who lived past infancy, Timur was survived in 1405/807 only by Miranshah (born about 1367/768) and Shahrukh (born 1377/779). Like the sources mentioned previously, although Timur himself, ꜤUmar-Shaykh, Miranshah, Shahrukh, and Muhammad-Sultan all had married Chingizid princesses, Husayn's genealogy dignifies only Timur and Miranshah with the title *küragan*.

The configuration of Husayn's genealogy and its political implications suggest Khalil-Sultan's brief rule in Samarqand from 1405/807 to 1409/811 as the most probable ambiance for its composition. Despite Timur's attempts to regulate his succession, he was far less successful in doing so than had been Chingiz Khan, and rancorous disputes broke out during these years among his descendants vying for the spoils of the warlord conqueror's empire (see table 4). Only with the accession of Shahrukh and his endeavors to implement a new basis for rule did this strife gradually abate. Among the causes of discord was without doubt Timur's passing

TIMUR'S GENEALOGY / 113

TABLE 4
Timur's Succession

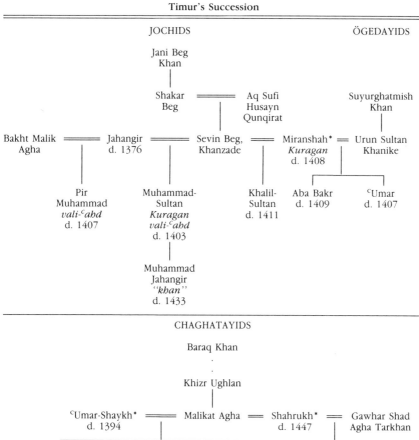

JOCHIDS		ÖGEDAYIDS

Jani Beg
Khan

Shakar ===== Aq Sufi   Suyurghatmish
Beg   Husayn   Khan
                   Qunqirat

Bakht Malik ===== Jahangir ===== Sevin Beg, ===== Miranshah* == Urun Sultan
Agha   d. 1376   Khanzade   *Kuragan*   Khanike
                                                                d. 1408

Pir   Muhammad-   Khalil-   Aba Bakr   ᶜUmar
Muhammad   Sultan   Sultan   d. 1409   d. 1407
vali-ᶜahd   *Kuragan*   d. 1411
d. 1407   *vali-ᶜahd*
                     d. 1403

Muhammad
Jahangir
"khan"
d. 1433

CHAGHATAYIDS

Baraq Khan

Khizr Ughlan

ᶜUmar-Shaykh* ===== Malikat Agha == Shahrukh* ===== Gawhar Shad
d. 1394   d. 1447   Agha Tarkhan

Pir Muhammad Iskandar   Bayqara   Ahmad   Ulugh Beg
d.1409   d. 1415   d. 1423   d. 1425   *Kuragan*
                                                          d. 1449

* Mother slave or concubine

over his sons Miranshah and Shahrukh—presumably because of the inferior status of their mothers—to designate his grandson Muhammad-Sultan heir apparent (*vali-ᶜahd*) before 1398/801.[115] Miranshah's assertion of what he perceived to be his patrimonial rights in this regard in opposition to his father's actions was portrayed as insanity, and his claims were largely neutralized until Timur died.

After Muhammad-Sultan succumbed to wounds received in the campaign against the Ottomans, Timur named his half-brother Pir Muhammad heir apparent on the eve of the projected invasion of China.[116] This final effort on Timur's part to establish his dynasty in the freeborn line of Jahangir further alienated the senior representatives of the other families, rendering his last will and testament a scrap of paper. No sooner had Timur's funeral cortege set out from the winter encampment at Utrar for Samarqand than Khalil-Sultan, with the complicity of a group of officers, seized control of the government (*hukumat va imarat*) of Transoxiana in Tashkent, and enthroned his nine-year-old nephew Muhammad Jahangir—"offspring of the heir [Muhammad-Sultan]" (*farzand-i vasi*)— as khan "in order to observe the will of the late Lord of the Fortunate Conjunction."[117]

This concoction may not appear quite so outlandish in light of the special Timurid notions of Chingizid legitimacy or in the context of the Qabul-Qachulay legend. First of all, Khalil-Sultan's behavior permits the assumption that Timur had not replaced the Ögedayid Sultan-Mahmud, who died in 1402/805, and had ruled independently without a khan during the last years of his life. Secondly, even though his mother was of Chingizid maternal descent and through her he was the uterine half-brother of Timur's first heir apparent Muhammad-Sultan, Khalil-Sultan did not claim the sovereignty in his own name, choosing instead to uphold the primacy of the principles of free birth, unigeniture, and dual kingship in elevating Muhammad Jahangir. He thereby negated the notion of corporate succession in the House of Jahangir implied by Timur's designation of Pir Muhammad as heir. Finally, Khalil-Sultan was apparently also counting on his tenuous Jochid ties to support his policy of ennobling a *qarachu* commoner with the imperial style.

The reactions of the princes elsewhere in Timur's empire between 1405/807 and 1409/811 further demonstrate the fragility of Timur's succession arrangements. For example, in Azarbayjan, Arabian Iraq, and Eastern Anatolia, Miranshah and his sons ᶜUmar and Aba Bakr, both born of a Chingizid princess, initially seem to have recognized neither Timur's designated successor—the Jahangirid Pir Muhammad—nor their own kinsman Khalil-Sultan. A heated rivalry subsequently flared between ᶜUmar in Azarbayjan and his father and elder brother in Arabian Iraq and Eastern Anatolia. Though agreeing to accept Aba Bakr's declarations of fealty, ᶜUmar nevertheless arrested his brother and interned him in Sultaniye. Miranshah, meanwhile, marched inconclusively on Khurasan, perhaps intending to link up with his other son Khalil-Sultan in Transoxiana to press his own candidacy.[118] Aba Bakr managed to escape from his jailers and join his father for whom he set up a golden throne, elevating Miranshah to the kingship (*padishahi*)—the long-delayed but short-lived realization of political ambitions unsuccessfully articulated in Timur's lifetime.[119]

Simultaneously, ᶜUmar's supporters in Tabriz reaffirmed their support for him as their "king and prince" (*padishah va padishahzade-yi ma*). A few days later, Aba Bakr decided to assume the sovereignty himself.[120] Unfortunately, the terminology associated with the maneuvers of the Miranshahids in the west does not clarify the issues raised by Khalil-Sultan's policies in Tashkent.

In Shiraz, Pir Muhammad, the eldest son of ᶜUmar-Shaykh, consulted with his principal officers on the question of Timur's succession. The most radical faction advocated a total rupture with Mongol tradition and the "Triumphant Türe" (*yasaq-i Mughul va Türe-yi Qahire*) altogether, and urged Pir Muhammad to request a diploma of investiture from the ᶜAbbasid shadow caliph in Egypt. Their singular recommendation is an important index of the degree to which Timur's polity was seen as rooted in the legal system identified with Chingiz Khan. A second group pragmatically favored allegiance to ᶜUmar Miranshahi, while yet another appealed to the seniority (*aqa'i*) of Miranshah. However, Pir Muhammad decided to yield instead to his uncle and stepfather Shahrukh as senior and paramount (*aqa va ulugh*) on the basis of the family ties between their two houses established by Timur, even though Shahrukh was about ten years younger than Miranshah.[121] Given that this report by Hafiz Abru represents the viewpoint of Shahrukh's court, it is nevertheless noteworthy that the options discussed by Pir Muhammad ᶜUmar-Shaykhi and his advisors in Fars did not include support for Pir Muhammad Jahangiri.

Finally, according to Hafiz Abru, Shahrukh declared himself independent in Khurasan and eastern Persian Iraq on learning of Timur's death.[122] In addition, Sharaf al-Din ᶜAli Yazdi claimed that even those officers who had consented to honor Timur's designation of Pir Muhammad Jahangiri as his heir recognized that Shahrukh was legally and rationally the conqueror's "real successor."[123] For his part, Shahrukh followed a cautious and conciliatory policy toward the other Timurid houses at the outset, while dealing ruthlessly and decisively with non-Timurid rebels in his own territories. The dominant impression is one of an astute politician biding his time in consolidating his position.

In 1409/811, Shahrukh ousted Khalil-Sultan from power in Samarqand and installed his own son Ulugh Beg as his deputy in Timur's capital. In an edict issued in the name of Shahrukh (*Shahrukh Bahadur sözidin, Ulugh Beg sözümiz*) and dated August 25, 1411/5 Jumada I 814, Ulugh Beg allowed the Muslim intellectuals and artisans forcibly settled in the city in Timur's time to return to their homes. According to the text of this document, the rationale behind this act of humanitarianism was to restore the efficacy of the Sacred Law of Islam.[124] Thus it was Shahrukh who began to carry out the definitive break with the Mongol past. Indeed, throughout the course of his long reign, a number of sources attest to his intentions to Islamize the ideology and the conduct of his administration.[125] History was literally rewritten by his court chroniclers who suppressed or deemphasized the Chingizid elements in their new versions of his father's biography. Despite his efforts in this regard, however, it is clear that the customary law and practice of the Turco-Mongol steppe empires was perceived as continuing to influence many aspects of life in Timurid lands in the fifteenth/ninth century.[126]

As a consequence of the disestablishment of the "Triumphant Türe" as the legal basis of the Timurid state, Shahrukh did away with the institution of the figurehead khan, struck coins in his own name with the Islamic title "the greatest sultan" (al-sultan al-a^{c}zam) and the Turco-Mongol epithet "hero" (bahadur), and issued documents on his own authority.[127] As noted above, Ulugh Beg included the name of his father Shahrukh on his documents, and, after Shahrukh's death, inscribed that of his late grandfather Timur on his coinage.[128] Moreover, according to a single, late, non-Timurid source, he maintained a Chingizid puppet in Samarqand as well.[129] Whether the testimony of this source is to be credited, in Shahrukh's new ideological system there was no longer any necessity to perpetuate Timur's legal fiction.

In contrast to his father, Shahrukh did not marry any of his sons to Chingizid princesses. Though he himself had wed Malikat Agha, the daughter of a Chingizid prince and widow of his brother ^{c}Umar-Shaykh, he did not utilize it for the title küragan; in the diplomatic correspondence from other sovereigns he is sometimes called Küragani, as if the term had become a dynastic name rather than a title.[130] It was not generally used by the epigones of Shahrukh until the second half of the fifteenth/ninth century when it was revived in the eastern part of the Timurid domains by Abu Sa^{c}id Miranshahi, who clearly entertained ambitions of restoring the fading political power and glory of the empire founded by his great-grandfather Timur.[131]

To conclude, this discussion of Timur's genealogy and its associated lore demonstrate that it is impossible to establish convincingly the authenticity of either. Although the broad outlines of Timur's emergence to power are discernible, the exact nature of his socioeconomic origins must remain obscure. It also shows, however, that there is ample evidence to suggest that both figured prominently in Timur's ideology of rule and conquest, particularly during the last fifteen years of his life. The quality of this evidence further indicates that the expression of his pretensions was designed to appeal to domestic as well as foreign audiences. Finally, it is clear that the importance of the Timurid family traditions as elaborated in the time of the warlord conqueror declined in the age of his successors, as Mongol notions of rule outwardly underwent a process of reconciliation with Islamic political principles.

Notes

¹ A. A. Semenov has produced the best edition of the inscriptions in "Nadpisi na nadgrobiyakh Timura i ego potomkov v Gur-i Emire," *Epigrafika Vostoka* 2 (1948): 49–62; 3 (1949): 45–54. Turkish translation: A. K. İnan, *Makaleler ve İncelemeler* (Ankara, 1969), 587–610.

² Hafiz Abru, *Majmaᶜ/Zubdat al-Tavarikh-i Baysungburi.* MS, Istanbul, Fatih, 4371/1, f. 598a; see also M. E. Masson, "Trety kusok nefritovogo namogil'nika Timura," *Epigrafika Vostoka* 2 (1948): 63–75.

³ Based on A. Z. V. Togan's oversight in "The Composition of the History of the Mongols by Rashid al-din," *Central Asiatic Journal* 8 (1963): 69–70, C. A. Storey and Y. E. Bregel, *Persidskaya literatura, bio-bibliograficheskii obzor,* trans. and rev. Y. E. Bregel, 3 vols. (Moscow, 1972), 819, incorrectly implies that Husayn's work is another copy of the *Muᶜizz al-Ansab*; see, for example, Osman F. Sertkaya, "Timurlü şeceresi," *İstanbul Üniversitesi Edebiyat Fakültesi Sanat Tarihi Yıllığı* 9–10 (1979–80): 241–58. Note that on 250–51, Sertkaya misreads the author's name in his seal (see figure 1) as "al-ᶜAshiq bi'llah Chin b. ᶜAli M(uhammad) Shah" for "al-Vasiq bi'llah Husayn b. ᶜAli Shah." See also Emil Esin, "The Bakhshi in the 14th to 16th Centuries, The Masters of the Pre-Muslim Tradition of the Arts of the Book in Central Asia," in Basil Gray, ed., *The Arts of the Book in Central Asia, 14–16th Centuries* (Paris and London, 1979), 290.

⁴ Emil Esin, "On the Genealogical Portraits, with Uyghur Inscriptions, of Mongol and Temurid Dynasties," Communication to the 22nd Permanent International Altaistic Conference, Ghent, May 27-June 2, 1979; Esin, "The Bakhshi," 290. It is noteworthy that the names of five of Shahrukh's sons—Ulugh Beg, Sultan Ibrahim, Baysunghur, Suyurghatmish, and Juki (born 1402/804)—are written in Uyghur, while two—Beg Ughli and Khan Ughli (born ca. 1403/805)—are written in Arabic.

⁵ Storey and Bregel, *Persidskaya literatura,* 818–19. See my forthcoming paper, *The Timurid Dynasty* (Papers on Inner Asia, Indiana University).

⁶ Hafiz Abru, *Majmaᶜ/Zubdat,* f. 9a (Nizam al-Din ᶜAli Shami), Felix Tauer, ed., *Zafar-name,* 2 vols. (Prague, 1937–56), 2:200, and 10b-14b.

⁷ Storey and Bregel, *Persidskaya literatura,* 797–807.

⁸ Ibid., 777–79; V. V. Bartol'd, *Sochineniya,* 9 vols. (Moscow, 1963–77), 2.2:141–42; 6:167–68; W. Barthold [V. V. Bartol'd], *Turkestan Down to the Mongol Invasion.* 3d ed. (London, 1968): 52, 56–57; B. A. Akhmedov, "Ulugbek i ego istoricheskii trud 'Tarikh-i Arbaᶜ Ulus,' " in S. K. Sirazhdinov, ed., *Iz istorii nauki epokhi Ulugbeka* (Tashkent, 1979), 29–36.

⁹ Bartol'd, *Sochineniya,* 5:167; 8:131n25.

¹⁰ Not J'NLMWNKT'Q as in A. Z. V. Togan, "Tahqiq-i nasab-i Amir Timur," in S. M. Abdullah, ed., *Professor Mohamed Shafi Presentation Volume* (Lahore, 1955), 108, 109, transcribed and vocalized as "Conelmu Neklak" and "Canelmu

118 / JOHN E. WOODS

Nektak" (!) in İsmail Aka's translation, "Emir Timur'un soyuna dair bir araştırma," *Tarih Dergisi* 26 (1972): 78, 80. See Anonymous, *Secret History of the Mongols*, transcription; Louis Ligeti, *Histoire secrète des mongols* (Budapest, 1971) [*Monumenta Linguae Mongolicae Collecta*, vol. 1]; Francis Woodman Cleaves, *The Secret History of the Mongols*, translation (Cambridge, Mass., and London, 1982), para. 23; translation, p. 5n13, and Rashid al-Din Fazl Allah, *Shuᶜab-i Panjgane*, MS, Istanbul, Topkapi Sarayi, III, Ahmet, 2937, f. 117b.

    ¹¹ Eiji Mano, "Amir Timur Kuragan—Timur ke no keifu to Timur no tachiba," *Toyoshi-Kenkyu* 34.4 (1976): 593, does not consider this part of the genealogy worthy of comment.

    ¹² *Secret History*, para. 43; Rashid al-Din Fazl Allah, *Jamiᶜ al-Tavarikh*, ed. Bahman Karimi (Tehran, 1959/1338), 185, 187, 189; Rashid al-Din, *Shuᶜab*, f. 100a.

    ¹³ Rashid al-Din, *Jamiᶜ*, 174.

    ¹⁴ *Secret History*, para. 46.

    ¹⁵ Rashid al-Din, *Jamiᶜ*, 185, 187, 189; Rashid al-Din, *Shuᶜab*, ff. 100ab.

    ¹⁶ Mongol *-tü* = Turkish *-chi*.

    ¹⁷ *Secret History*, para. 202; Rashid al-Din, *Jamiᶜ*, 604.

    ¹⁸ *Secret History*, para. 120. The other Barulas mentioned are Qubilai and Qudus. See Togan, "Tahqiq," 109, and Mano, "Amir Timur," 598.

    ¹⁹ Anonymous, *Muᶜizz al-Ansab*, MS, Paris, Bibliothèque Nationale, ancien fonds, persan, 67, ff. 8a, 80b.

    ²⁰ Husayn, *Nasab-name*, MS, Istanbul, Topkapı Sarayı, 2152, (*Jung-i Baysun-ghuri*, ff. 32ab, 33ab, 36ab, 37ab, 38ab, 39b, 42a, 43ab) f. 43a; Sharaf al-Din ᶜAli Yazdi, *Zafar-name*, ed. A. Urunbaev (Tashkent, 1972), f. 26b.

    ²¹ *Secret History*, paras. 202, 243. According to *The Secret History*, para. 242, Chaghatay's troop allotment was eight thousand, while Rashid al-Din, *Jamiᶜ*, 409, states that it amounted to half that number.

    ²² Rashid al-Din, *Jamiᶜ*, 409, 541; *Shuᶜab*, f. 117b.

    ²³ *Muᶜizz al-Ansab*, f. 29b.

    ²⁴ For the limitations of formal Ilkhanid historiography in this respect, and the emergence of a codified historical consciousness in Eastern Iran and Central Asia, see my article, "The Rise of Timurid Historiography," *Journal of Near Eastern Studies* 46 (1987): 81–108.

    ²⁵ Yazdi, *Zafar-name*, Tashkent, ff. 24a-25a; Anonymous, *Shajarat al-Atrak*, MS, London, British Library, Add. 26190; ff. 35a-36a; translation: Col. Miles, *The Shajarat ul Atrak, or Genealogical Tree of the Turks and Tatars* (London, 1838), 55–57 (with slightly different details).

    ²⁶ Rashid al-Din, *Jamiᶜ*, 193 ff. Qutula Khan's role is also minimized in *Secret History*, paras. 48 ff.

    ²⁷ Yazdi, *Zafar-name*, Tashkent, 26a; *Shajarat al-Atrak*, f. 38a; translation, 61.

    ²⁸ Abu al-Ghazi Bahadur Khan, *Shajare-yi Turk*, ed. and trans. I. P. Desmaisons, *Histoire des Mongols et des Tatares* (St. Petersburg, 1871–74), text, 65; translation, 69.

    ²⁹ *Muᶜizz al-Ansab*, ff. 8a, 80b-82a.

    ³⁰ Ibid., f. 10a, gives the year of Yesügey's death as 562, so it is possible that 560 is a scribal error in the Tashkent facsimile edition of the Prologue.

[31] Yazdi, *Zafar-name*, Tashkent, f. 51b; *Shajarat al-Atrak*, f. 39b; translation, 64, mentions another son Buyusam (BYWSM?). Neither is found in *Mu^cizz al-Ansab* or Hafiz Abru, *Majma^c/Zubdat*.

[32] Yazdi, *Zafar-name*, Tashkent, f. 61b; *Shajarat al-Atrak*, ff. 108b-109a; translation, 195–97.

[33] Yazdi, *Zafar-name*, Tashkent, f. 75b; *Shajarat al-Atrak*, f. 165b; translation, 347.

[34] Mu^cin al-Din Natanzi, *Muntakhab al-Tavarikh-i Mu^cini*, ed. Jean Aubin (Tehran, 1957/1336), 103—Mano, "Amir Timur," 599, characterizes Qarachar's authority in the Chaghatayid appanage khanate as only that of a majordomo; Hafiz Abru, *Majma^c/Zubdat*, f. 11a.

[35] *Mu^cizz al-Ansab*, f. 82b.

[36] According to Hafiz Abru, *Majma^c/Zubdat*, f. 11a, Qarachar Noyan died in 1243–44/640 corresponding to the Year of the Hare (March 14, 1234-March 13, 1244/21 Ramazan 640-1 Shavval 641), while the date 1255–56/652 given in Yazdi, *Zafar-name*, Tashkent, f. 77a, in fact corresponds to the Turco-Mongol years of the Ox and the Tiger.

[37] Yazdi, *Zafar-name*, Tashkent, ff. 82b; *Shajarat al-Atrak*, f. 169a; translation, 355.

[38] *Mu^cizz al-Ansab*, ff. 83b ff.; Hafiz Abru, *Majma^c/Zubdat*, ff. 11b ff. Hafiz Abru asserts that Qul was the third son of Qarachar, not his grandson.

[39] Hafiz Abru, *Majma^c/Zubdat*, f. 11b: *naslan ba^cd nasl va khalafan ba^cd salaf bi mansab-i hukumat-i [Qubbat al-Khazra-yi Kish] mawsum gashtand*.

[40] Only *Shajarat al-Atrak*, f. 169b; translation, 356, gives Ichil this title.

[41] Yazdi, *Zafar-name*, Tashkent, ff. 77b-78a, 83a (the last reference claims that Ichil Noyan had gone to Iran in the time of Hülegü, at least a decade earlier); *Shajarat al-Atrak*, ff. 170b-171a; translation, 359.

[42] Togan, "Tahqiq," 108. For the manuscript (Istanbul, Topkapı Sarayı, Revan Köşkü, 1518), see Storey and Bregel, *Persidskaya literatura*, 306–7.

[43] Togan, "Tahqiq," 108, inexplicably reads "*sipurd*" (*vermişti*, "he delivered") for "*gardid*" ("he migrated").

[44] *Mu^cizz al-Ansab*, f. 95b; Hafiz Abru, *Majma^c/Zubdat*, f. 13a.

[45] Yazdi, *Zafar-name*, Tashkent, ff. 79b, 83a; *Shajarat al-Atrak*, f. 174b; translation, 367.

[46] Yazdi, *Zafar-name*, Tashkent, f. 81a; *Mu^cizz al-Ansab*, ff. 177b-178a. The *Mu^cizz al-Ansab*, f. 44a, lists Timur Barlas and Amir Husayn Qaraunas among his amirs! Mano, "Amir Timur," 600–601, thinks the break in the narrative occurs after the account of Ichil.

[47] Yazdi, *Zafar-name*, Tashkent, f. 83a; Ahmad Ibn ^cArabshah, *^cAja'ib al-Maqdur fi Nawa'ib Timur*, ed. ^cAli Muhammad ^cUmar (Cairo, 1979/1399), 3, calls Timur's grandfather Abaghay, "paternal uncle"; see Gerhard Doerfer, *Türkische und mongolische Elemente im Neupersischen*, 4 vols. (Wiesbaden, 1963–75), 1:107–8, and Sir Gerard Clauson, *An Etymological Dictionary of Pre-Thirteenth-Century Turkish* (Oxford, 1972), 5.

[48] *Mu^cizz al-Ansab*, ff. 95b-96a; Hafiz Abru, *Majma^c/Zubdat*, f. 13a. Mano (1976), 602, questions the historicity of Burgul and suggests that the life-style of

Taraghay may simply have been projected onto his father; on Taraghay, see also
ᶜAbd al-Rahman Ibn Khaldun, *Al-Taᶜrif bi Ibn Khaldun*, ed. Muhammad al-Tanji
(Cairo, 1951), 382.

⁴⁹ See Woods, "Timurid Historiography," 105.

⁵⁰ Yazdi, *Zafar-name*, Tehran, 1:9, 36, 463; *Muᶜizz al-Ansab*, ff. 89b, 90b;
Hafiz Abru, *Majmaᶜ/Zubdat*, f. 12b; see also Natanzi, *Muntakhab*, 206: *tuman-i
Shahr-i Sabz kih aban ᶜan jadd miras-i Barlasiye bud*; Hafiz Abru,
Majmaᶜ/Zubdat, f. 98b (Shami, *Zafar-name*, 2:13).

⁵¹ Yazdi, *Zafar-name*, ed. Muhammad ᶜAbbasi, 2 vols. (Tehran, 1957/1336),
2:518–19, but see Mano, "Amir Timur," 602; *Muᶜizz al-Ansab*, f. 89b; Hafiz Abru,
Majmaᶜ/Zubdat, f. 12b.

⁵² Shami, *Zafar-name*, 1:9–10, 14, 58, 65. See Mano, "Amir Timur," 597.

⁵³ Ruy Gonzalez de Clavijo, *Embajada a Tamorlán*, ed. F. Lopez Estrada
(Madrid, 1943), 150: "*fue omne fildalgo de linaje destos chacataes, pero fue de
pequeno estado*"; Jean of Sultaniye, "Mémoire sur Tamerlan et sa cour par un
dominican en 1403," ed. H. Moranvillé, *Bibliothèque de l'Ecole des Chartes* 55
(1894): 441: "*de petite condicion et de petite renommée . . . bien qu'il soit de
commune bonne ligniée.*" The tradition transmitted by the Russian chronicles,
compiled in the mid-fifteenth/ninth century, seems to reflect the Jochid view of
Timur as an usurper: *ne tsar' be rodom', ni syn' tsarev', ni plemeni tsar'ska, ni
knyazh'ska, ni boyar'ska, no tako iz' prosta edin' sy' ot' khudykh' lyudei*; see
Sofiiskaya vtoraya letopis', 124 (*Polnoe sobranie russkikh letopisei*, vol. 6 [St.
Petersburg, 1853]) and, with slightly different language (*ot' prostykh' nishchikh'
lyudei*), *Patriarshaya ili nikonovskaya letopis'*, 158 (*Polnoe sobranie russkikh
letopisei*, vol. 11 [St. Petersburg, 1897]).

⁵⁴ Ibn Khaldun, *Taᶜrif*, 382.

⁵⁵ Ibn ᶜArabshah, *ᶜAja'ib*, 4, 6–7.

⁵⁶ Yazdi, *Zafar-name*, Tehran, 1:18; see Ibn Khaldun, *Taᶜrif*, 382–83.

⁵⁷ Yazdi, *Zafar-name*, Tehran, 1:8; *Muᶜizz al-Ansab*, f. 98a (this reference
states that Haji Mahmud Shah Yasavuri was Timur's maternal cousin).

⁵⁸ Ibn Khaldun, *Taᶜrif*, 373; Ibn ᶜArabshah, *ᶜAja'ib*, 7; Jean of Sultaniye,
"Memoire," 447.

⁵⁹ Ibn ᶜArabshah, *ᶜAja'ib*, 7–8.

⁶⁰ Barthold, *Turkestan*, 52–53 = Bartol'd, *Sochineniya*, 1:100–102.

⁶¹ V. Barthold, *Four Studies on the History of Central Asia*, trans. V. and T.
Minorsky. 3 vols. (Leiden, 1956–62), 2:14–15 = Bartol'd, *Sochineniya*, 2.2:38–39;
see also W. Barthold, *Zwölf Vorlesungen über die Geschichte der Türken Mit-
telasiens* (Hildesheim, 1962), 213 = Bartol'd, *Sochineniya*, 5:168–69, 2.1:741–42.

⁶² Shami, *Zafar-name*, 1:46; Natanzi, *Muntakhab*, 247; Yazdi, *Zafar-name*,
Tehran, 1:120.

⁶³ Shami, *Zafar-name*, 1:65; Yazdi, *Zafar-name*, Tehran, 1:173; see also
Natanzi, *Muntakhab*, 427.

⁶⁴ Masataka Takeshita of Tokai University kindly prepared a complete English
translation of this important article for me; it has served both as a model and a
point of departure for this paper. For a similar interpretation, see Hans R. Roemer,

"Timur in Iran," in Peter Jackson and Laurence Lockhart, eds., *Cambridge History of Iran* (Cambridge, 1986), 6:44.

65 Doerfer, *Elemente*, 1:475–77.

66 Natanzi, *Muntakhab*, 280; Hafiz Abru, *Majmaᶜ/Zubdat*, f. 9a (Shami, *Zafar-name*, 2:200). According to Yazdi, *Zafar-name*, Tehran, 2:521, in 1405/807 he was survived by fifty-three lineal descendants, including three children, twenty-seven grandchildren, and twenty-three great-grandchildren.

67 For a similar type of composition, see F. Keshavarz, "The Horoscope of Iskandar Sultan," *Journal of the Royal Asiatic Society* (1984):197–208, and L. P. Elwell-Sutton, "A Royal Timurid Nativity Book," in R. M. Savory and D. A. Agius, eds., *Logos Islamikos, Studia Islamica in Honorem Georgii Michaelis Wickens* (Toronto, 1984), 119–36, for the recently discovered nativity book of Timur's grandson Iskandar b. ᶜUmar-Shaykh.

68 ᶜAbd al-Husayn Nava'i, *Asnad va Mukatabat-i Tarikh-yi Iran az Timur ta Shah Isma'il* (Tehran, 1962/1341), 99: *che ma khud az dudman-i ilkhaniye bashim*; for other examples, see 96, 109. Note that the anonymous author of the *Muᶜizz al-Ansab* (ff. 2ab) gives the title khan to both Timur and Shahrukh.

69 See, for example, Ibn ᶜArabshah, ᶜAja'ib, 20, 52, 233, 319–20, and Shami, *Zafar-name*, 1:12.

70 Shihab al-Din Ibn Fadl Allah al-ᶜUmari, *Masalik al-Absar fi Mamalik al-Amsar*, ed. and trans. Klaus Lech, *Das mongolische Weltreich* (Wiesbaden, 1968) *Asiatische Forschungen* 22, text, 41, 47; Rashid al-Din, *Jamiᶜ*, 541.

71 Natanzi, *Muntakhab*, 206; Hafiz Abru, *Majmaᶜ/Zubdat*, f. 98b (Shami, *Zafar-name*, 2:12–13).

72 Natanzi, *Muntakhab*, 291, 319, 332.

73 Hafiz Abru, *Majmaᶜ/Zubdat*, ff. 328ab (Shami, *Zafar-name*, 2:169–70).

74 Hafiz Abru, *Majmaᶜ/Zubdat*, ff. 237b, 249a (Shami, *Zafar-name*, 2:88–89, 99); *Muᶜizz al-Ansab*, ff. 105b, 129b, 133b, 138b, 142a. For a narrative description of this dual court system around the time of Timur's birth, see Abu ᶜAbd Allah Muhammad Ibn Battutah, *Tuhfat al-Nuzzar fi Ghara'ib al-Amsar wa ᶜAja'ib al-Asfar*, ed. and trans. C. Defremery and B. R. Sanguinetti, *Voyages d'Ibn Batoutah*. 4 vols. (Paris, 1853–58), 3:11–12; for a normative account of the *yarghu* and the *yarghuchi* in late Ilkhanid times, see Muhammad Nakhjavani, *Dastur al-Katib fi Taᶜyin al-Maratib*, ed. ᶜAbd al-Karim ᶜAlizade, 2 vols. (Moscow, 1964–76), 2:29–35.

75 Note, however, that coinage issued in Timur's name in Anatolia after 1402/805 does not refer to Sultan-Mahmud and names Timur *khan*; see, e.g., Ibrahim and Cevriye Artuk, *İstabul Arkeoloji Müzeleri teşhirdeki İslami sikkeler kataloğu*, 2 vols. (Istanbul, 1970–74), 1:439 (Germiyan); 443–44 (Qaraman); 2:459 (Ottoman).

76 *Muᶜizz al-Ansab*, f. 82a. For references in Shami, see note 52 above.

77 See note 45 above for references.

78 Natanzi, *Muntakhab*, 102, 113, 199; Hafiz Abru, *Majmaᶜ/Zubdat*, ff. 66b-67a (Shami, *Zafar-name*, 2:9).

79 See my article "Turco-Iranica II: Notes on a Timurid Decree of 1396/798," *Journal of Near Eastern Studies* 43 (1984):332–33, for references.

80 *Shajarat al-Atrak*, ff. 181ab; translation, 381–82.

81 Ibn Khaldun, *Ta^crif*, 372–73; Jean of Sultaniye, "Mémoire," 444, 445, 447, 461.

82 Nasir al-Din Muhammad Ibn al-Furat, *Ta'rikh al-Duwal wa al-Muluk*, ed. C. K. Zurayk, vols. 7–9 (Beirut, 1936–42), 9:7, 14, 24, 358; compare Ibn Khaldun, *Ta^crif*, 382 "guardian" (*kafil*).

83 'Aziz Astarabadi, *Bazm u Razm*, ed. Kilisli Rifat (Istanbul, 1928), 460.

84 Yazdi, *Zafar-name*, Tehran, 1:155; Ibn ^cArabshah, *^cAja'ib*, 7; Clavijo, *Embajada*, 152.

85 Shami, *Zafar-name*, 1:169–70; Yazdi, *Zafar-name*, Tehran, 2:9 ff.

86 *Mu^cizz al-Ansab*, ff. 101b, 115b, 123b, 134b, 140b.

87 L. Fekete, *Einführung in die persische Paläographie, 101 persische Dokumente*, ed. G. Hazai (Budapest, 1977), 63–65, 71–73; Sylvestre de Sacy, "Mémoire sur une correspondence inedite de Tamerlan avec Charles VI," *Mémoires de l'Institut Royal de France, Academie des Inscriptions et Belles-Lettres* 6 (1822):473–78, 479; Nava'i, *Asnad*, 54, 127; Gottfried Herrmann, "Zur Intitulatio timuridischer Urkunden," *Vortrage des XVIII. deutschen Orientalistentages*, ZDMG, Supplement, 2 (Wiesbaden, 1974), 504–5; S. Lane-Poole, *The Coinage of Bukhárá (Transoxiana) in the British Museum from the Time of Timur to the Present Day* (London, 1882), 4–20; Shami, *Zafar-name*, 1:9; see also Ahmad al-Qalqashandi, *Subh al-A^csha fi Sina^cat al-Insha'*, 14 vols. (Cairo, 1913–19), 7:307, 320, 325, 326.

88 Natanzi, *Muntakhab*, 197, 261 (*taqallub*).

89 Ibid., 125; Yazdi, *Zafar-name*, Tehran, 1:67; Haydar Mirza Dughlat, *Tarikh-i Rashidi*, MS, London, British Library, Or. 157, f. 17a; translation: N. Elias and E. Denison Ross, *A History of the Moghuls of Central Asia* (London, 1898), 23.

90 Natanzi, *Muntakhab*, 125; Dughlat, *Rashidi*, f. 30b; translation, 38.

91 Natanzi, *Muntakhab*, 296 = Hafiz Abru, *Majma^c/Zubdat*, ff. 143 ff. (Shami, *Zafar-name*, 2:29–30).

92 Natanzi, *Muntakhab*, 300–301 = Hafiz Abru, *Majma^c/Zubdat*, f. 145b (Shami, *Zafar-name*, 2:31–32); Shami, *Zafar-name*, 1:65; Yazdi, *Zafar-name*, Tehran, 1:173, 174.

93 ^cAla' al-Din ^cAta Malik Juvayni, *Tarikh-i Jahan-Gusha*, ed. Mirza Muhammad Qazwini, 3 vols. (London and Leyden, 1912–37), 1:31; 2:218; Shihab al-Din ^cAbd Allah Shirazi, *Tajziyat al-Amsar va Tazjiyat al-A^csar (Tarikh-i Vassaf)*, lithograph (Bombay, 1852–53/1269), 50; see also Ibn Khaldun, *Ta^crif*, 381–82; *Mu^cizz al-Ansab*, f. 81b.

94 Ibn Battuta, *Tuhfat*, 3:4; al-^cUmari, *Masalik*, 67, 78, 81.

95 Natanzi, *Muntakhab*, 427. See also Peter Jackson, "The Dissolution of the Mongol Empire," *Central Asiatic Journal* 22 (1978):212 quoting Juzjani, *Tabaqat-i Nasiri*, British Library MS. Add. 26189, f. 225b (variant of the printed text, Kabul, 1963–64/1342–43, 2:176) for an instance of a similar practice attested from classical Mongol times.

96 Natanzi, *Muntakhab*, 93.

[97] Hafiz Abru, *Majma^c/Zubdat*, f. 3a (Shami, *Zafar-name*, 2:187).

[98] Yazdi, *Zafar-name*, Tehran, 1:228.

[99] Ibid., 1:229; Hafiz Abru, [*Jughrafiya-yi Tarikhi*], MS, Tashkent, IV AN UzSSR, 5361, ff. 412ab (Hafiz Abru, *Panj Risale-yi Tarikhi*, ed. Felix Tauer, *Cinq opuscules de Hafiz-i Abru concernant l'histoire de l'Iran au temps de Tamerlan* [Prague, 1959] [Českolovenská Akademie Ved, Archiv Orientání, Supplementa, 5], 61–62); Fasih al-Din Ahmad, "Fasih-i Khvafi," *Mujmal-i Fasihi*, ed. M. Farrukh, 3 vols. (Mashhad, 1960–62/1339–41), 3:131; Ibn ^cArabshah, ^c*Aja'ib*, 8, 24–25.

[100] Nava'i, *Asnad*, 54–63; see also Shami, *Zafar-name*, 1:118.

[101] Hafiz Abru, *Majma^c/Zubdat*, f. 233a (Shami, *Zafar-name*, 2:77).

[102] Shami, *Zafar-name*, 1:111–12; Yazdi, *Zafar-name*, Tehran, 1:330; Hafiz Abru, *Majma^c/Zubdat*, ff. 224b-225a (Shami, *Zafar-name*, 2:69).

[103] Shami, *Zafar-name*, 1:118. There is no hint of this religious justification in Timur's commemorative inscription of 1391/793; see A. I. Ponomarev, "Popravki k chteniyu nadpisi Timura," *Sovetskoe Vostokovedeniya* 3 (1945): 222–24.

[104] Astarabadi, *Bazm*, 460.

[105] Sari ^cAbd Allah Efendi, *Munsha'at-i Farsi*, MS, Istanbul, Es^cad Efendi, 3333, ff. 6a-10a, published by A. Z. V. Togan in "Timurs Osteuropapolitik," *Zeitschrift der Deutschen Morgenländischen Gesellschaft* 108 (1958):295–96.

[106] Haydar Ivughli [Evoğlu], *Nuskhe-yi Jami^ce-yi Murasalat-i Ulu al-Albab*, MS, London, British Library, Add. 7688, ff. 26b-27b, published in Nava'i, *Asnad*, 75–79. See the important statement in al-^cUmari, *Masalik*, 20, on the Hülegü'id usurpation not quoted in Jackson, "Dissolution."

[107] Jackson, "Dissolution," 212.

[108] Note in this connection the prominence given to the Ögedayids in the Tashkent manuscript of Rashid al-Din's *Jami^c al-Tavarikh*, considered to date no later than the beginning of the fifteenth/ninth century. See Storey and Bregel, *Persidskaya literatura*, 307, and Bartol'd, *Sochineniya*, 8:179n282.

[109] For the meaning of *ilkhan* as subordinate or lieutenant khan, see Doerfer, *Elemente*, 2:207–9, and Jackson, "Dissolution," 231–32, quoting Rashid al-Din, *Jami^c*, 530.

[110] Osman Sertkaya, *Islami devrenin uygur harfli eserlerine toplu bir bakış* (Bochum, 1977), 9, 15; Sertkaya, "Timurlü şeceresi," 250–51; Esin, "The Bakhshi," 290.

[111] Sertkaya, "Toplu bir bakış," 9; Sertkaya, "Timurlü seçeresi," 251.

[112] A. Z. V. Togan, *On the Miniatures in Istanbul Libraries* (Istanbul, 1963), 11; Esin, "The Bakshi," 290; ^cAbd al-Hayy Habibi, *Hunar-i ^cahd-i Timuriyan va mutafarri^cat-i an* (Tehran, 1976/2535 [1355]), 565–72, essentially a paraphrase of Togan.

[113] The lineages of ^cUmar-Shaykh and Miranshah in Husayn's genealogy were elaborated in the second half of the fifteenth/ninth century under their descendants Sultan-Abu Sa^cid (d. 1469/873) and Sultan-Husayn (d. 1506/912). The same is also to be seen in the *Mu^cizz al-Ansab*.

[114] *Mu^cizz al-Ansab*, f. 100b; *pisar-i buzurg-i Amir Sahib-Qiran Jahangir Mirza bude'ast*. According to Shami, *Zafar-name*, 1:58, and Yazdi, *Zafar-name*,

Tehran, 1:149, however, ᶜUmar-Shaykh was sixteen in 1370/771, indicating that he was born in 1354/755, while Yazdi, *Zafar-name*, Tehran, 1:201, reports that Jahangir died at age twenty in 777, the Year of the Dragon which began on March 12, 1376/19 Shavval 777, placing his birth in 1356/757.

115 Shami, *Zafar-name*, 1:192; Ghiyas al-Din ᶜAli Yazdi, *Ruz-name-yi Ghazavat-i Hindustan*, ed. L. A. Zimin, *Dnevnik pokhoda Timura v Indiyu* (Petrograd, 1915), 124.

116 Taj al-din Salmani, *Shams al-Husn*, ed. and trans. Hans R. Roemer, *Šams al-Ḥusn, Eine Chronik vom Tode Timurs bis zum Jahre 1409* (Wiesbaden, 1956), ff. 33a, 42b; Yazdi, *Zafar-name*, Tehran, 2:466, 479—not mentioned in Hafiz Abru, *Majmaᶜ/Zubdat*, f. 375a, but see ff. 387ab.

117 Hafiz Abru, *Majmaᶜ/Zubdat*, f. 365a: *Muhammad Jahangir-ra bi khaniyat qabul kard va khud bar masnad-i hukumat va imarat qarar girift*; Yazdi, *Zafar-name*, Tehran, 2:505 (not mentioned in Salmani, *Shams*): *Muhammad Jahangir . . . bi ism-i khani namzad kardand . . . ism-i u-ra bi al-rasm bar sadr-i manashir va ahkam sabt mikardand*. The numismatic evidence in Lane-Poole, *Coinage of Bukhárá*, 21, shows only the use of the title *sultan* for Muhammad Jahangir.

118 Salmani, *Shams*, f. 64b.

119 This is confirmed by an important coin in the collection of Robert C. Grossman of Skokie, Ill., bearing the legend *Miranshah Kuragan, Abu al-Muzaffar Aba Bakr*.

120 Hafiz Abru, *Majmaᶜ/Zubdat*, ff. 378b-79b: *ism-i saltanat bi nam-i khud gardanid va tuy-i bi 'azamat farmud va bar takht nishast*.

121 Ibid., f. 372ab.

122 Ibid., f. 364a.

123 Yazdi, *Zafar-name*, Tehran, 2:479: *va dar vaqiᶜ varis-i mulk va takht-i Sahib-Qiran-i saᶜid sharᶜan va ᶜaqlan Amirzade Shahrukh'ast*.

124 Jalal al-Din Yusuf Jami, "Yusuf-i Ahl," *Fara'id-i Ghiyasi*, MS, Tehran University, 4756, pp. 671–77; esp., 673: *hamigi himmat bar ihya-yi rusum-i dini va ahkam-i qavanin-i umur-i sharᶜi masruf'ast*. On the protocol of this document, see Herrmann, "Intitulatio," 505 ff.

125 See, for example, Ibn ᶜArabshah, ᶜ*Aja'ib*, 320; Dughlat, *Rashidi*, f. 51a; translation, 69–70; and Nava'i, *Asnad*, 134, 164.

126 See, for example, Fazl Allah Khunji-Isfahani, *Tarikh-i ᶜAlam-ara-yi Amini*, MS, Istanbul, Fatih, 4431, f. 180b.

127 For example, Lane-Poole, *Coinage of Bukhárá*, 22–34; Jean Deny, "Un soyurgal du Timouride Šahruh en écriture ouigoure," *Journal Asiatique* 245 (1957):255; Jami, *Fara'id*, MS, Preussischer Staatsbibliothek, 110, f. 311b.

128 Lane-Poole, *Coinage of Bukhárá*, 38; Minorsky in Barthold, *Four Studies*, 2:Appendix A, 178, summarizing Bartol'd, "Monety Ulugbeka," *Sochineniya*, 4:362–66: *Timur Kuragan himmatidin, Ulugh Beg Kuragan sözümiz*.

129 Barthold, *Four Studies*, 2:85–86 = Bartol'd, *Sochineniya*, 2.2:98–99, quoting Dughlat, *Rashidi*, f. 52b; translation, 72; see also Dughlat, *Rashidi*, ff. 58ab; translation, 83–84. It should be noted, however, that when 'Abd al-Latif revolted against his father Ulugh Beg, he elevated an unspecified khan "after the custom of Timur" (*bi yusun-i Hazrat-i Sahib-Qiran*) to issue the sentence legitimating

his act of patricide; see Kamal al-Din ^cAbd al-Razzaq Samarqandi, *Matla^c-i Sa^cdayn va Majma^c-i Bahrayn*, ed. Muhammad Shafi^c (Lahore, 1941–49), 991. On a coin in the Grossman collection, ^cAbd al-Latif gives his *nasab* as ^cAbd al-Latif b. Shahrukh b. Timur.

[130] Nava'i, *Asnad*, 165, 172, 174, 180, 187, 189.

[131] Lane-Poole, *Coinage of Bukhárá*, 40–41, 50; A. N. Kurat, *Topkapı Sarayı müzesi arşivindeki Altın Ordu, Kırım, ve Türkistan hanlarına ait yarlık ve bitikler* (Istanbul, 1940), 120.

6
ULRICH HAARMANN

Albert-Ludwigs-Universität, Freiburg im Breisgau
Federal Republic of Germany

Regicide and the "Law of the Turks"

WE OWE Martin Dickson important
insights into the rules and dynamics of Turkish statecraft. In the introduction to his 1958 Princeton dissertation on "Shah Tahmasb and the Uzbeks" (which to our greatest regret was never published) as well as in his concise contribution to the 25th International Congress of Orientalists in Moscow[1] on "Uzbek Dynastic Theory in the Sixteenth Century," he studied the modes of distributing and legitimizing power in a post-Chingizid, specifically Turkish polity: the Uzbek confederacy that was to dominate Transoxania and Turkestan in the sixteenth century barred Safawid expansion to the northeast, and provided the framework for the silver age revival of orthodox Islam in Bukhara and Samarqand.

———————— I ————————

In this connection it may not be inappropriate to turn one's attention to a so-called "law (or custom, in Arabic: asa[t] = Yasa) of the Turks" to be encountered in the very first phase of Mamluk history. This asat al-Turk entails the following norm: He who kills the king will be king himself.

This "law" is mentioned within the context of the assassination of Sultan al-Malik al-Muzaffar Qutuz after his triumphal victory over the Mongol army led by Ketbogha Noyon at ᶜAyn Jalut in October 1260. The amir Rukn al-din Baybars al-Bunduqdari, who had fought with exceptional bravery in this decisive battle against the Tatars, had the feeling that Qutuz would not duly recompense him for his achievement and, preempting a similar fate for himself, slew Qutuz during a hunting expedition at Qusayr al-Salihiyya, on the road from Damascus to Cairo on the fringe of the desert, at the time when the victorious army was slowly returning to Egypt.[2] Baybars was now declared new sultan and received the homage of the assembled great amirs.

There are two closely related reports on these events that are of particular interest to us. One is by Muhyi al-din Ibn ᶜAbd al-Zahir (1223/620–1292/692) and forms part of his *vita* of Baybars, *al-Rawd al-zahir fi sirat al-Malik al-Zahir*.[3] This work was written during Baybars's lifetime and is correspondingly uncritical toward the more problematic and sinister chapters in his biography. The other historian is Ibn ᶜAbd al-Zahir's maternal nephew Shafiᶜ b. ᶜAli (1252/649–1330/730), who very deliberately tries to bring light to all those passages in which his uncle and respected master (*al-sahib Muhyi al-din*[4]) had preferred not to be explicit or even to manipulate historical truth.[5] So we learn from Shafiᶜ b. ᶜAli[6] that Baybars had by no means, as Ibn ᶜAbd al-Zahir maintains, killed Qutuz single-handedly, but rather had schemed his assassination in collusion with Qutuz's sword-bearer, a certain ᶜAla' al-din Anas[7] (or Qanas?[8]), by luring the sultan, a passionate hunter, insidiously away from the camp. And it was Anas, not Baybars, who seems to have struck the first blow; Baybars only completed the gruesome deed. Qutuz was buried ignominiously on the spot still in his clothes; "until today no one knows exactly where his grave is."[9]

Also in another respect that is of direct relevance to our subject, Shafiᶜ b. ᶜAli provides important additional detail and a picture somewhat different from the one given by Ibn ᶜAbd al-Zahir: The consensus of the assembled grandees who had to choose a successor for Qutuz had been— on this point both chroniclers agree—to elect Sayf al-din Balaban al-Rashidi al-Salihi, "the most venerable" (*akbaruhum qadran wa-aᶜlahum dhikran*)[10] candidate from among their own ranks. Al-Rashidi had only recently been released from prison by Qutuz. Suddenly, however, the *atabak* Faris ad-din Aqtay al-Mustaᶜrib intervened and interrupted the process of nominating al-Rashidi by asking:

> "What are you about to do with him?" Pointing at al-Rashidi, they answered: "We are making him sultan." He then retorted: "What does *the law of the Turks* say?" They answered: "That kingship should go to him who has killed." He then replied: "And who is the one who has killed?" "He," they answered, pointing at al-Malik al-Zahir [Baybars]. He (= Faris ad-din) then took him by his hand and made him sit as king [on the royal cushion].[11]

In an earlier passage of his work Shafi^c replaces this dialogue (fictitious as it is likely to have been) between Faris al-din al-Atabak and the magnates by a brief speech delivered by Faris al-din: "^{c}Amirs, if al-Malik al-Muzaffar [Qutuz] had left a son I would be the first to fight for his installation [as new sultan]. But now this has happened [and cannot be remedied] *and the law of the Turks says that he who kills the king shall be king himself.* Why else should he who killed this king personally have taken this risk—[only to see] that kingship should go to someone else? You all know that it was this amir Rukn al-din [Baybars] who killed him.' Thereupon he took [Baybars] by his hand, seated him on the royal cushion (*tarraha*), and he received the royal title, *laqab* [al-Malik] al-Qahir, which was then changed to [al-Malik] al-Zahir."^{12}

In Ibn ^{c}Abd al-Zahir's version, the basis of the two texts just quoted, there is a statement made by Faris al-din al-Atabak which is not in the form of a conversation between him and the Mamluk grandees. Addressing those present he said, " 'Listen, my friends! By God, if al-Malik al-Muzaffar [Qutuz] was still alive, or if he had left a son, we would owe fealty to him (*labu fi ^{c}unuqina yamin*) and I would be the first to fight [even] you with my sword [to support his claim]. But as things are now (*as-sa^{c}a*) this matter has happened, and there is no doubt that he who killed him and put his life at stake and carried out this grave act did not do it to the benefit of someone else. He did not risk his life (*wa-la badhala nafsahu wa-khatara biha*) only to see that the rule (*al-amr wa'l-nahy*) goes to another person. For he who killed him has the first claim for his position.' The sultan replied: 'It was me who committed this deed.' The assembly agreed upon this, and the sultan stood up and took his seat on the royal cushion."^{13}

The "law of the Turks" is not explicitly mentioned in Ibn ^{c}Abd al-Zahir's rendering of this event.

Numerous questions are raised by this text, some of them very specific (was Faris al-din's initiative masterminded by Baybars?), others rather general. What role did the *asat al-Turk* play in Mamluk history? There is, indeed, another implicit reference to this Turkish convention in early Mamluk history. When Sultan al-Ashraf Khalil, the son of Sultan Qalawun and conqueror of ^{c}Akka, was assassinated by a group of rebellious amirs around Baydara and Lajin (the future sultan al-Malik al-Mansur), the following gruesome scene took place: Baydara hit his defenseless victim with the sword yet only managed to cut off his hand. Now Lajin, in collusion with Baydara, sarcastically asked his fellow conspirator: "Is this the blow of someone who wants to be king?" (*man yuridu 'l-mulk takunu hadhihi darbatuhu?*)^{14} Thereupon Baydara hit Khalil a second time, again not strongly enough to kill him. In the end the chief of the guard, a certain Sayf al-din Bahadur, brutally pierced the throat of the poor sultan.

In this context one will note that both Baybars and Baydara, both gaining the sultanate as successful regicides (even though this triumph lasted only a few hours in Baydara's case) adopted the regnal title al-Malik al-Qahir. Did Baybars relinquish it and change it to the less martial al-Malik al-Zahir after his power was consolidated? Or was the renunciation of this title not rather, as the contemporary historian Ibn Wasil maintains,[15] caused by Baybars's fear from a bad omen that was associated with this very name?

Both Ibn ʿAbd al-Zahir and Shafiʿ b. ʿAli agree, if only rhetorically, on the primacy of the dynastic principle, familiar from the Ayyubids, over the asat al-Turk. However, this priority of hereditary succession over usurpatory practices did not last into later Mamluk history. It was rather reversed in the course of time. Gradually succession by sons and brothers—so natural and acceptable to fourteenth-century observers[16]—was replaced by the rigorous application of a new motto: al-mulk ʿaqim, "kingship has no progeny,"[17] a nonspecific formula that no longer necessitated the "ceremonial" assassination of the ruler by his would-be successor. This was first mentioned in the early fourteenth century in connection with Baybars (II) al-Jashnkir's brief sultanate. It began to fully assert itself in the Circassian period, at the latest after the demise of Barquq's son Faraj and the humiliating abdication of the sultan-caliph al-Mustaʿin in 1412. Were the Circassian Mamluks (also Baybars II had been a Circassian) particularly adamant about this norm? Certainly, by the end of the fifteenth century, the succession of the son (instead of a genuine, i.e., first-generation Mamluk) was generally regarded as illegitimate.[18]

———————— II ————————

There is a historical precedent to the invocation of this asat al-Turk, in which, however, no Turks are explicitly mentioned. It goes back to the late tenth/fourth century and takes us to Upper Mesopotamia during the period of the Hamdanid (Arab)-Marwanid (Kurdish) contest over the control of Diyar Bakr.

In 990–91/380 Badh, the Kurdish tribal ruler of Diyar Bakr and former Buyid vassal, perished in his fight against the ʿUqaylids, then the allies of the Hamdanids, in the vicinity of Mosul.[19] Badh's nephew (through his sister), Abu ʿAli al-Hasan b. Marwan, who had failed to rescue his uncle during the decisive battle,[20] entered the fortress of Mayyafariqin held by Badh's wife, informed her of the death of her husband, and contrived to marry her in his stead.[21] Within a short period he furthermore managed to regain the territories formerly held by Badh, to take revenge on the Hamdanid princes (one of whom is rescued only at the intervention of the Fatimids[22]), and to stand up successfully against the Byzantines between the Upper Euphrates and Lake Van with whom he concludes an honorable truce for ten years in 992/382.[23]

In his internal politics Abu ᶜAli was, however, less fortunate. In his residence at Mayyafariqin he had to face an insubordinate citizenry, headed by the shaykh al-balad, a certain Muhammad b. Abi 'l-Saqr.[24] The people of the city still seem to have cherished loyalties to the vanquished Hamdanids.[25] His orders were not obeyed. Without his consent heavy punishment was meted out to some of his own men (jundi aw kurdi).[26] Much to the dismay of his loyal counsel, the chamberlain Mammā (Mamma), his prestige as a ruler was in jeopardy. At Mamma's advice, in 994–95/384, he used the opportunity of the absence of many inhabitants from the town on the occasion of one of the two feasts—the chronicler of Mayyafariqin, Ibn Azraq al-Fariqi, leaves open whether it was the ᶜId al-Adha (January 15, 995) or the ᶜId al-Fitr (November 8, 994)[27]—and threw the unruly shaykh al-balad, the paragon of urban resistance and pro-Hamdanid sentiment, from the wall of the city, killing him and also many others. An exodus from Mayyafariqin begins. Many citizens were never to return to their hometown for fear of Abu ᶜAli, who by now had gained full control of the city.

In order to further enhance his position in the region to the north of the Buyid domains Abu ᶜAli contracted his marriage with Sitt al-nas bint Saᶜd al-Dawla, a Hamdanid princess. That this liaison could also be seen as an effort on the part of the Hamdanids to regain control over the lost province of Diyar Bakr becomes evident from an anecdote in which the young bride, on her way from Aleppo to Edessa and Amid, was forewarned of a horseman who would make her a widow even before the nuptial night, whereupon one of her companions, a granddaughter of the celebrated adib al-Khatib ibn Nubata (946/335–984/374, who was born and died in Mayyafariqin),[28] cheered her up reminding her that "you are about to take the lands of your father and your grandfather back into possession."[29]

In 997/387 Abu ᶜAli left Mayyafariqin to meet his future wife halfway in Amid—foolishly, as it turned out, leaving his chamberlain Mamma behind. In his company were his brothers and, in Mamma's lieu, his son Sharwa as hajib. Eager to seat his personal protector Abu Mansur Saᶜid b. Marwan on the throne in Abu ᶜAli's place, Sharwa sought contact with the shaykh al-balad of Amid, ᶜAbd al-Barr, head of the market of victuals in the city. He warned him treacherously that he and persons like him would suffer from the Marwanid ruler—who might be looking benevolent yet in reality was cunning and brutal—the same fate that had happened to Muhammad b. Abi 'l-Saqr and the people of Mayyafariqin "who were, after all, less partisan against him [Abu ᶜAli] than you and more ready to suffer.''[30] All taken by fright, ᶜAbd al-Barr, who had been prepared to serve Abu ᶜAli loyally, confronted the people of Amid, who in full alarm now gave him a free hand to act. ᶜAbd al-Barr suggested the following stratagem:[31] "When [Abu ᶜAli] enters the gate, I shall make him unaware of you by pouring money over him (*bi-'l-nithar*) [as the common token of welcome]. In this moment [when he lifts his arm to ward off the coins] you shall hit him with your swords. We shall close the gate and thus seal his fate. *And whoever kills him first shall be the prince of the city (wa-man basharahu minkum bi-'l-qatl kana amir al-madina).*''

This plan was indeed successfully carried out. Abu ᶜAli's brother Abu Mansur Saᶜid Mumahhid al-dawla—the first Marwanid to adopt a *laqab* (Buyid style, as one should add) as Ibn Azraq al-Fariqi makes us aware[32]—succeeded as a ruler[33] in Mayyafariqin, although, as Ibn al-Athir is eager to point out, initially only as figurehead without any effective power (*wa-lam yakun lahu fihi illa 'l-sikka wa-'l-khutba*).[34] This lack of political ambition in no way impeded (or even rather may have furthered) the rise of Mumahhid al-dawla to become one of the most luminous patrons of medicine in medieval Islam; Jibril b. ᶜUbaydallah, a descendant of Bukhtishuᶜ, Yahya b. Jarir and Mansur b. ᶜIsa, they all sought the proximity of this Marwanid ruler.[35]

In Amid, however, the regicide, a certain Abu Tahir Yusuf b. Damna (was he a Kurd, a Turcoman, or an Arab?) was indeed to triumph, if only after he had assassinated ᶜAbd al-Barr, whose daughter he had been given in marriage and who had initially taken over the command of the city after Abu ᶜAli's death. To what degree Ibn Damna asserted his rights, on the basis of the "Turkish law," by killing ᶜAbd al-Barr, cannot be determined. Ibn Damna then, to quote Ibn al-Athir, "brought his relations with Mumahhid al-dawla (who married the Hamdanid princess in his brother's stead) in order, concluded an armistice with the king of the Byzantines and the lord (*sahib*) of Egypt (this was the derogatory term customary for the heretic-Ismaᶜili Fatimids) as well as with other rulers, and his fame spread around."[36]

--------------- III ---------------

Is there any common denominator for the two contexts in which we have heard explicitly of the application of the "law of the Turks"? Evidently it was a custom not limited to ethnic, Turkish, quarters. The Marwanids were Kurds, and Abu ᶜAli's murderer may even have been an Arab. If we keep in mind that the term "Turk"—at least in the Mamluk period— was often understood to encompass ethnic groups that were not Turkish strictly speaking yet in their life-style and certainly in the perception of outside observers closely assimilated to Turkdom—such as Kurds and outside observers closely assimilated to Turkdom—such as Kurds and Circassians—one is tempted to suggest that we rather face a custom of nomadic tribesmen of the vast regions to the North (the Dasht-i Qipchaq, the homeland of the Bahri Mamluks) and to the South (Eastern Anatolia, Armenia and Adharbayjan, the Kurdish territories) of the Caucasus. The term *asa*, derived from Mongol *yasa*, might even point to an origin further to the East in Central Asia. Direct connections between the two episodes will, however, be as difficult to establish as it will be desirable to find a broader and more representative documentation on the "law of the Turks."

One may nevertheless recall in this connection that the first, albeit abortive, application of the "law of the Turks" in Mamluk history may well not have been the killing of Qutuz by Baybars, but rather the murder of Turanshah, the son of al-Salih Ayyub, by al-Faris Aqtay (not to be confused with al-Faris Aqtay al-Musta^c^rib mentioned above), the leader of the Bahri Mamluks who, however, did not succeed in gaining the sultanate for himself, because—in this early stage of Mamluk history—one evidently preferred not to put the strongest of the oligarchs on the throne.[37] This murder, on May 2, 1250/28 Muharram 648, four weeks after Turanshah's triumphant victory over the French king Louis IX at al-Mansura, marked the effective termination of Ayyubid sway over Egypt. The unfortunate Turanshah may well have understood what was at stake when al-Faris Aqtay approached him brandishing his sword in the shallow waters of the Nile. Before he had been summoned to the Nile to take the place of his deceased father in a period of grave peril for Ayyubid Egypt and Islam altogether, he had held the remote fief of Hisn Kayfa right in the Ayyubid-Kurdish heartland on the Upper Tigris (i.e., exactly the region in which also the Marwanids had flourished). But, for the time being, this connection cannot be more than speculation.

Notes

[1] In *Trudy 25-ogo Mezhdunarodnogo Kongressa Vostokovedov* (Moscow, 1963), 3:208–17.

[2] al-Maqrizi, *Kitab al-Suluk li-ma^c^rifat duwal al-muluk*, ed. Muhammad Mustafa Ziyada (Cairo, 1936), 1:330, 4–6; see also the reference in Shafi^c^ b. ^c^Ali b. ^c^Abbas al-Katib: *Husn al-manaqib al-sirriyya al-muntaza^c^a min al-sira al-zahiriyya*, ed. ^c^Abd al-^c^Aziz b. ^c^Abdallah al-Khuwaytir, al-Riyad (1976/1396), 31n1.

[3] Ed. by ^c^Abd al-^c^Aziz al-Khuwaytir, al-Riyad (Beirut, 1976/1396); see also a précis of Baybars's career based on this source compiled by the editor: Abdul-Aziz Khowaiter, *Baibars the First: His Endeavours and Achievements* (London, 1978).

[4] Cf., e.g., *Husn al-manaqib*, 31, 18.

⁵ On Shafi^c's chronicle see note 2 above; for his criticism of his uncle and model see Ulrich Haarmann, *Quellenstudien zur frühen Mamlukenzeit* (Freiburg, 1970), 145–47; Baybars used to sit with Ibn ^cAbd al-Zahir and listen to what his secretary had written on him since their last meeting. In the end Ibn ^cAbd al-Zahir was regularly remunerated for his pleasant and complimentary writing—no wonder that such a relationship did not allow for the presentation of the unvarnished truth! On this subject we now have also Peter M. Holt, "Three Biographies of al-Zahir Baybars," in D. O. Morgan, ed., *Medieval Historical Writing in the Christian and Islamic Worlds* (London: School of Oriental and African Studies, 1982), 19–29, esp. 26f; and Peter M. Holt, "Succession in the Early Mamluk Sultanate," in *Zeitschrift der Deutschen Morgenländischen Gesellschaft*. Supplement VII: XXIII. *Deutscher Orientalistentag vom 16. bis 20. September 1985 in Würzburg.* Ausgewählte Vorträge. (Stuttgart, 1989), 144–48, esp. 145. In the latter article, Holt ends the relevant passage by writing: "Furthermore one wonders if there is any evidence of a Turkish tribal custom of regicide or chief-killing such as is alleged in this passage"; my article here is intended to turn the attention to this question and to show possible parallels inside and outside of Turkish quarters.

⁶ *Husn al-manaqib*, 31, 21: Ibn ^cAbd al-Zahir states that "al-Malik al-Zahir grabbed the hand of Qutuz and killed him with nobody participating in the murder."

⁷ Ibid., 31, 12. This form (one also reads Anas) is given in most of the Mamluk sources describing these events; cf. the different reports by other contemporary as well as later chroniclers as they are presented in Peter Thorau, *Sultan Baibars I. von Ägypten. Ein Beitrag zur Geschichte des Vorderen Orients im 13. Jahrhundert* (Wiesbaden, 1987), 99–101. See also the remarks in Robert Irwin, *The Middle East in the Middle Ages: The Early Mamluk Sultanate 1250–1382* (London and Sydney, 1986), 37.

⁸ *Husn al-manaqib*, 155, 6.

⁹ Ibid., 31, 14–15.

¹⁰ Ibid., 31, 26–32, 1.

¹¹ Ibid., 155, 12–22.

¹² Ibid., 32, 4–9.

¹³ *al-Rawd al-zahir*, 69, 2–8.

¹⁴ Khalil b. Aybak al-Safadi: *al-Wafi bi-'l-wafayat*, vol. 13, ed., Muhammad al-Hujayri (Wiesbaden, Beirut, 1984/1404), 400, lines 6–10 (biography of Sultan al-Ashraf Khalil).

¹⁵ See his *Mufarrij al-kurub fi akhbar bani Ayyub*, MS Paris No. 1703, f. 164r-v; see the reference in Thorau, *Sultan Baibars*, 104n60.

¹⁶ Cf. the remark by the Mamluk grandee Tashtamur Hummus Akhdar after al-Malik al-Nasir Muhammad's death when one of the later sultan's sons was about to be stripped of some of his privileges in Khalil b. Aybak al-Safadi's *al-Wafi bi-'l-wafayat*, ed. Wadad al-Qadi (Wiesbaden/Beirut, 1982/1402), 16:440, 16f.

¹⁷ See Peter M. Holt, "Some Observations on the ^cAbbasid Caliphate of Cairo," in *BSOAS* 47.3 (1984); Ulrich Haarmann, "Der arabische Osten im späten Mittelalter," in U. Haarmann, ed., *Geschichte der arabischen Welt* (Munich, 1987),

229; Jean-Claude Garcin, "The Mamluk Military System and the Blocking of Medieval Moslem Society," in Jean Baechler, John A. Hall, and Michael Mann, eds., *Europe and the Rise of Capitalism* (Oxford, 1988), 120.

[18] Arnold von Harff, *The Pilgrimage of Arnold von Harff, Knight from Cologne . . . in the Years 1496 to 1499*, trans. and ed. Malcolm Letts (The Hakluyt Society. 2d series, vol. 94), Nendeln/Liechtenstein [2] (1967), 104n1, 121; Haarmann, "Der arabische Osten," 229.

[19] See H. F. Amedroz, "The Marwanid Dynasty of Mayyafariqin in the Tenth and Eleventh Centuries A.D.," in *JRAS* (January 1903): 123–54, here 124; Heribert Busse, *Chalif und Grosskönig. Die Buyiden im Irak (945–1055)* (Beirut, 1969), 73. Badh figures prominently in the writings of Abu Ishaq al-Sabi' and, as a corollary, even of al-Qalqashandi, cf. *Subh al-a^{c}sha fi sina^{c}at al-insha* (Cairo 1913/1331–1919/1338), 7:104, 14f. and 8:347, 10f.; see also Walther Björkman, *Beitrage zur Geschichte der Staatskanzlei im islamischen Ägypten* (Hamburg, 1928), 125, 138. I owe this reference to Dr. Ludger Ilisch, Basel.

[20] Ibn al-Athir, *al-Kamil fi 'l-tarikh* [2] (Beirut 1979/1399), 9:71, 8–9.

[21] Ibn Azraq al-Fariqi, *Tarikh al-Fariqi* [2], ed. Badawi ^{c}Abd al-Latif ^{c}Awad (Cairo, 1959, Beirut, 1974), 60, 12; *Kamil*, 71, 18.

[22] *Kamil*, 72, 4–5.

[23] *Tarikh al-Fariqi*, 61; *Kamil*, 94, 17–19.

[24] *Tarikh al-Fariqi*, 68, 6.

[25] See the remark by Amedroz, "The Marwanid Dynasty," 124.

[26] *Tarikh al-Fariqi*, 67, 6–8.

[27] Ibid., 68, 1–2. See also *Kamil*, 72, 10–11.

[28] See Carl Brockelmann, *Geschichte der arabischen Litteratur* (Leiden, 1943), 1:92; Ibn Nubata spent most of his life as preacher at the Hamdanid court in Aleppo. He personalizes the close ties between Mayyafariqin and the Hamdanid capital.

[29] *Tarikh al-Fariqi*, 73, 10–11.

[30] Ibid., 76, 5.

[31] Ibid., 76, 9–11. See also *Kamil*, 72, 15–21 (without the crucial quotation) and Haarmann, *Quellenstudien*, 146n6.

[32] *Tarikh al-Fariqi*, 77, 11.

[33] See the brief sketch on his rule (and sad end) by Amedroz, "Marwanid Dynasty," 126–31.

[34] *Kamil*, 9:73, 6–8.

[35] Busse, *Chalif und Grosskönig*, 517–18.

[36] *Kamil*, 9:73, 11–12.

[37] The event is described in detail (with indication of the relevant sources) in R. Stephen Humphrey's, *From Saladin to the Mongols: The Ayyubids of Damascus 1193–1260* (Albany, N.Y., 1977), 302–3.

7

LEILA AL-IMAD

Department of History, East Tennessee State University
Johnson City, Tennessee

Women and Religion in the Fatimid Caliphate: The Case of al-Sayyidah al-Hurrah, Queen of Yemen

FROM THE point of view of strict religious duties and obligations, Muslim men and women were treated as equals by the Prophet and by the Qur'an. In *surah* 9:71–72, specific reference is made to this point: "And the believers, men and women, are protecting friends one of another; they enjoin the right and forbid the wrong, and they establish worship and they pay the poor due, and they obey Allah and his messenger. . . . Allah promiseth to the believers, men and women, Gardens underneath which rivers flow, wherein they will abide—blessed dwellings in Gardens of Eden. And—greater (far!)—acceptance from Allah. That is supreme triumph."

The Qur'an does not restrict women only to the role of passive acceptance of religion. They are in fact called upon to "establish worship" and to spread the religion of Allah and to teach it. In this respect Islam differs from Judaism. The dicta of rabbinic Judaism specifically mention that men should not teach their daughters the Torah.[1] This view is also found in the New Testament (I Timothy 2:12): "I do not permit a woman to teach or to have authority over men."[2]

Not only did Islam permit women to spread the religion but also it accorded them an equal standing with men as far as this matter was concerned. In a well-known hadith, the Prophet said that women should not be barred from entering mosques to listen to preachers or to attend prayers, so long as they were segregated from men, a practice which may be found in other religious communities of his time.[3]

With the religious splits in Islam, women's status also changed, particularly in matters of inheritance. The Qur'an specifically states that in matters of inheritance a son's share is double his sister's, an uncle inherits if no male heirs are available, and so on. The Shiʿites introduced equal divisions of property among survivors, and in cases where no male heir was available, the Shiʿites gave the property equally to the daughters of a deceased male. Except for mutʿah marriages, this was looked upon as an improvement in women's status. The Ismaʿilis, an offshoot of the Shiʿites whose tolerance has been noted by many historians, improved women's lot by encouraging them to pursue knowledge.

Further encouragement of religious careers for women came with the accession of the Fatimid caliphate, in which the Ismaʿili daʿwa entered a new phase. The daʿwa became an open one rather than an underground movement calling on its followers to believe in a hidden imam. Now the imams became caliphs, and the duʿat had a reason to proselytize in the name of al-Mahdi and his successors. The Fatimid policy of tolerance, whether religious or bureaucratic, gave rise to a multitude of talented individuals who became staunch supporters of the daʿwa. The Ikhwan al-Safa' best expressed this tolerance: "It befits our brothers that they should not show hostility to any kind of knowledge or reject any book. Nor should they be fanatical in any doctrine, for our opinion and our doctrine embrace all doctrines, and presume all knowledge."[4] The Fatimids encouraged knowledge and encouraged those who sought it by building libraries and fostering the art of reading. They benefited from this by exposing their subject peoples to their own religion and their own theory of state. Women as well as men were encouraged to use books. The Fatimids organized sessions for both men and women whereby the duʿat taught the Ismaʿili religion. These sessions were organized according to social strata. The historian Maqrizi relates that there were special majalis (as they were called) for the house of ʿAli, for the leaders in society, for court servants, for commoners, travelers, and "the women who were attached to the court, mainly women slaves."[5] Women on the whole attended al-Azhar mosque for prayer and for instruction.

The Fatimids were very keen on educating everyone they could because Ismaʿilism preached equality for believers regardless of whether one came from the upper crust or was a laborer or craftsman. This trend in Ismaʿilism was attacked by many theologians such as al-Ghazali, who admitted that "the chief danger of the heresy (Ismaʿilism) lay in its attraction for the labouring and artisan classes."[6] The Ismaʿilis, mainly through the works of Ikhwan al-Safa', contributed to a flowering of Islamic culture.[7]

Women, not having been excluded from the pursuit of religious education, could not have been barred from teaching what they learned or

from actually spreading the Isma^{c}ili-Fatimid da^cwa. That women partici-
pated in spreading the da^cwa has been established; what actually is very
difficult to ascertain is what rank they achieved and how influential such
a tiny minority of women was, a minority which could not have exceeded
a half dozen. Such women no doubt came from influential upper-class societies. They were to a certain degree an educated elite. The little that is
known about them has come down to us through male historians who
could not absolutely ignore these women. On the other hand, historians
accorded them minimal attention. Although Islam produced women
warriors such as Khawlah bint al-Azwar and women poets such as al-
Khansa', alas no women historians are known to us. Thus no complete
picture of the achievement of many women who were worthy of mention
has survived.

Before describing the role of women in spreading the da^cwa one
should describe the Fatimid da^cwa's structural organization and the ranks
of da^cis. The Isma^{c}ilis/ Fatimids divided the then-known world into twelve
regions or *jaza'ir*, where they sent their religious dignitaries to propagate
the teachings of the imam. The main areas of activity were Yemen, al-Kufa,
Khurasan, Transoxiana, Sind, North Africa, and Salamiyya, Syria. These
dignitaries "are arranged in different grades according to the state of their
knowledge."[8] It is important to note that a da^ci was capable of
proselytizing without necessarily having attained to the highest grades of
knowledge. Many of the da^cis who lived during the Fatimid hegemony
had a double task: not only did they try to obtain converts and spread
the word about the Isma^{c}ilis; they also had to defend the Fatimid caliphate,[9] a task that the Sulaihid queen, al-Sayyidah al-Hurrah, tried to
achieve. The officers in any given *jazirah* or "sector" were of the following ranks: first, a local *hujjah* under whom were several da^cis, "the
more important of whom were called *balagh*, the lesser ones being the
mutlaqs."[10] In the absence of the above-mentioned *hujjah* and da^ci
balagh from a given sector, the da^ci *mutlaq* was promoted to the chief
office of the da^cwa. The da^ci *mutlaq* had two assistants: the *ma'dhun
mutlaq* and *ma'dhun mashhur*. The ordinary believer or *mu'min* and the
mustajib or seeker (candidate to join the da^cwa) were listed as part of the
hierarchy. They were of higher rank and were differentiated from other
Muslims, or ^cammat al-Muslimin.[11] Add to all this the office of da^ci al-
du^cat, which was a bureaucratic position in the Fatimid state and which
was of lesser rank than *qadi al-qudat*. Da^ci al-du^cat was the head of Is-
ma^{c}ili propaganda and the chief liaison officer between the caliph and his
followers. His duties were to oversee preaching in the different *majalis*.
These *majalis* or *karrasat* were lessons written by da^ci al-du^cat and were
sent to the various du^cat to be recited on assigned dates. The da^ci al-du^cat

also headed Dar al-Hikmah and Dar al-ᶜIlm[12] and was entrusted with collecting *al-najwa*, a monetary contribution equivalent to three and one-third *dirhams* per believer, and equivalent to the *zakat* among other Muslims.

Prior to the establishment of the Fatimid caliphate, Yemen had become a center for Ismaᶜili propaganda. "By 881 the daᶜi Ibn Hawshab, with the help of ᶜAli ibn Fadl, the Qarmatian had been able to establish his base in Yemen."[13] Thus the Yemeni *daᶜwa* was well entrenched when the Sulaihid dynasty ruled over Yemen as nominal vassals of the Fatimids. The founder of the Sulaihid dynasty, ᶜAli ibn Muhammad, the *qadi* of Haraz, was from the clan of Yam, a subdivision of the Hamdanids. It was this man, under the influence of the Shiᶜa missionaries, who decided in 1037/428 "to set up the rule of the Fatimids in Yaman."[14] He united the whole of Yemen under his rule. His son, al-Mukarram, became the ruler after his father's death, but he was not a capable ruler. He gave up his position in favor of his wife, Queen Sayyidah al-Hurrah Arwa. The epithet al-Hurrah or "liberated" reflected her actual position as the liberated woman of her era. Al-Hurrah was born in 1052/444 and was brought up in the Sulaihid court by Asma, the mother of al-Mukarram. She subsequently married al-Mukarram and bore him four children. Queen Sayyidah was a very able woman whose independence shocked the medieval Islamic world. Not only did she assume management of affairs of state, she also demanded from al-Mukarram "full freedom of action" without having to answer to him or to any of his men. In order to ensure her independence, she decided to move her residence from Sanᶜa' to Dhu-Jibla, which subsequently became the capital. Her move was absolutely calculated: first she left her husband behind, thus assuring that he would be unable to influence or meddle in her affairs; second, Dhu-Jibla was the Sulaihids' first residence and where their supporters resided; third, her move made those supporters more zealous in their support.

Her political career was as celebrated as her religious one. Having been brought up by the queen mother in the court of ᶜAli ibn Muhammad, the defender of the Isma'ili *daᶜwa* and the Fatimid caliphate, she was given instruction in the faith. Her reign came at a time in Fatimid history when a split was taking place that was essentially both political and religious. The death of the Fatimid caliph al-Mustansir ushered in a period of unrest. His son and designated heir, Nizar, was hailed as the Imam in Syria and Iran, while in Egypt, Yemen, and Sind, al-Mustaᶜli with the help of the army commander, al-Afdal, became the caliph and his son al-Amir followed him. Another problem arose later: al-Amir's son, al-Tayyib, who was still a minor at the death of his father, had been entrusted to "Daᶜi Ibn Madyan, the Bab of the Imam, and a council of *daᶜi*s trustees (*mustauda*ᶜ)."¹⁵ He was taken into concealment and "nothing more was heard from him."¹⁶ The *wazir* ᶜAbd al-Majid, who was entrusted to run affairs of state by al-Amir, tried to influence Queen Sayyidah to change the *da*ᶜ*wa* in Yemen in favor of the Fatimid caliph al-Hafiz. But she insisted on keeping the *da*ᶜ*wa* for al-Tayyib, thus steering Yemen away from the direction the *da*ᶜ*wa* took in Egypt and elsewhere.

With the disappearance of the old school of Ismaᶜili thought in Egypt, Yemen became the refuge for the propagators of the old school.¹⁷ In Yemen, the aim of the *da*ᶜ*wa* had been to convert the masses rather than to try to convert only prominent members of the upper classes. This policy proved very successful, for Yemen until then had a large number of Ismaᶜilis.¹⁸ Because of the nature of her followers, Queen Sayyidah had no problem amassing support for the imamate of al-Tayyib, who went into concealment. Although Queen Sayyidah was not officially accepted as a *da*ᶜ*iyah*, when her husband died with no male heirs she assumed the religious leadership of the Ismaᶜili community although her husband, al-Mukarram himself, had bequeathed the position to Saba', son of Ahmad ibn al-Muzaffar ibn ᶜAli, the Sulaihi. According to Maqrizi and ᶜUmarah al-Yamani, there is no doubt that al-Amir, the Fatimid caliph, did accept al-Sayyidah al-Hurrah as *da*ᶜ*iyat al-Yaman*. In 1123/517 al-Amir sent his envoy to "Hurrat al-Yaman," as she was called, with numerous gifts of jewelry, clothing, and fine foods. Most importantly he sent "twelve lessons of the *da*ᶜ*wa* which were to be read every Thursday. These religious instructions were signed by the caliph."¹⁹

Al-Amir, in a letter accompanying the lessons, gave al-Sayyidah al-Radiyyah or al-Sayyidah al-Hurrah several titles of interest to us: Sayyidat Muluk al-Yaman, ᶜUmdat al-Islam, Khalisat al-Imam, Nasirat al-Din, ᶜIsmat al-Mustarshidin, Waliyyat Amir al-Mu'minin. These titles are more than enough to lead us to conclude that she was indeed the propagator of the Ismaᶜili faith. Her actual rank, while unknown to us, must not have exceeded that of a *da*ᶜ*i mutlaq*, although ᶜImad al-Din Idris, in ᶜ*Uyun al-Akhbar*, relates that she was elevated by al-Mustansir from the rank of *da*ᶜ*i* to that of *hujjah*, a matter that caused a great deal of controversy among the Ismaᶜili religious hierarchy of that time. It is related that al-Khattab ibn Hasan al-Hajwari al-Hamdani, an Ismaᶜili *da*ᶜ*i*, responded to the objections to having a female in a position of *hujjah* by saying

> that the human body is nothing except a cloth or a cover for humanity. We find that many who appeared to us in female covering were of the highest and most noble position, such as al-Zahra' al-Batul, Khadijah ibnat Khulayyid, and Maryam ibnat ᶜImran. It is up to all of you to recognize the signs of their

mission and to obey them as all who believe should obey, without questioning the gender of those who carry the message.[20]

The Sulaihid queen must have contested the position of da^ci of Yemen with the above-mentioned Saba', due to the fact that Saba' had asked al-Mustansir leave to have Sayyidah al-Hurrah marry him so that he could at least practice his da^ci position. She declined at the beginning, then accepted. Saba' came to her capital, Dhu-Jibla, to get married; but he was so intimidated by her that he spent only one night there and left without consummating the marriage. He eventually acquiesced and gave her absolute religious leadership of the Isma^{c}ilis in Yemen.

Two very important questions arise here: why didn't her husband, al-Mukarram, who initially gave her the temporal rule, not give her the religious scepter which he held too? The second question is why did the caliph al-Mustansir want her to marry Saba'? Both questions can be answered simply: the religious leadership of the community could not be entrusted to women, a situation that still persists in the twentieth century. The queen was in fact capable as an individual even when much of her kingdom was split into small principalities. She still exercised some kind of suzerainty over these entities. She even led her own army and regained her capital when it was captured by rivals.

The Fatimids, who saw that her temporal authority was slipping, sent their own emissary, Najib al-Dawlah, in 1119/513 to help subdue the principalities. He did so but was shocked, when he attempted to dethrone her and assume power in 1124/519, by "the strong support [she received from] the various princes of the country [and] . . . was forced to desist from his design."[21] He also tried to call on the Yemenis to follow the Nizari da^cwa, but Sayyidah had him arrested with the caliph al-Amir's permission and shipped him via Aden to Egypt, where he died.

Sayyidah al-Hurrah's influence was much greater than the Fatimid caliph ever dreamt it would be. Not only was she a political and religious leader, she was also, in the words of ^{c}Umarah al-Yamani, "a complete woman, a reciter ($qari'ah$), a scribe ($katibah$) with a superb memory for incidents ($akhbar$), poetry (ash^car), and history ($tarikh$)."[22] She died in 1138/532. With her death Sulaihid rule of Yemen came to an end.

From the case of the Sulaihid queen one gathers that women had a hard time making it as religious leaders on the actual political scene. Given that virtually all those educated in religious matters were male, Sayyidah stands out as an exemplary wife and mother of four children, capable of handling affairs of state and spreading the da^cwa. The Tayyibi da^cwa continued after her death, although it did not enjoy the support of any of the rulers of Yemen.[23] Thus her religious influence did not end with her dynasty.

Notes

[1] Quoted in Rosemary Radford Ruether, "The Feminist Critique in Religious Studies," *Soundings* 64 (1981): 388.

[2] Ibid.

[3] Roger Arnaldez, "Statut juridique et sociologique de la femme en Islam," *Cahiers de civilisation medievale* 20 (1977) 132.

[4] Bernard Lewis, *The Origins of Ismailism* (Cambridge: W. Heffer, 1940), 94.

[5] Taqi al-Din al-Maqrizi, *al-Mawaᶜiz wa al-Iᶜtibar fi dhikr al-khitat wa al-athar* (Cairo: Bulaq Press, 1874/1270), 1:391.

[6] Lewis, *Origins*, 93.

[7] Syed Mohammed Taqi, "Ismailites: Their Contribution to History," *Pakistan Historical Society: Proceedings of the Pakistan Historical Conference* 8 (1958): 89.

[8] Husayn F. al-Hamdani, "A Compendium of Ismaᶜili Esoterics," *Islamic Culture* 2 (1937): 216.

[9] Husayn F. al-Hamdani, "Some Unknown Ismaᶜili Authors and Their Works," *Journal of the Royal Asiatic Society* (1933): 365: "The Daᶜwa which once aimed at the destruction of the Abbasid Khilafa, now defended the claims of the Fatimids. . . . It became then the duty of the Daᶜwa to assume the task of defending the faith as well as to help the state."

[10] Abbas Hamdani, "Evolution of the Organizational Structure of the Fatimi Daᶜwah: the Yemeni and Persian Contributions," *Arabian Studies* 3 (1976): 91.

[11] Ibid.

[12] Hasan Ibrahim Hasan, *Tarikh al-Dawlah al-Fatimiyyah* (Cairo: Maktabat al-Nahdah al-Misriyyah, 1958), 345. Edward G. Browne, *A Literary History of Persia* (Cambridge: Cambridge University Press, 1969), 1:411: "The primary aim of the daᶜi is, indeed, mainly to secure from the proselyte this allegiance, ratified by a binding oath and expressed by periodical payment of the tribute money."

[13] Aziz Esmail and Azim Nanji, "The Ismai'lis in History," *Ismaili Contributions to Islamic Culture*, ed. Seyyed Hossein Nasr (Tehran: Imperial Iranian Academy of Philosophy, 1977), 233.

[14] F. Krenkow, "Sulaihi," *Encyclopedia of Islam*, 1st ed. (Leiden: E. J. Brill, 1934), 4:515.

[15] Husain F. al-Hamdani, "The History of the Ismaᶜili Daᶜwa and its Literature During the Last Phase of the Fatimid Empire," *Journal of the Royal Asiatic Society* (1932): 128.

[16] Ibid.

[17] Ibid.

[18] S. M. Stern, "The Early Ismaᶜili Missionaries in North West Persia," *Bulletin of the School of Oriental and African Studies* 23 (1960): 81.

[19] Taqi al-Din al-Maqrizi, *Ittiᶜaz al-hunafa' bi-akhbar al-a'immah al-Fatimiyyin al-khulafa'* (Cairo: Lujnat Ihya' al-Turath al-Islami, 1973), 3:103.

[20] Husayn ibn Fayd Allah al-Hamdani and Hasan Sulayman Mahmud, *al-Sulayhiyyun wa al-harakah al-Fatimiyyah fi al-Yaman* (Cairo: Maktabat Misr, 1955), 144.

21 F. Krenkow, "Sulaihi," *EI*¹ 4:515.

22 Najm al-Din ᶜUmarah al-Hakami al-Yamani, *Kitab Tarikh al-Yaman* (London: Edward Arnold, 1892), 28.

23 S. M. Stern, "The Succession to the Fatimid Imam al-Amir, and the Claims of the Later Fatimids to the Imamate, and the Rise of the Tayyibi Ismaᶜilism," *Oriens* 4 (1931): 193–255.

II

8
ANDRAS HAMORI

Near Eastern Studies Department, Princeton University
Princeton, New Jersey

A Sentence of Junayd's

IN HIS later writings ever more the guide to a void beyond thought, Heidegger came to express for our time—and, as mystics will, to repeat in varied forms—an old temptation of thought: that Being is essentially self-disclosing, that its disclosure needs and uses human existence for its truth ("die Botschaft die uns als Botengänger braucht"),[1] and that Being summons man.

It is a therapeutic orientation of thought. And as therapy goes with at least a dream of health, a vision of being perfectly at home in the body and the world, so too the old temptation goes, more often than not, with a vision of wholeness: man's turning wholly to the ground of disclosure, freed of inauthentic concerns, so that disclosure and man's openness to what is disclosed (which is called Truth—$\mathrm{\alpha\lambda\acute{\eta}\theta\epsilon\iota\alpha}$ al-ḥaqq) are like the parts of the Roman fountain in Conrad Ferdinand Meyer's poem, where

jede nimmt und gibt zugleich
Und strömt und ruht.

One way to deal with the mode of ultimate transparency in the discourse of Being is to regard it as something that weaves in and out of historical time, as in the work of great poets, or the experiences of great mystics. But one shall be tempted, when entertaining a vision of such transparency, to locate it outside of time altogether. For Hegel—who perhaps (as in Kojève's reading) tried to hold on to the old temptation but demystify it, too—perfect transparency in the self-disclosure of the Absolute comes with the writing of the Phenomenology even as the Napoleonic Wars are writing the end of history, and so, properly speaking, of time. For Junayd, writing in ninth-century Baghdad, the event of ultimate transparency occurs *before* historical time begins in a kind of prelude in heaven.

Junayd's thoughts on this matter are found most clearly in the first part of a short text known as *Kitab al-mithaq*, "On the Covenant."[2] In this Junayd comments—extremely boldly—on a rather cryptic and non-committal verse of the Qur'an (7:172):

> When your Lord took from the loins of the children of Adam their seed and made them bear witness and obligate themselves [He asked:] "Am I not your Lord?" They said: "Yes indeed; we bear witness." Thus you will not be able to say at the Resurrection: "We did not know anything about this."

The literal point of this verse—to warn the unbelievers that pleas of ignorance or lack of proof will not be accepted—is of no interest to Junayd. He turns this prelude in heaven into a center of his thought because he finds in it the discourse of Being. Abdel-Kader, in whose view "Junayd interpreted the Qur'an verse on the *Mithaq* through the neo-Platonic doctrine of the pre-existence of the soul" quotes the following paragraph (*Enn.* V 1, 4. 14) from Plotinus:[3]

> Before we had our becoming here, we existed There, men other than now; we were pure souls. Intelligence inbound with the entire of reality, not fenced off, integral to that All. . . . Then it was as if One voice sounded. One word was uttered and from every side an ear attended and received and there was an effective hearing; now we are become a dual thing, no longer that which we were at first, dormant, and in a sense no longer present.

The quotation is indeed well chosen, for it illustrates not only Plotinus's doctrine of the preexistence of the soul, but also his vision of the original transparency of the discourse of Being. But Junayd held a different view of the relation between Being and beings, and this is what I hope to outline in these pages. In good epistolary style, the invocation of the *Kitab al-mithaq* already points to discourse as the main theme of the text:[4]

> Praise be to God who made the shining forth (*ibzagh*) of His bounty, which He bestowed upon His servants into their guide to knowledge of Him, through His conferral on them of the benefit of acts of understanding and imagination (*afham wa-awham*) by which they might understand how to give answer (*yafhamuna biha raj^c al-khitab*).

"Giving answer" refers to the primordial scene which is described so:

He summoned them, and they replied at once. This reply was His act of generosity bestowed upon them, an act in which He answered for and through them (*ajaba ʿanhum*) when He gave them existence, so that they were the call emanating from Him (*fa-hum al-daʿwah minhu*). He made Himself known to them when they were but conceptions of His will. He transferred them by His will [to a different mode of existence], then He made them into something like seeds which He brought forth (*akhraja*) by His will as human.[5] He then deposited them in the loins (*sulb*) of Adam. Thus we read in the Qur'an: "When your Lord took from the loins of the children of Adam their seed and made them bear witness and obligate themselves [He asked] 'Am I not your Lord?' "

Here the text becomes difficult to render because it plays on words, exploiting that in Arabic "to be found" is the idiom for "to exist." For the places where Junayd uses the verb in the active, R. C. Zaehner proposes a transitive use of "exist" ("He existed them," etc.).[6] But a literal translation perhaps best puts across the drift of this portion of the text:

In this passage God tells us that He addressed them when they were not found except through His finding them, when they found the Truth without finding themselves, so that in this the Truth was with the Truth (*fa-kana al-haqq bil-haqq fi dhalika*), found in a sense which none but He can know and none but He can find.

This is hermeneutics at its boldest. The Qur'anic background shelters it; the primordial setting of the moment when the Truth was with the Truth seems to make it remote and relatively safe to speak about. But we should not underestimate the dangerousness (or centrality in Junayd's thought) of this prelude in heaven, nor should Junayd's own counsels of sobriety blind us to its meaning. The Truth was with the Truth, and not as the Logos was with God in John but through the presence of man open to Being and to nothing else. This thought grows from the same seedbed as the thought of Ibn ʿArabi, in whose theory of divine names the essential self-disclosure of Being appears most emphatically, and in whose theory of the Perfect Man we have a version of the way Being needs and uses man and discourse: "die Botschaft die uns als Botengänger braucht." Unlike Junayd, Ibn ʿArabi offers of course a vast elaboration of detail, and is quite content to shout heresy from the rooftops. A truly fundamental difference between them lies in Ibn ʿArabi's doctrine of the Perfect Man in whom the discourse of Being achieves total transparency and who exists in historical time. But in meditating the essential self-disclosure of Being the cautious Junayd and the irrepressible Ibn ʿArabi are akin. Junayd's "the Truth was with the Truth" cannot be reconciled with a tame interpretation of the hadith in which God says "I was a hidden treasure and wished to be known": it cannot be reconciled with the notion of a contingent relation between man and God.

What Junayd says about the self-disclosure of being and its need of human finitude is sheltered by a Qur'an verse, and it is also followed by a careful analysis of the experiences of the mystic, whose lengthy correctness perhaps camouflages the heart of the matter. But Junayd's famous sobriety is no camouflage. His thought, if understood, would have scandalized the guardians of religion for the masses, but it must also disappoint adepts of a mystical *Schwärmerei*. The phrasing of the crucial sentence embodies this scandalous sobriety. In the prelude in heaven, at the moment of the total transparency of discourse, man is not merely the object of address: he disappears into the summons of Being. "So that they were the call emanating from Him," *fa-hum al-daʿwah minhu*. Man as object of the call is totally transparent; he is the call itself. But man must also be thought of as subject that gives answer. "He answered for and through them," *ajaba ʿanhum*. Is the transparency of the self-disclosure of Being still there? Why does Junayd write that "they were the call," but not that "they were the response?"

The asymmetry makes perfect sense once we make a phenomenological translation of the mystical language. For whatever the value of thinking about Being detached from beings, it is a fact that the perfection of a thing—dogwood blossom or cracked bathroom tile—at times calls out to us and catches us up in a fusion of joyful perception and unfocused desire.

The conjunction of such perception and such desire is as a summons, and some will say it is a summons. For the mystic, the perception is mine but the intentionality is on the part of Being. It is possible to imagine oneself utterly absorbed in this experience, so that "you are the music while the music lasts." "They did not find themselves except insofar as He found them."

But in fact the luminosity of the experience depends on a tension that cannot be smoothed over (except of course by falling back into routine). One can test this, in a modest sort of way, by experiment. The experiment resembles the contemplation of those trompe-l'oeil pictures that can be read in two different ways and seem abruptly, if we prolong our gaze, to flip from one interpretation to another, or the contemplation too long of a printed word that at last dissolves into squiggles and dots and straight lines, and escapes usefulness. In our experiment we look at a familiar object and give it leave to detach itself from its nexus of uses—give it leave in fact to detach itself from our life. (The experience will be real, but will not of course seem an epiphany: the experimenter cannot after all ignore that the intentionality is his.) Abruptly we succeed, the object shines, is complete, in itself. No sooner does this happen than we want to recuperate the object, but in some way other than the nexus of its uses. This is impossible; certainly outside of art it is impossible.

The experience depends on the lack of adequate response, on the fact that the object calls out to me most when I sever my history and my projects from it. Perhaps this is because I know that my history will in fact be severed from it, but we need not concern ourselves here with the ground of the experience. What matters for our reading of Junayd is that in such contemplation—switching back now to the mystic's language— Being and finitude (for it is my finitude that permits the intentional severance, too) shine forth together, as they must. This essential tension is embodied in the asymmetry between Junayd's phrases. "They were the call emanating from Him," but not "they were the reply." I can feel transparent to the summons, but without the screen of my finitude there is no reply at all.

Another theorist of mysticism might have objected: "Let us cultivate openness to Being and eliminate this obscure desire that seems to respond to its call. We shall then have pure absorption in the call of Being." I do not know what this tranquil openness would mean. At any rate, Junayd is not interested in it. He does not lose from sight that the asymmetry is necessary for the discourse of Being.

In the prelude in heaven, man is, to begin with, nothing but transparence—a servant of discourse of Being. Next (but the temporal sequence is only a metaphor) Being replies for and through man, but in this, to reverse the old trope, Being is dipped into the dying vat of finitude. "Am I not your Lord?" God answers for man, and man, offering lack and shadow, will serve the discourse of Being.

In the rest of the text, which deals with mystical practice in the world we know, Junayd is on religiously safe ground. He proclaims that the mystic retains his individuality no matter what rank of gnosis he attains. It never occurs to him to say what would condemn him in the eyes of the orthodox: that the ontological difference between Being and beings can be erased. Nor can it occur to him—as we see from the prelude in heaven—but the stress on the mystic's finitude does camouflage the real scandal of Junayd's thought: that this finitude is necessary so that God might properly be called *al-ḥaqq*, the Truth.

Notes

[1] End of "Aus einem Gespräch von der Sprache," *Unterwegs zur Sprache*, 4th printing (Pfulligen, 1971), 155.

² Arabic text in A. H. Abdel-Kader, *The Life, Personality and Writings of al-Junayd*, "E. J. W. Gibb Memorial" Series, NS XXII (London, 1976), 40–43, of the Arabic numeration. Dr. Abdel-Kader's English translation is on 160–69. The translations in this essay are my own.

³ Abdel-Kader, 79. The quotes from *The Essence of Plotinus*, ed. G. H. Turnbull (New York: Oxford University Press).

⁴ Cf. "Let there be a clear indication of your intention at the beginning of your letter," *Al-risala al-ᶜadhra*', ed. Kurd ᶜAli in *Rasa'il al-bulagha*' (Cairo, 1954), 236. Cited by van Gelder, whose translation I quote, in *Beyond the Line* (Leiden, 1982), 57.

⁵ *As human*: I follow Abdel-Kader's cautious translation of *khalq*. But *akhrajahum bi-mashi'atihi khalqan* raises the question of how fully the sense "brought them out as created things" should be meditated.

⁶ *Hindu and Muslim Mysticism* (London, 1960), 147.

9
ANNEMARIE SCHIMMEL

Harvard University
Cambridge, Massachusetts

Khankhanan ʿAbdur Rahim and the Sufis

ONE OF THE MOST fascinating characters in Mughal, and perhaps in Indo-Muslim, history is Khankhanan ʿAbdur Rahim, Akbar's commander-in-chief, who conquered Gujarat and Sind for the Mughal empire and spent the last decades of his life in the Deccan to fight first with the rulers of Ahmadnagar and then with Malik ʿAmbar, a specialist in guerrilla warfare. The son of Bayram Khan, thanks to whom Humayun reconquered northwestern India after his Persian exile, ʿAbdur Rahim was born on December 17, 1556, four years before his father's assassination. He was educated under Akbar's tutelage, and accompanied him to Gujarat during the first campaign to become governor there; later, he subdued a rebellion and annexed the province for good to the Mughal empire.

For some time after 1583 he was Prince Salim's (the later Jahangir) tutor, and manifold were his relations with the Mughal house: his mother, a Mewati lady, was the sister of one of Humayun's wives, while his father's first wife, Salima Begum, was later married by her cousin Akbar to become the most powerful woman in the imperial household. ʿAbdur Rahim himself was married to the sister of Akbar's foster brother Mirza ʿAziz Koka, whose daughter married Salima's son, Prince Murad, and one of his daughters became the wife of Akbar's third son, Prince Daniyal. Like his brother Murad, Daniyal died in 1604 from alcoholism, leaving his young wife and two little sons with the Khankhanan. Finally, the daughter of his eldest son, Jahangir's favorite Iraj Shahnawaz, became the wife of Prince

Shahjahan. The fact that ᶜAbdur Rahim took a rather undecided stance in Shahjahan's rebellion in 1623 caused him many difficulties and is probably the reason for some negative remarks by historians of a later period about his untrustworthiness. For during his lifetime—up to 1623—he was, despite some critical remarks about his alleged cunning, the best loved nobleman among the Mughals, greatly admired not only for his military prowess but also for his many other skills: a poet in Persian, Turki, and Hindi, and translator of Babur's Turki memoirs into Persian (1589). He was proverbial for his boundless generosity which allowed him to patronize more than a hundred poets and to keep a most remarkable library in which calligraphers and painters worked together to produce copies of classical works; it also contained autograph copies of the poems of a good number of those Persian poets who had sung encomia for him. They came from near and far, and his house was compared to the Kaᶜba to which everyone turns. Some poets, like Naziri and Ghururi, saw in his name, ᶜAbdur Rahim, a fitting allusion to the mystery of God's name *rahim*, "compassionate," which manifested itself in him.

ᶜAbdur Rahim's achievements until 1616 are described in the nearly 3,000 pages of the *Ma'athir-i Rahimi*, composed by a Persian immigrant, ᶜAbdul Baqi Nihavandi.[1] This author attached himself to the Khankhanan in Burhanpur, a city which he adorned with many buildings, gardens, and water supplies during his long stay. ᶜAbdul Baqi's work is a useful account of the martial and even more the cultural activities of his patron even though its use of historical dates is sometimes not too reliable. The learned author finished his work before the Khankhanan's star began to sink, for it happened during the last ten years of his life that he was afflicted in various ways, both (partly by his own mistake) on the political and on the personal level.

One of the greatest shocks he had to bear was the death of two of his sons in 1619. The elder one, Iraj Mirza, had distinguished himself as a valiant officer, yet, he died not in the battlefield but, like so many Mughal nobles, from misuse of alcohol. A few months later the Khankhanan's youngest son, Rahmandad, born from a Sindhi mother in 1600, passed away, exhausted after fighting and struck by a sudden cold. As he was his father's favorite, one had to find a way to inform the Khankhanan, for even the emperor was shocked by this event. In his *Tuzuk*, Jahangir writes: "It appeared very grievous to me, and what must it have been to the heartbroken old father? Hardly had the wound from the calamity of Shah Nawaz Khan healed, when he received this fresh wound. I trust that God Almighty may give him patience and resignation."[2] The person who was elected to bring the sad news to ᶜAbdur Rahim was a Sufi from

Burhanpur, ᶜIsa Jund Allah, with whom the commander had developed a warm friendship. This brings to mind an aspect of his personality which has rarely been touched upon, i.e., his relation with the mystics of his time. For not in vain was he called by Muhibb ᶜAli Sindhi, one of his court poets, *dostdar-i darvishan*, "who is a friend of the dervishes."[3]

It is known that he acquired in 1587 a fine copy of the *Maktubat-i sadi*, the famous Hundred Letters, by Sharafuddin Maneri, the Firdausiyya saint of Bihar (d. 1381). This work was one of the favorites of Indian Muslims because of Maneri's clear exposition of the true path of the Sufis in a strictly *shariᶜa*-bound attitude—without intoxication and rapture but full of the awareness of the guiding Divine Light. This, of course, would be insufficient to prove the Khankhanan's interest in Sufism. A more important witness is Badauni, whose chronicle *Muntakhab at-tawarikh* is highly critical of many of his contemporaries but who held the commander in high esteem and praised him for keeping company with pious people and Sufis; however, he reproachingly tells that even this good man fell a victim to the miracle mongery of a would-be saint, one Biyabani, and "swallowed the deception."

An interest in Sufism in ᶜAbdur Rahim is not surprising—his father Bayram Khan had also been a firm believer in certain mystics and attended their meetings although he professed the Shia creed as was natural for a Qaraqoyunlu Turcoman. In the case of ᶜAbdur Rahim, however, there is no clear indication about the form of Islam he professed. His enemies accused him of being a Shiite practicing *taqiya*, dissimulation, and therefore spread rumors that he was secretly in league with the Shia rulers of the Deccan whose kingdoms he was supposed to conquer. His sons, on the other hand, are described as Sunnis.

Was he perhaps a member of Akbar's *din-i ilahi*? It seems that the emperor tried to win him over, along with Raja Man Singh who, like ᶜAbdur Rahim, belonged to the *nauratan*, the Nine Jewels at court. But he apparently never became an official member of this circle although he is addressed in a *firman* by Akbar not only as someone who "fulfills the duties of *farzandi*," "being a 'son' of the emperor," but also the etiquette incumbent upon a *murid*, a "disciple," of Akbar.[4] Yet, this may have been a mere form of address.

One thing that can be said against both his joining the *din-i ilahi* and belonging to the Shia faction is the fact that he had a rather intense correspondence with Ahmad Sirhindi, the *mujaddid-i alf-i thani*, whose anti-Akbarian political statements as well as his exalted mystical self-consciousness are well expressed in his 534 letters, many of which were directed to Mughal nobles. Ten letters of the Mujaddid to the Khankhanan are extant; they were probably written between 1600 and 1615. One of them (no. 23) is in Arabic and speaks of the necessity of finding a true spiritual guide whose company works like red sulphur, the ingredient in alchemy supposed to transform copper into gold. In the postscript to this letter the Mujaddid tells his correspondent that it is a terrible idea to have a panegyrist with the nom-de-plume of *Kufri*, "the one connected with *kufr*, infidelity," and urges him to change this poet's name into something more acceptable. As Kufri died in 1606, a *terminus ante quem* is given. Other, Persian, letters warn the Khankhanan of overstressed interest in speculative mysticism, one letter (no. 198) beginning with the words: "May the *Futuhat al-makkiyya* be the key to the *futuhat-i madiniyya!*" That is, "may you stop reading Ibn ʿArabi's *Futuhat* and turn to the *sunna* of the Prophet of Islam," whose importance and central place in Islam is always emphasized in the letters. Sirhindi also warns the Khankhanan, who had, it seems, inquired about the meaning of some Qur'anic punishments, never to doubt the wisdom of this or that Qur'anic statement, as illogical it may seem to the intellect: "It is the decree of the Mighty, the Wise!" and one has to accept it without questioning, whether one likes it or not, "and someone who wants to understand rationally all the rules of the *shariʿa* and compare them with rational proofs, is a denier of prophethood."

There are also other scenes in the letters: Sirhindi likes to remind his "brother, capable of manifesting perfections" (no. 23) of his previous generosity toward the poor, needy, and dervishes, and urges him to continue with this kind of charity because, as he repeatedly states, "This world is the seedbed of the next world," as the Prophet had said. He even calls the Khankhanan a "faithful friend of the Naqshbandiyya" and follower on the path—a statement which would certainly speak against any Shia leaning of the commander, given Sirhindi's (and most Naqshbandis's) aversion to Shia thought and lore.

It seems possible that the connection between the Khankhanan and the Mujaddid was made, or at least strengthened, by Husamuddin ibn Qadi Nizami Badakhshani, a faithful follower of Sirhindi's own master, Khwaja Baqi Billah, who accompanied the Khankhanan in the Deccani wars. And when ʿAbdur Rahim died in Delhi in early 1627, it was the foremost disciple of Sirhindi in the Burhanpur area, Molla Hashim, who wrote an oft-quoted chronogram for his death.

One of Sirhindi's letters (no. 214) mentions the gratitude of the son of Hajji Sultan Thanesari to the Khankhanan, and this remark leads us back to the days when he was setting out for the conquest of Sind after pacifying Gujarat. In 1590, Akbar had changed the Khankhanan's fief from Jaunpur to Multan and Bhakkar, and he had forfeited a part of Bhakkar for the benefit of Mir Maᶜsum Nami Bhakkari, the historian, poet, and calligrapher, who had been serving with Nizamuddin Bakhshi, ᶜAbdur Rahim's trusted friend and helper in Gujarat. Mir Maᶜsum, who later composed and calligraphed many inscriptions of Akbar and Jahangir in Fathpur Sikri and other places, was granted leave by the emperor to go home and see his aged mother, and the Khankhanan helped him in getting settled in his hometown Bhakkar in Upper Sind. He himself came about the same time to Sind, in the late summer of 1590, and met in Bhakkar one of the former stars of Akbar's translation bureau, Hajji Sultan of Thanesar, whose Persian rendering of the *Mahabharata* was so correct that he, as Badauni says, "even rendered the accidental dirt of flies" in his translation. This scholar had incurred the emperor's displeasure due to some cow slaughtering and had been banished to Bhakkar. Now the Khankhanan used his influence to have him relocated in his hometown, an act for which his descendants remained ever grateful.

There are different versions of the spiritual aspects of the conquest of Sind. The most frequently told one is that the Khankhanan paid a visit to Qadi ᶜOthman in Bhakkar, a stern ascetic noted for his piety, and sat with him in utter humility. Somewhat later, pious people saw in a vision how the Qadi brought the Khankhanan into the presence of the Prophet while the ruler of Sind, Mirza Jani Beg Tarkhan, was brought by Makhdum Nuh, the great Suhrawardi saint of Hala in Sind. The Sindis implored the Prophet not to let the Mughals take over their country, and the Prophet advised them not to fight against the Khankhanan. But Mirza Jani Beg did not heed the advice and Sind was conquered after hard fighting in October 1591.

Another version of the legend tells that Makhdum Nuh had just died when the Mughal army arrived, and it was said that whosoever would be the first to recite the *Fatiha* for the deceased saint would win Sind. Both the Khankhanan and Mirza Jani Beg hastened to Hala, but the Mughal commander was faster to reach there, and therefore became victorious. But as Makhdum Nuh, the first translator of the Qur'an into Persian, had died on July 30, 1590, and the Khankhanan arrived in Bhakkar only on August 25, it would have been difficult for him to be in Hala a month earlier.

However, this story points to his close connection with Sufi saints, a connection which apparently grew stronger during his long stay in Burhanpur. This city, founded in 1380 by the Faruqi rulers of Khandesh, was named after the Chishti saint Burhanuddin Gharib (d. 1340) who is buried in Khuldabad and was noted for his excessive love of music and whirling dance. Burhanpur, strategically situated close to the northern fringe of the Deccan, attracted many people from other parts of the subcontinent, among them a considerable contingent of weavers and Sufis from the area around Thatta. They migrated from Sind to Central India when Humayun was seeking shelter in Sind (where his son Akbar was born in 1542 in the city of Omarkot). The Sindi Sufis belong mainly to the Qadiriyya order which had been established in northern Sind and the southern Panjab in the late fifteenth century. Among them, ᶜIsa Jund Allah was certainly the most outstanding figure; born after the family left Sind, he attached himself also to the Shattariyya order, centered in Gwalior. In Burhanpur, he composed a number of treatises, among them a small treatise on *wahdat al-wujud*, Ibn ᶜArabi's system of "Unity of Being"; he attracted many disciples who popularized his teaching in central and northern India. The Khankhanan befriended him and attended the *samaᶜ* sessions in his *dargah*, for he was a great lover of music and mystical poetry in the vernacular. It was this close relationship that led his friends to choose the Shaykh ᶜIsa as messenger when Rahmandad had suddenly passed away. When the shaykh himself died two years later, in 1621, the Khankhanan erected a fine mausoleum for him.

ᶜIsa Jund Allah, however, was only one in the great number of mystics in Burhanpur. Among them one finds even a noble and pious lady, called Bubu Rasti, who was famous for her interpretation of classical Persian Sufi texts, in particular ᶜIraqi's *Lamaᶜat*, which she used to read and interpret for her disciples and admirers, to whom the Khankhanan seems to have belonged. Other friends of his, such as Muhammad Sharif Khan, a descendant of the great Kubrawi saint of Kashmir, Sayyid ᶜAli Hamadhani, spent "most of his time with great and venerable shaykhs and ecstatic people,"[5] and quite a few of the poets who attached themselves to him are classified as darvish or as inclined toward Sufism.

The relations between Burhanpur and the descendants of Burhanuddin Gharib continued, and an interesting document, which was recently discovered by Carl Ernst in Khuldabad, shows that the Khankhanan was in more than one way interested in Sufism. The document, called *Fath al-auliya*, "The Conquest of the Saints," was written in 1620, at the time when Malik ᶜAmbar besieged Burhanpur and the Khankhanan was near despair. After dealing with Burhanuddin Gharib and other Deccani saints it shows the relations of the rulers with the shrines and speaks of the gifts of the Mughals to Khuldabad, which are meant to establish their sovereignty over that place. But it may well be that at least one intention of the author, who dedicated his treatise to Jahangir and the Khankhanan, was to secure the spiritual support of the Deccani saints for those in charge of the besieged city.

The Khankhanan loved poetry and was a fine poet himself. He left short verses and fragments in Persian, some of which have become almost proverbial. He also, like his father, wrote in Turki, but he is known even better for his delightful Hindi verse. One has to remember that during his lifetime the mystical poetry in the Indian vernaculars became quite important: not only was the first mystical *dohas* in Sindi composed by Qadi Qadan in the early sixteenth century, but the rebellious Pathan leader, Bayezid Ansari, called *Pir-i raushan*, composed his religious treatise in his native Pashto, and when the Khankhanan lived, in the late 1580s, in his birthplace Lahore, he may have well met the first major Panjabi mystical poet, Madho Lal Husayn, who died in this place in 1593. Hindi poetry flourished among the *bhakti* poets, and when reading ᶜAbdur Rahim's short *dohas* and his verse in *bhairavi*, one immediately senses a deeply religious feeling in them. It seems ironical that Akbar's successful commander is one of the few Muslim "devotional poets" mentioned in a collection, *Cultural Leaders of India*,[6] and the Hindu author of the article shows with abundant love the role of the Khankhanan for the development of Hindi devotional verse. He mentions his friendship with Tulsidas, the author of the famous version of the Ramayan, and sees even a possible influence of ᶜAbdur Rahim's *bhairavi* on this mystical Hindu writer.

ᶜAbdur Rahim's proverbial generosity, his love of giving and of helping those in need, and his gentleness, which seems so surprising in a man of his profession, can perhaps be explained by his deep love of the mystical aspect of religion, be it the Sufi or the bhakti approach. He admitted in true Sufi fashion that he was well aware of being only an instrument in the hands of the Divine Giver. We read that a Hindu poet, Ganga Kavi, asked him once why he lowered his eyes when giving, and he replied in Hindi verse:

It is someone else that gives.
And He gives day and night.
But people erringly think
That it is I who give,
And therefore my eyes remain lowered in
embarrassment.

It seems correct when his biographer ᶜAbdul Baqi Nihavandi has called him "a dervish in a prince's disguise," and he and many of the poets who wrote in his honor have highlighted the modesty and humility which he showed not only in the presence of great saints but also to the poor; he would easily forgive a servant's faults or mistakes (including the forging of his signature on a paycheck) and was always ready to give people pleasant surprises, never withholding anything.

In a time when the ruling classes did not care much for the life of an enemy or evildoer, and cruelty went along with utterly refined taste, the Khankhanan stands out as someone who, to all accounts, tried to be helpful, even though later his adversaries claimed that he wanted "to hurt his enemy under the guise of friendship." (Did he perhaps try to win over those whom he could not overcome otherwise?) In the notes he prepared for himself while serving at Akbar's court in the late 1580s, he remarked that one could certainly reach nowhere without any ruse, but, as he was quick to add, "one should use ruses only as a shield, not as a sword," that is, only in defense. And his approach to life is perhaps best summed up in the Hindi lines which certainly sound rather like a Sufi song than the words of a successful conqueror:

> Give up haughty airs, Rahim;
> Adopt the ways of the humble.
> Be soft of speech. Walk in humility,
> And everywhere you'll find, it is your own
>   native place.

Notes

[1] ^cAbdul Baqi Mihavandi, *Ma'athir-i Rahimi*, ed. M. Hidayat Husain (Calcutta, 1930–31).

[2] Jahangir, *Tuzuk* (Lahore: Sang-e Meel Publications, 1974), 2:176–77.

[3] *Ma'athir-i Rahimi*, 3:489.

[4] Ibid., 2:118.

[5] Ibid, 3:1676.

[6] *Cultural Leaders of India* (Delhi, 1978).

10
PETER HEATH

Department of Asian and Near Eastern
Languages and Literatures
Washington University, St. Louis, Missouri

Disorientation and Reorientation in Ibn Sina's *Epistle of the Bird*: A Reading

THE *EPISTLE OF THE BIRD* (*Risalat at-tayr*) is one of several short allegories composed by Abu ᶜAli al-Husayn ibn Sina ("Avicenna," d. 1037/428). Since first offered in a modern edition by F. Mehren almost a century ago, it has been considered one of Ibn Sina's *traités mystiques*: a corpus of texts whose ideas and rhetoric appear more mystical in nature than philosophical.[1] The general question of the nature and extent of the philosopher's "mysticism" has attracted a respectable degree of scholarly attention and produced a sizeable body of learned discussion.[2] But the *Epistle* itself has remained little studied. One reason for this is the narrative's difficulty; although quite short, the work is by no means easy to understand. What follows here is an attempt to do just this: to understand and explicate the text. This essay falls into four parts. First, it presents a new, exact translation of the *Epistle*. Second, it offers a reading which attempts to clarify its many riddles, puzzles, and mysteries. Third, it sums up what appears to be the narrative's general intent. And finally, it briefly raises the question of whether this now-explicit intent is the work's only, or even most important, thematic dimension.

——————— I ———————

The Epistle of the Bird[3]

In the name of God, the Merciful, the Compassionate
My success is only through God, on Him I rely,
in Him I trust

1 Will any of my brothers lend me ear long enough for me to tell him something of my sorrows? For perhaps through sharing, some of their burdens may be lifted from me. Indeed, a friend cannot purify his brother of impurity as long as he does not—in good times and in bad—preserve his own clarity from the muddiness of sorrow.

2 And where do you have a genuine friend? Friendship has been made a business to which one turns when a motive of personal gain makes one appeal to a friend, while its responsibilities are rejected when one is free of need. A comrade will not be visited unless a sudden problem visits; a friend will not be remembered unless a wish is remembered.

3 Brothers are only those whom divine kinship has joined together, whom celestial closeness has made intimate, who have observed realities with the eye of insight, who have polished the filth and rust of doubt from their inner heart, who will be joined together only by God's herald (calling):

4 "Come, Brothers of Truth![4] Open your hearts and join together![5] Let each of you unveil the innermost part of his heart to his brother, so that you may examine each other and perfect each other!

5 "Come, Brothers of Truth! Cover yourselves, just as hedgehogs cover themselves! Reveal your interiors and conceal your exteriors! For, by God, your interior is manifest and your exterior is hidden /43/.

6 "Come, Brothers of Truth! Shed your skins as snakes do! Crawl as worms crawl! Be scorpions whose weapons are in their tails! For Satan deceives Man only from behind. Gulp down poison and you will live! Prefer death and you will attain life! Fly! Do not take a nest to which you constantly return, for the hunting grounds of birds are their nests. And if want of wings hinders you, then become a thief, and you will snatch success. The best of the vanguard are those strong of flight.

7 "Be ostriches who gulp down hot stones,[6] vipers who swallow hard bones, salamanders who descend upon blazing flames with confidence, and bats who do not emerge in the day. The best of birds are bats.

8 "Come, Brothers of Truth! The richest of men is he who dares the morrow, and the most dismal failure is he who falls short of his goal.

9 "Come, Brothers of Truth! It is no wonder when an angel avoids an evil deed, or a beast commits a foul act. Rather, the wonder is Man when he rebels against sensual desires even though his form has been fashioned to prefer them completely,[7] or when he renders total obedience to them even though his character has been enlightened by reason. By Everlasting God! How far above an angel is a man steadfast in eliminating sensual desire, whose foot does not slip from its path. And lower than a beast is the person unable to resist any sensual desire which calls him."

10 But I return to the beginning of my discourse:

11 A party set out hunting. They set up snares, arranged nets, prepared bait, and hid themselves in the grass. I was among a flock of birds. When they caught sight of us, they whistled, seeking to call us. We sensed plentiful food and friends; doubt did not enter our breasts, nor did suspicion sway us from our course. We hastened /44/ towards them and descended, all together, amongst the snares. Suddenly rings encompassed our necks, nets entangled our wings, and snares caught our legs. We tried to move, but our difficulties only increased. So we resigned ourselves to destruction, our individual sorrow precluding each of us from caring about his brother. We strove to discover stratagems for escape for a time, until we were made to forget the form of our predicament. We became accustomed to nets and content with cages.

12 Then one day, I looked through the net and caught sight of a company of birds that had removed their heads and wings from the net. They emerged from their cages, flying with the remnants of the snares still on their legs. But these did not burden them, for deliverance filled them with determination. Nor did the birds feel them, for life had become clear for them. And they made me remember what I had been made to forget, and made loathsome that to which I had grown accustomed. I almost melted with remorse; my soul almost slipped away with regret. I called from behind my cage for them to approach and inform me of the means of relief, for length of captivity had tamed me. Remembering the treachery of the hunters, however, they only fled farther away. Then I adjured them in the name of ancient friendship, sustained comradeship, and remembered vows, which instilled trust in their hearts and expelled suspicion from their breasts. They presented themselves to me, and I asked them about themselves. They related that they had been afflicted with that with which I was afflicted, and that they had despaired and grown accustomed to affliction.

13 Then they tended to me. The snare was removed from my neck, the net from my wings, and the door of the cage was opened. And it was said to me, "Take advantage of deliverance!" I asked them to release my foot from its ring, but they said, "If we were able to do that, we would have hastened to release our own legs first. How can one himself ill cure you?"

14 Then I rose flying away from my /45/ cage. And it was said to me, "Before you are regions from whose danger we will not be safe unless we advance through them singly. Follow our courses; we will save you and guide you along the right path."

15 The flight led us between two slopes of the mountain of God, in a valley grassy and fertile—no, rather, barren and desolate—until its sides fell behind us. We proceeded along its face and attained the mountain's summit. And there before us were eight lofty mounts whose pinnacles were far beyond the reach of eyesight. We said to each other "Hurry! For we will not be secure until we have crossed them safely."

16 So we embraced resolution until we surmounted six of the peaks and reached the seventh. When we entered its boundaries, we said to each other, "Do you want a rest?" Fatigue had weakened us, a vast expanse lay between us and our enemies, and we saw that we could allot our bodies a measure of rest. For indeed, flight at a relaxed pace leads more surely to salvation than pushing oneself to exhaustion.

17 We stopped at its pinnacle. And there were gardens, with grassy meadows, flourishing fields, fruit-laden trees, and flowing rivers, whose delight quenched your gaze; with forms whose splendor confounded the intellect and astonished the mind, who filled our ears with rapturous melodies and heartrending songs, and our nostrils with fragrances unapproached by noble musk and fresh ambergris. We ate of its fruits and drank from its rivers and tarried there until we had cast off weariness.

18 Then we said /46/ to each other, "Hurry! For there is no trap like security, nor any haven like caution, nor is any fortress impregnable to evil thoughts. Our stay in this region has stretched to the verge of negligence; behind us, our enemies follow our path and seek our halting place. If residing in it is pleasant, nothing is as pleasant as safety."

19 So we resolved to travel on and departed from the area; and we alighted on the eighth mountain. It was a towering peak whose tip penetrated the clouds of the sky, and on whose slopes lived birds. Never have I encountered sweeter melodies, lovelier colors, more elegant forms, or pleasanter companionship than theirs! When we alighted in their vicinity, we knew of their beneficence, their kindness, and their cordiality, that which en-

compassed us; and of assistance, that which whose slightest part we could not recompense, even if we devoted ourselves to it for the period of our lifetime—no, even if we stretched it out twice-over!

20 When gaiety had established itself between them and us, we informed them of what had befallen us. They shared in our anxiety and related, "Behind this mountain is a city over which the Greatest King rules. Any wronged person who seeks his protection and puts his trust in him will find his distress lifted away by his might and support."

21 We trusted in their counsel, and headed toward the city of the King until we alighted in his outer courtyard, awaiting his permission to enter. Then the order of permission for new-arrivals emerged, and we were admitted into his palace. Before us lay a courtyard whose vastness description does not encompass. When we crossed it, the curtain was raised before us, revealing another courtyard, spacious and luminous such that, beside it, we thought the first constricted—no, we considered it small! Finally, we arrived at the chamber of the King. When the curtain was raised before us, and our eyes beheld the King in his beauty /47/, our hearts were captivated by him; we were overcome by an amazement which hindered us from presenting our complaint. He perceived what had befallen us and restored our composure with his kindness until we dared to address him.

22 When we related our story before him, he said, "Only those who knotted the snares will be able to undo them from your feet. I will send to them a messenger who will demand from them your satisfaction and the removal of the nets from you. So depart, well-blessed!"

23 And now we are on the way with the messenger, and my brothers are clinging to me, demanding from me the tale of the splendor of the King before them. So I will describe him extremely briefly:

24 "He is the King who, whatever you have attained in your mind of beauty unblended with ugliness, and perfection unmixed with fault, in this you have hit upon a complete picture of him. Every perfection, in reality attains to him; every fault, if only in metaphor, is banished from him totally. His beauty has a face, his generosity a hand. Whoever serves him gains the utmost happiness; whoever forsakes him forfeits the next world and this."

25 How many a brother, when my story struck his ear, then said, "I see that your mind is touched; you have become slightly deranged. No, by God, you did not fly! Rather, your mind flew. Nor were you hunted! Rather, your heart was hunted. How does a human being fly! Or a bird speak? It is as if bile has become predominant in your temperament, or

dryness has gained mastery over your brain! You should drink cooked epithymun; start bathing in tepid fresh water; inhale nymphea oil; go easy on food, choose healthy ones /48/; avoid sexual indulgence; leave off staying up late at night; reduce thought! We have known you to be reasonable in the past and have observed you to be astute and intelligent. By God, examining our minds, they are worried about you. And because of the imbalance of your state, our own has become unbalanced."

26 How much they say, how little it avails! The worst of speech is that which is wasted! One seeks recourse from God and freedom from man; whoever believes otherwise has lost in the next world and this.

27 "Those who do wrong will come to know which reversal they will suffer."[8]

Thus is *The Epistle of the Bird* completed.
Praise to God is abundantly sufficient.

II

As can be seen from the above translation, the *Epistle* falls into three main parts: a prologue (1–9), the bird allegory itself (10–24), and an epilogue (25–27).

In the first and last parts, Ibn Sina himself (or, more correctly, his narrative *persona*) dominates the narrative, while the middle part is narrated from the point of view of the bird. One might think that the prologue and epilogue would serve as a frame for the allegory in between, that they would be buffers of familiarity that would lead the reader in and out of the dark and mysterious forest of allegory. But this is not the case. Each part of the work has its own difficulties and enigmas. This is especially true of the prologue, by far the most confusing and opaque part of the *Epistle*. Thus although there does appear to be a growing trend of coherence running through the work, with the prologue offering the most perplexities, the allegory being easier to comprehend, and the epilogue still clearer, the *Epistle* remains a difficult work. Because of a lack of an immediately obvious logical connection among the contents of the three parts, because of the abruptness of the transitions between them, and because of the conundrums that each part in itself presents, the reader is constantly forced to readjust his sense of context, not only within each section but among them as well. This is not a narrative whose beginning and middle set riddles and whose end offers solutions. Rather, it is one each of whose parts presents its own riddles without offering any solutions, either to them or to those found in other sections. In this context, the apparent lack of coherence among the three parts of the *Epistle* becomes simply one more unsolved riddle.

Balancing one's feelings of confusion or disorientation, however, is the text's strong emotional appeal. A depth of feeling, a powerful sense of sadness and loss, a wrenching yearning, and even undertones of anguish permeate the narrative. The *Epistle*, one feels, reflects an important, even crucial, inner experience. If there are confusions, they are those of senses, emotions, and thoughts in tumult. This, one feels, is not a dry intellectual exercise, but a *cri du coeur*. This emotional dimension becomes the work's saving grace. Without it, one would hardly bother with its complexities; with it, solving the riddles and resolving the complexities become a worthwhile, if sometimes difficult, task.

The Prologue

Ibn Sina begins the prologue by drawing a distinction between the true friend, or spiritual brother, and the false friend (1–3). False friendship, he says, is based on the idea of one-sided exploitation; showing friendship only for the sake of ulterior motives. True friendship or brotherhood, on the other hand, is founded upon mutual understanding of divine realities; its purpose is not individual material gain, but reciprocal spiritual purification of base "impurity" (*al-shawb*) from the heart. Brothers are those who have "polished the filth (*al-wasakh*) and rust (*ar-rayn*) of doubt from their inner hearts (*al-sarira*)," those joined and united by "divine kinship" (*al-qaraba al-ilahiya*) and "celestial closeness" (*al-mujawara al-ᶜalawiya*).

Why does Ibn Sina draw this distinction? Because he himself is afflicted by sorrows and anxieties that only the concern and company of a true friend can assuage. Furthermore, it is of the utmost importance that these sorrows be relieved. For unless one can preserve his own "clarity" (*al-safa'*) of heart and mind from the spiritual "turbidness" (*al-kadar*) that such sorrow causes, he cannot carry out the important task of helping fellow participants in the process of spiritual progress. In other words, one's own internal confusion or disturbance levies its toll on the efforts of the group, interrupting a cycle of mutual spiritual purification. Thus Ibn Sina's cry for help; for only a true brother, a selfless friend, can succeed in alleviating his cares. A false friend will not only fail this task, but through egoism and lack of true understanding, will even increase the sufferer's anguish.

In these opening lines, then, Ibn Sina presents us with two dichotomies. That between the false friend and the true brother (the selfish exploiter and the pure sharer), and that between a pure, clear heart and one polluted by impurity and the filth and rust of doubt. Naturally, these two dichotomies run on lines of equivalence. A true brother is he who possesses a pure heart, while a false friend has a heart sullied by self-interest and doubt. It is thus one's internal state, one's spiritual awareness, that defines brotherhood, not external conditions. In this regard, a good action done by one of impure heart is a chance affair, in no way part of the conscious cycle of mutual purification intended by Ibn Sina.[9]

Besides this pair of conceptual dichotomies, we should notice another, this one grounded in the rhetorical structure of the text. This is the dichotomy between the narrator and his readers. On the one hand we have the narrator, aware of the nature and meaning of true friendship, yet in need of a friend; cognizant of the importance of clarity of heart, yet afflicted—for some reason—by cares and sorrows. On the other hand we have us, the readers, the narrator's audience. If the narrator is knowledgeable but depressed, we are sympathetic but ignorant. While our hearts naturally sympathize with the narrator's sad state, wish to respond to his plea for a true friend, and are attracted by his call for spiritual purity, we unfortunately suffer from confusion concerning the real nature or purpose of the classifications that Ibn Sina is setting forth. What does the idea of true brotherhood really entail? What are the spiritual realities to which he refers? How exactly does one proceed to purify one's heart and soul? Do true brothers such as those to which Ibn Sina refers really exist; if so, who are they?

Ibn Sina thus entices the reader into his text on both emotional and intellectual levels. His appeal for help stirs one's sympathies. But the extension of sympathies is stymied by one's intellectual ignorance. To overcome this ignorance, the reader must turn his mind fully to the text; this in turn deepens his emotional involvement—and so on, in an ever-deepening process of dialectic.

Having created this dichotomy between the knowing but sad narrator, and the ignorant and thus inconsequently sympathetic reader, Ibn Sina proceeds to introduce a link between them in the figure of the "herald of God" (munadi-llah). Unfortunately, at first glance one cannot say that this link clarifies matters. God's herald—presumably the Active Intellect, the intermediary between the Divine and mundane, whose function is to encourage, inspire, and direct those aspiring to intellectual and thus spiritual perfection—issues a series of exhortations to the "Brothers of Truth." But instead of drawing aside the veil of confusion as to just who and what this group is, his exhortations serve to mystify even further.

The herald of God urges one to imitate a diverse group of creatures: hedgehogs, snakes, worms, scorpions, ostriches, and so forth. But the symbolic significance and, in many cases, even the literal context of their specific traits remain unclear. What does God's herald mean when he exhorts one to cover oneself like a hedgehog, gulp down hot stones like an ostrich, or fly like a bird but not return too often to the nest? Why indeed are bats the best of birds? Do salamanders really descend upon blazing flames? To such questions we must now turn.

The herald of God addresses his exhortations to the "Brothers of Truth," a group which is presumably equivalent to Ibn Sina's previously mentioned class of pure-hearted brothers. One further assumes that these exhortations are intended to encourage and instruct those aspiring to spiritual perfection. This assumption is supported by the first and last parts of the exhortations themselves.

The first exhortation urges one to open his heart fully to his brother so that mutual contemplation may ensue. When each brother sees his own heart reflected in that of another, he is able to view it more objectively and thus cleanse it more fully. Mutual contemplation leads to mutual perfection (4). As a later exhortation (9) points out, that Man is able to undertake such a process is due to his unique cosmological status. A beast is unable to distinguish between right and wrong; all of its actions are intrinsic to its nature. To expect the lions to spare lambs, for example, is nonsensical, for it is lions' nature to consume lambs. Similarly, for all of their other differences, angels resemble animals in that they too are ethically one-dimensional. To praise angels for purity of heart is tautological; created pure, they are constitutionally unable to sin.

But Man (as our daily experience so fully confirms) has capacities for both good and evil. In this sense, he is a composite of both animal and angelic natures, of matter and spirit, of sensual and rational perception. Because of this, he represents an arena of cosmological struggle. His material or bestial self attempts to drag him downward toward the status of animals, while his spiritual, rational self urges him upwards to aspire to the state of angels. The message of the herald of God here, therefore, is that only by allowing Divine enlightenment (i.e., God's herald) to enter his soul, only by becoming a Brother of Truth, can Man master the dark exoteric forces of his sensual, material self and realize the potential for perfection that his rational, spiritual self offers. This struggle is not easy; one's foot can easily "slip from its path" (9). Hence the importance of having brothers to offer support along the way. Still, the struggle is worth undertaking, for many are the rewards that await one who emerges from it victorious. As Ibn Sina says: "The richest of men is he who dares the morrow" (8).

Having grasped this general context of spiritual struggle, one can begin to unravel the riddles of the other parts of the prologue. As long as one keeps in mind the nature of the opposing forces (spiritual vs. material), and the fact that the victory of the one over the other presumes the necessity of struggle, the conundrums of the exhortations become easier to crack.

All the animal traits that Ibn Sina selects for symbolic comparisons are similar to Man's innate capacity for spiritual perfection in two ways. First, they are unique to that species of animal. No other creature besides the hedgehog has quills, no other besides the snake sheds its skin, no other besides the ostrich gulps down rocks. Second, in spite of the uniqueness and remarkableness of these features, they are—like Man's capacity for perfection—natural to these various creatures. It is natural for birds to fly, vipers to swallow their prey bones and all, and salamanders to descend upon flames and emerge unscathed (natural, at least, according to the popular scientific wisdom of the time). In accomplishing these apparent marvels, these creatures are only exercising natural capacities. The important difference between them and Man is that while they do so as a matter of course, Man is usually unaware of his innate capacity for spiritual perfection. In most cases, he must be awakened to its existence.

Let us now review the remaining exhortations in the light of the above remarks and attempt to elucidate the symbolic and, where necessary, literal meaning of their imagery. To begin: "Cover yourselves, just as hedgehogs cover themselves!" (5) What does God's herald mean by this?

The trait that is unique to the hedgehog is its quills. No other animal shares this feature. In their normal, lowered (potential) position, these quills resemble ordinary hair. But in their true, raised (actual) state, the once-hidden quills now cover what was before the hedgehog's outer layer. The animal's presumed interior has in fact revealed itself to be its exterior. In this process of revelation, one's perception of reality has been reversed. What one first considered to be reality (quills equal hair) has proven to be a false perception, while what was at first hidden has been proved to be the truth.

It is in this regard that Man resembles the hedgehog. Normally one considers Man's external, corporal aspect as his truest, most real dimension. But this is not the case, since Man's most distinctive and remarkable feature is his interior, spiritual dimension. A Brother of Truth is one who realizes this, one who is ready to reverse commonly held priorities of innerness and outerness, one who can distinguish what is truly real from what is only apparently real. When urged to cover himself like a hedgehog, he recognizes that he is being urged to identify himself with and develop that part of himself that is most truly real: his soul.

A Brother of Truth is thus one who recognizes that he is able to slough off his outer dimension just as snakes shed their skins. But of course he cannot expect this task to be easy. He must be ready for hard work. He must be prepared to be like a worm, who, though a soft spineless creature, is able to make its slow way through solid earth by dint of relentless persistence. Moreover, throughout his progress, a Brother of Truth must be constantly on his guard. Since flesh is weak, his spirit must be like a scorpion, ever ready to sting those parts of himself that he thinks he has purified himself of and left behind, but which are nevertheless always ready to sneak up from behind and hinder spiritual progress (6).

Again, a Brother of Truth must realize that this process involves being able to reverse or invert previously held assumptions. To strengthen spirit, one must offer matter poison; one can only obtain spiritual life at the cost of material death. One must reach a state where the soul flies from the body like a bird from the earth. But this flight does not come suddenly of itself; it is the result of long, exhausting effort. One cannot return to one's previous states (or nests), for lack of progress is equivalent to backsliding. Instead one works steadily on. If birdlike soaring is at times too difficult, one relies on thieflike stealth. The important thing is continual progress toward the final goal. Those who keep trying, whose flight becomes strong through continual practice, eventually join the vanguard (6).

During this whole process, a Brother of Truth understands that he is not attempting anything unnatural. Strange as it may seem to the uninitiated, engaging in the process of spiritual purification is only the exercising of an innate and unique natural talent. It is no more unnatural than the difficult-to-believe, but completely natural, traits of other animals, whether it be ostriches gulping down hot stones, vipers digesting bones, salamanders penetrating blazing flames, or bats flying only at night, a time when most creatures rest. Indeed, the best of birds are bats (7).[10]

Viewed according to this reading, the seeming conundrums of the exhortations become comprehensible. What the herald of God is calling for is that the Brothers of Truth appreciate the part of human nature that has true value, the spiritual dimension; that they recognize that this dimension is unique to Man; and that fulfilling or perfecting this potential is life's true purpose. Remaining immersed in the material level of being, says God's herald, is only death in the semblance of life.

Having thus adumbrated in this rather obscure speech of the herald of God the themes with which he wishes to deal, Ibn Sina now presents them in a more organized form in his bird allegory. We observed before that the prologue does not form a lucid introduction to the realm of allegory we now enter. But it does provide a useful prelude of sorts. After we have struggled along its twisting, hard-to-discern paths, the allegory itself stretches out like a wide, well-marked highway.

The Allegory

Since the metaphorical correspondences one faces in this part of the *Epistle* are more organized, they are more immediately comprehensible. In fact, one quickly grasps the gist of the allegory: the bird represents the rational soul; the hunters and their snares represent the material world, or, more exactly, the vegetable and animal souls with their senses, passions, and imaginings; the various regions through which the flock travels represent the heavenly spheres of the celestial Souls and Intelligences; and the Great King represents the Necessary Existent, God. In short, this is a version of part of the basic Neoplatonic myth: the story of the descent of the soul into its material, corporal prison, its lapse into oblivion, the moment of its reawakening, and the account of its journey toward reunion with its Divine Source. Since this myth also forms the basis of other of Ibn Sina's allegories, we shall refer to them here when appropriate or useful.[11]

In *Hayy ibn Yaqzan* Ibn Sina personifies human passions and instincts as evil companions, eager to lead the unwitting narrator astray.[12] Here he presents them as clever hunters who cunningly lure into captivity a flock of naive and unsuspecting birds. And such is the nature of this captivity that the birds become accustomed to it and forget that they were ever free. "We became used to nets and content with cages" (11).

Both the events and imagery of this sequence resemble that of Ibn Sina's "Ode on the Soul." Here too the soul is likened to a bird, a dove in this case. Here too its descent into matter is presented as a tragedy:

It descended upon thee out of the regions above,
That exalted, ineffable, glorious, heavenly Dove.
Unwilling it sought thee and joined thee, and yet,
    though it grieve,
It is like to be still more unwilling thy body to leave.
It resisted and struggled, and would not be tamed in haste,
Yet it joined thee, and slowly grew used to this desolate waste,
Till, forgotten at length, as I ween, were its haunts and its troth
In the heavenly gardens and groves, which to leave it was loath.[13]

The "Ode" is interesting in that besides describing the soul's descent into the body, it poses the question of why it was forced to do so. Our allegory, however, does not take up this question; instead it concentrates on the process of release.

The bird/soul's captivity entails its not only forgetting its own true nature and place of origin, but also that of its comrades ("our individual sorrow precluding each of us from caring about his brother" [11]). Deliverance from this sorry state comes through recollection; recollection comes through remembrance. The sight of a group of birds who have liberated themselves reminds the narrator of his former freedom and inspires him to strive to regain it. Ibn Sina thus retouches the theme of needing an "other," a Brother of Truth, to begin and facilitate the process of spiritual purification.

Just whom the philosopher has in mind here is uncertain. It is of course possible that he had in mind some esoteric group, such as the Isma^cilis, or perhaps some circle of mystics. More likely, however, is that he was referring to the philosophical tradition of which he was part.[14] Through the process of learning, studying, meditating on, discussing, and regenerating this tradition, one's soul awakens and perceives its true origin, realizes the loneliness and lowliness to which it has fallen, and begins to work toward reinstatement. Whatever its intended identity, this group of birds effects the narrator's reawakening and release. And they also become his guides during his flight towards salvation. But although they can guide, they cannot carry. Each individual soul must forge its own path.

Having achieved initial release, the bird and his new-found companions begin their ascent. But although they have escaped from their nets and cages, they have not yet totally escaped the bondage of the sensations and passions of the material world. They still have the remnants of their snares and ropes dangling from their legs.

They fly up the slope of what Ibn Sina calls the "mountain of God, in a valley grassy and fertile—no, rather, barren and desolate" (15). At first this phrase seems contradictory and puzzling. But here Ibn Sina is pointing out the change of perspective that ascent through the sublunary realm of transient generation and corruption entails. From the perspective of earth, the realm immediately above seems to have positive aspects. This is because it is closer to the region of Absolute Form than earth itself. As one traverses it, however, and comes to look down on it from above, its negative aspect, the desolation and waste that increased immersion in matter entails, is what becomes more noticeable and highlighted. One sees then that, as Ibn Sina says in *Hayy ibn Yaqzan*, "This clime is desolate, a dung-heap, filled with discord, strife, controversy, and commotion; it borrows its splendor from a distant place."[15] The beauty of creation thus comes from its formal aspect, which emanates from above. Seen from below, the sublunary region's formal aspect attracts and enchants; seen from above, its material aspect puts off and repels.

From the peak of the first mountain (the sphere of the moon), the birds see eight more peaks (the spheres of Mercury, Venus, the Sun, Mars, Jupiter, Saturn, the Fixed Stars, and the Starless Heaven). Undaunted by this sight, they continue their ascent. It is not until they reach the seventh peak, that of the Fixed Stars, that they pause to rest. Even in this lofty and wondrous realm, however, they must still be on their guard. Otherwise, they may be lured back to their previous state of sensual captivity. They must be "scorpions whose weapons are in their tails." This is because the pleasures of this realm are still sensual. It has textures pleasing to the touch, sights beautiful to the eye, sounds lovely to the ear, fragrances pleasant to the smell, and food and drink delightful to the taste. Even in the highest realms of the heavenly spheres, the sensual temptations of the material world remain dangerous. Perceiving these dangers, the birds urge each other on and resume their journey.

They next arrive at the outermost heavenly sphere, the Starless Heavens. And here for the first time, they encounter other beings: birds (souls) like themselves whose forms, colors, and songs enchant the wanderers. This region is the closest in creation to that of Absolute Form; its inhabitants are the "spiritual beings of the angels (*ar-ruhiyun min al-mala'ikah*)" whom Ibn Sina mentions in *Hayy ibn Yaqzan*.[16] But even this realm of almost pure Form does not satisfy the travelers; for they still have not achieved complete release. On the advice of the heavenly birds, they continue their journey until they at last come to the abode of the Great King who rules from beyond the spheres. Arriving at his palace, they await permission to enter, according to courtly protocol. Being invited in, they cross great courtyards, each surpassing the other in magnitude and glory. Finally, they reach the throne room of the Great King. At first, they are dazzled by his beauty, but later the narrator attempts to describe him (24).[17]

Although the Great King is all-beautiful and described as perfect, he is apparently not all-powerful. He himself cannot directly free the pilgrims from their ultimate material snares; only those who set the snares can do this. But He can arrange that this occurs. He sends a messenger to return with them and give the necessary orders.

Here is another logical paradox in the Neoplatonic cosmological scheme. Although the Great King is the pinnacle of existence, he is not its omnipotent master. He is bound by the limits of the hierarchical cosmic structure of which he is the prime source; he is limited by the forms He himself produces. As in the case of the above-mentioned question of why the soul is initially sent down into matter in the first place, the question of this apparent limitation in the powers of the Great King (God) is here neither stressed nor pursued.

As for this messenger, it seems certain that Death is intended here. After reaching an advanced state of spiritual progress, one sees Death as an ally whose arrival is welcomed rather than an enemy whose onslaught against bodily matter is feared or hated. This is because only Death can fully and finally release the soul from material bondage.[18]

The Epilogue

From the heights of spiritual glory to which he has led us, Ibn Sina ends the *Epistle* by plunging us down to the depths of irony and sarcasm, for on describing his experiences to his fellows, to his "friends," he finds himself accused of mental derangement. And his narrative suffers the cruelest fate possible for an allegory; it is taken literally. Men cannot fly, he is told, nor birds talk. And his states of spiritual anguish, yearning, and joy are merely the results of physical disorder. We thus have the irony of having the greatest physician of the Middle Ages portraying himself as being prescribed physical remedies.[19] Moderation in all things, good food, plenty of sleep, not too much thinking, all these, he is told, will return him to his senses. More than this, the very complaint with which he began the *Epistle* is reiterated and turned against him. His wild ravings and apparent illness is upsetting his friends and causing them distress. So that rather than easing his sorrows through sharing them with a friend, Ibn Sina is himself accused of causing his friends sorrow and worry. As one would expect, his reaction to this charge is bitter. He gives up his friends and seeks refuge in God. And with this, the *Epistle* ends.

III

The meaning of the text should now be clear; its riddles, difficulties, and conundrums solved. What we have here is a particular representation, an *exemplum*, of the general Neoplatonic myth of the drama of the soul. This is a version of the story of the soul's blissful primordial union with the World Soul; the tragedy of its separation, individual descent, and isolation in the world of matter; the account of its joyful rediscovery of its original nature and source; and the epic of its heroic quest to return to and regain its original estate. But why, one might ask, did Ibn Sina not simply relate the myth itself? Why did he cloak it in symbols, metaphors, and riddles? And why did he make his narrative so difficult to understand?[20]

Ibn Sina would reply, I think, in two ways. First, he might say that this is his version of the myth. This was one way he felt he could best express it. Second, he would perhaps say that the meanings of myths cannot be taught; they must be discovered. The emotional, intellectual, and spiritual reverberations that myths provoke cannot be instilled from without; rather they must be induced from within. The symbolic and allegoric mode of the *Epistle*, with all of its difficulties and riddles, imbues the work with an aura of mystery and immanence. It also presents a challenge. To discover the text's meaning, the reader must tread slowly and warily; he must pause, study, reflect. In this way, he is seduced into the world of the text. Without perhaps entirely realizing it, he embarks on a project of retrieving, gathering, and reconstructing the details of a myth much of whose force and potency stem from its very emphasis on the idea of primordial recollection and remembrance. In the process of identifying with the *dramatis personae* of the narrative—whether Ibn Sina himself or the bird—and in the process of meditating upon and solving the text's metaphoric mysteries and symbolic complexities, the reader ends by becoming a full and active participant in charting out a conceptual universe whose nature, details, and modes of thought had hitherto been unknown and unimagined.

The reader begins the process of striving to understand the text, making sense of its details, clarifying its enigmas, and grasping its meaning with the idea that he is translating the text, transferring it from its own terms and reformulating it in terms of his own conceptions of reality. But what really happens—or what should happen—is the reverse. In the course of his reading, it is really the reader who becomes translated and transmuted, for the process of his reading and thinking ends with he himself being stripped of his former conceptions of reality and adopting those of the text. At least, this is the *Epistle's* intention. By the end of the work, the myth is reality, while one's former conception of reality is now reduced to the status of myth.

The test as to whether this process of seduction and transformation, of disorientation and reorientation, has been successful comes at the narrative's end. By then, it is intended that the reader is so affected by his reading and unraveling that he does not sympathize with, or even comprehend, Ibn Sina's "friend" when he says: "No, by God, you did not fly! Rather, your mind flew. Nor were you hunted! Rather, your heart was hunted." Instead the reader trusts, sympathizes with, and believes the "herald of God" when he exclaims: "Fly!"

———————— IV ————————

Before leaving the text, one further question deserves attention. Is the subject of the *Epistle* only that discussed above, or does it have another, simpler, more basic theme?

Traditionally, allegories end happily.[21] Since their intent is to move from the confusion of ignorance to the order of enlightenment, they customarily end with a sense of completion and fulfillment. In allegory, true knowledge is bliss. But in the *Epistle*, the situation is different. Returning to the plane of everyday reality, Ibn Sina does not meet an appreciatively receptive audience. Instead he encounters a crowd of doubters and skeptics: fools who neither believe his tale nor comprehend its implications. Hence to the initial query: "Will any of my brothers lend me ear long enough for me to tell him something of my sorrows?" the *Epistle's* final answer appears to be a resounding "No!" If "Brothers of Truth" are those who "observe realities with the eye of insight," few seem to have surrounded Ibn Sina!

The bitterness of the epilogue seems to be more than just a reaction to returning to the world of material imperfection after a sojourn in that of spiritual perfection, a kind of mystical postpartum depression. Rather, it is part of a tone of profound dissatisfaction with the nature of Man and a disillusionment with the potentiality of his attaining a common, social level of perfection that runs throughout the text. If one is to achieve some measure of perfection, one must, it appears, attain it individually. Furthermore, it seems that in this project, the group serves more to hinder than help. So we have a paradox. At the same time that Ibn Sina calls for a perfect companion, a "Brother of Truth," someone who will participate and aid in the process of attaining perfection, he also continually suggests that such perfect companionship, i.e., membership in a group striving for perfection, is totally impossible.

This conclusion does not stem only from the work's ending. It emerges continually throughout the narrative's presentation of the interplay between individuality and sociability, solitude and companionship, division and unity. Consider the following scheme an attempt to trace these dichotomies in the *Epistle*. After each element, or moment, is an assessment (plus or minus) of how the reader is intended to react to the situation.

   i. Individual narrator's state of solitude and sorrow (minus)

   ii. Possibility of solace in companionship (plus)

  iii. Realization of rareness of genuine friends, as described by the herald of God (minus)

  iv. Group of hunters set snares (minus)

   v. Group of birds enticed and entrapped (minus)

  vi. Individual bird in state of solitude and oblivion (minus)

 vii. Another group of birds helps individual bird escape (plus)

viii. But group still has remnants of snares on their legs (minus)

  ix. Possibility of common final release through ascension (plus)

   x. But necessity of advancing singly during the journey (minus)

  xi. Temptation of backsliding during rest stop (minus)

 xii. Members of group urge on each other (plus)

xiii. Meeting with group of heavenly birds, who are friendly and helpful (plus)

xiv. But inability of this group to do more than offer advice (minus)

 xv. Arrival at their final destination and audience with the Great King, the symbol of final unity (portrayed, notice, as an individual) (plus)

 xvi. His inability to provide immediate help (minus)

xvii. His sending a messenger to secure their complete release (plus)

xviii. The group's lack of knowledge concerning the Great King (minus)

xix. Its rejection of the narrator's description and tale (minus)

xx. The narrator's rejection and turning away from the group (minus)

Of these twenty elements, thirteen are negative. And two of the remaining seven positive moments are only presented as possibilities, not realities. Hence, although the *Epistle* begins by suggesting that the group should be a positive entity, that it should encompass and nurture the individual and promote his development and deliverance, in reality, the narrative almost always portrays it failing or, even more, obstructing this task. If salvation is to be achieved, one concludes, it is to be done so individually; in spite of the group, not because of it.

The *Epistle of the Bird* thus appears to have two dimensions. One, the conscious plan of the text is that the narrative, with its stylistic difficulties, rhetorical obscurity, metaphorical riddles, and symbolic allegory, should serve as a *kone*, an object of meditation aiming at provoking the attentive reader into shedding one plane of awareness and adopting that of another. The other, latent, dimension is the narrative as a complaint; an expression of and perhaps meditation on both the fact and the inevitability of spiritual solitude. For at the same time that the *Epistle* points out and emphasizes the usefulness and desirability of group membership, of striving and working toward perfection in concord with others, it continually discounts this project's possibility of success. The *Epistle's* rhetoric and intent, therefore, rest on a paradox. The very thing that it calls for (perfect spiritual companionship), is something that it in the end despairs of finding. But then, most birds only fly so high.

Notes

[1] For the Arabic texts and French paraphrases of most of this corpus, see A. F. Mehren, *Traités mystiques d'Abou Ali b. Sina ou d'Avicenne* (Leiden: Brill, 1889–99). To these texts, one should add Ibn Sina's "Ode on the Soul" (see note 13 below). Also useful is the collection of texts in Hasan ᶜAsi, *at-Tafasir al-Qur'aniyya wa-l-lugha as-sufiyya fi falsafat Ibn Sina* (study and texts) (Cairo: al-Mu'assasa al-jamiᶜiyya li-d-dirasa wa-n-nashr wa-t-tauziᶜ, 1983). This collection should, however, be used with care since not all texts in it are by Ibn Sina.

[2] The best introduction to Ibn Sina's thought is Dimitri Gutas, *Avicenna and the Aristotelian Tradition: Introduction to Reading Avicenna's Philosophical Works*, Islamic Philosophy and Theology 4 (Leiden: Brill, 1988). For Gutas's views on the place of allegory in Ibn Sina's methods of exposition, see ibid., 297–318. For a general account of Ibn Sina's mysticism—or lack of same—see Gutas's section "Mysticism," 79–83, in Muhsin S. Mahdi, Dimitri Gutas, et al., "Avicenna," *Encyclopedia Iranica*, ed. Ehsan Yarshater (London and New York: Routledge & Kegan Paul, 1982–), 1:66–110. Seyyed Hussein Nasr, *An Introduction to Islamic Cosmological Doctrines*, rev. ed. (Boulder, Colo.: Shambhala, 1978), 181–96, and Parviz

Morewedge, "The Logic of Emanationism and Sufism in the Philosophy of Ibn Sina (Avicenna)," *JOAS* 91.4 (1971): 467–76 and 92.1 (1972): 1–18, provide useful surveys of the problem and its literature. See also T. Sabri, "Avicenne philosophe et mystique dans le miroir de trois récits: Hayy b. Yaqzan, l'Oiseau, Salaman et Absal," *Arabica* 27.3 (1980): 257–74.

³ This translation is based on a collation of the Arabic text published by Mehren in *Traités mystiques*, 2d fascicule, 42–48 (of the Arabic text) and that published by L. Cheikho in *al-Mashriq* 19 (1901): 882–87. In general, I have followed Mehren. But in several places, Cheikho's text's reading seems better (Cheikho also offers many personal amendments to his text, but these I have declined to follow). There exist two Western versions of the *Epistle*. One is a French paraphrase offered by Mehren (pp. 27–32 of the above-mentioned 2d fascicule). The other is Henri Corbin's translation, first presented in his *Avicenne et le récit visionaire*, 3 vols. (Tehran and Paris: Institut Franco-Iranien and A. Maisonneuve, 1952–54). I have consulted the new edition of the English translation of this work: W. Trask, trans., *Avicenna and the Visionary Recital*, Bollingen Series 66 (New York: Pantheon Books, 1960). Here Corbin's translation is on pp. 186–92. Because Mehren's effort is professedly only a paraphrase, and because Corbin based his effort mainly (if not totally?) on Persian translations of the *Epistle*, I offer a new translation of the original Arabic here. The pagination of Mehren's Arabic text is inserted between slashes in the translation. I have numbered the paragraphs on the left-hand side of the translation for easy reference in my analysis.

⁴ The Arabic here is *wayl-ak*, which literally means "Woe unto you!" Here it is used as an exhortation: "Woe unto you if you do not!" "Come!" presents a better translation of the sense and intent of the phrase than the archaic and at any rate quite strong (in modern English) "Woe unto you!"

⁵ Reading Cheikho's (and Mehren's B² variant) *tadammu* (gather together) instead of Mehren's preference, *tasabu* (act childishly, or rejuvenate yourselves).

⁶ Reading Cheikho's *taltaqimu* (gulp down) rather than Mehren's *taltaqitu* (gather).

⁷ Reading Cheikho's *suyigha* (were formed, fashioned) rather than Mehren's *duyiᶜa* (were lost, wasted).

⁸ Qur'an 26:227.

⁹ In the framework of Ibn Sina's philosophical terminology, "brothers" help each other strengthen the powers of each others' rational souls, while those of impure hearts are immersed in the preoccupation of their animal souls.

¹⁰ Bats are the best of birds because medieval zoologists and ornithologists considered them the species of birds in the hierarchy of Creation closest in attribute to the genus of Animal (of which they are in truth members!). See Zakariyya ibn Muhammad ibn Mahmud al-Qazwini, *ᶜAja'ib al-makhluqat wa-ghara'ib al-mawjudat*, 4th ed. (Cairo: Mustafa al-Babi al-Halabi, 1970), 274–75. They are also another example of initial, exterior impressions being deceptive. Bats appear weak at first, because they are blinded by light. But no creature compares with them in nighttime navigation.

¹¹ See Plotinus, *The Enneads*, trans. Stephen MacKenna, 3d rev. ed. (London: Faber and Faber Limited, 1957), esp. "Fourth Ennead," VIII, "The Soul's Descent

182 / PETER HEATH

into Body," 357–64. See also A. H. Armstrong on Plotinus in *The Cambridge History of Later Greek and Early Medieval Philosophy*, ed. A. H. Armstrong (Cambridge: Cambridge University Press, 1970), 250–63. Neoplatonism shares this myth with gnosticism and hermeticism. The gnostic versions of this myth are essentially dualistic, however. It is sometimes more difficult to distinguish between hermetic and Neoplatonist versions, but in general the trend of the first is occultist and theurgic while that of the second philosophic (in the more traditional sense of the word). See Hans Jonas, *The Gnostic Religion*, 2d ed. (Boston: Beacon Press, 1963), 42–47, 154–73.

   12 See Mehren, *Traités*, 1st fascicule (Arabic), 1.

   13 Ibn Sina's "Ode on the Soul" has not—as far as I know—been critically edited in a reliable fashion. This translation is from E. G. Browne, *A Literary History of Persia* (London: T. Fisher Unwin, 1906), 2:110–11. For a version of the Arabic text, see al-Qazwini, *ᶜAja'ib*, 201–2.

   14 Here I agree with Gutas's general argument in *Avicenna and the Aristotelian Tradition*, 1–8.

   15 Mehren, *Traités*, 1st fascicule (Arabic), 9–10.

   16Ibid., 13.

   17 For other descriptions of the Great King in Ibn Sina's writings, see that in *Hayy ibn Yaqzan*, Mehren, *Traités*, 1st fascicule (Arabic), 20–21 (Corbin, *Avicenna and the Visionary Recital*, 149–50). See also the description in Ibn Sina's *Kitab al-isharat wa-tanbihat*, ed. Sulayman Dunya (Cairo: Dar al-maᶜarif, n.d.), 3:124.

   18 In reading the identity of the messenger to be Death, I endorse the view proposed by Mehren (cf. *Traités*, 2d fascicule, 26 and 31n2 of the French) rather than the more optimistic, but in my view clearly erroneous, interpretation of Corbin, who sees the messenger as a representation of the Active Intellect (cf. *Avicenna and the Visionary Recital*, 194–95). Nor do I agree, by the way, with Corbin's rather simplistic view (followed by S. H. Nasr in *Islamic Cosmological Doctrines*) that Ibn Sina's *Hayy*, the *Bird*, and *Salaman and Absal* are consecutive moments in a single narrative sequence or portrayal of Man's spiritual development. Pushing the texts into this framework glosses over too many of their individual characteristics.

   19 According to Ibn Sina's medical masterpiece *al-Qanun fi-l-tibb*, both nymphea oil and epithymun are effective mild tonics against general discomfort and melancholy, see *al-Qanun*, repr. of Bulak ed. (Beirut: Dar Sadir, n.d.), 1:375 and 1:25 respectively.

   20 Here I am not referring to Ibn Sina's adherence to the Aristotelian theory of levels of exposition—demonstration, dialectic, rhetoric, sophism—for which see Gutas, *Avicenna and the Aristotelian Tradition*, 297–318, and Ismail M. Dahiyat, *Avicenna's Commentary on the Poetics of Aristotle: A Critical Study with an Annotated Translation of the Text* (Leiden: Brill, 1974), 31–44. Rather, I am inquiring into the question that given that symbolic exposition is intended for those unable to follow rational demonstrations, why then should Ibn Sina's *Epistle* be so enigmatic and difficult.

   21 For the genre of allegory, see Morton W. Bloomfield, ed., *Allegory, Myth, Symbol*, Harvard English Studies 9 (Cambridge: Harvard University Press, 1981),

Angus Fletcher, *Allegory: The Theory of a Symbolic Mode* (Ithaca, N.Y.: Cornell University Press, 1964), Stephen J. Greenblatt, ed., *Allegory and Representation* (Baltimore: Johns Hopkins University Press, 1981), and Jon Whitman, *Allegory: The Dynamics of an Ancient and Medieval Technique* (Cambridge: Harvard University Press, 1987).

11

FRANCIS E. PETERS

Department of Near Eastern Languages and Literatures
New York University, New York

Hermes and Harran: The Roots of Arabic-Islamic Occultism

THE OCCULT is what is hidden. But not to everyone. Wherever there is something hidden, there is necessarily someone who knows. Nor is the occult something that is merely ignored. It has, by implication, been concealed, by some agent and to some purpose, to all except those same inevitable knowers. Thus to ignore the occult would be folly, the equivalent, in parabolic terms, of failing to submit a bid on the Pearl of Great Price.

The occult is doubly occult: it is a hidden knowledge of hidden truths or powers. These latter were concealed, it is agreed, by the Maker of Truths who appears to have been generally reluctant to cast his Pearl before swine, while those who do possess them are careful to keep a close guard on their treasure. Indeed, in many societies those "knowers," who everywhere and always constitute an elite, banded together in guilds and brotherhoods to stand guard over the extremely useful and valuable knowledge that was theirs.

The secret knowledge these adepts possessed—*gnosis* for the Greeks, *hikmah* to the Arabs—was more than useful; it was highly sensitive and indeed dangerous, having passed, as it did, from the dimension of the divine, the Other, into the realm of the human. The clergy—and this was the normal form of self-association among the Knowers—were the conductors of this divine electricity. They were not consumed by their knowledge: they could enter the Holy of Holies, handle the Sacred Species with impunity, go up to the Sacred Mountain, eat of the Tree of

Knowledge, even peer into the Abyss. If the clergy grew rich on their privy knowledge of what they discerned in the Abyss and then passed it out in regulated dosages to the profane and unknowing laymen, they probably deserved their tithes: they were daredevil tightrope walkers on what their societies generally conceded were high-voltage lines. For our own part, we are more inclined to regard the priestly guilds of Egypt and Babylonia and Israel as confraternities of skilled technicians or even as mere charlatans who knew full well that there was no power in those circuits. To us their fees appear exorbitant and their priestly secrecy no more than oppression since we have, at least on the philosophical level, a very different view of knowledge: science is an open and public enterprise, self-achieved rather than bestowed, dialectical, cumulative.

These latter notions are not entirely nor even chiefly our own. We got them from the Greeks, who had an intelligentsia but no dominant clergy on the Jewish or Babylonian model. For the garrulous Hellenes talk and reasoning were both expressed by the same word, *logos*. Like us they cherished a moving and perhaps even naive belief in the value of education, and they thought that wisdom was something that could be learned not by passing through dark rites but by attending open lectures, or through public debates and discussions on the subject. Whatever else wisdom was, it was not revealed; it had to be acquired by what the Arabs later called a "striver," a *mujtahid*.

Or nearly so. The Greeks no less than their eastern contemporaries knew there was electricity in the universe. For them, however, it was more a question of each man watching his own step rather than running the power lines through a temple-conductor. But the gods assuredly had access to a knowledge of things unknown to men, the future, for instance, and so the Greeks too indulged, not terribly consequentially, in the minor occult arts of divination by natural signs and dreams. There were seers and prophets in Athens even in its glory days. The Athenians hearkened but continued to go to school.

The records indicate that there was a Babylonian enrolled in the most prestigious Athenian school of all, Plato's own Academy. This is an interesting and suggestive piece of information since toward the end of Plato's life near the midpoint of the fourth pre-Christian century there are indications of an increased interest among Greek intellectuals in what other peoples liked to think was *their* wisdom. Earlier the Greeks had dismissed such claims with an almost Chinese disdain for the wit and wisdom of the "barbarians." The Greeks were curious about foreigners and were eager, as no other people in the world were eager, to learn *about* others. The notion of learning *from* those non-Hellenes remained, however, simply laughable.

Times and attitudes were changing in fourth-century Athens, however, and the young Aristotle was willing at least to entertain the notion of a history of wisdom that began before the Greeks and included such an unlikely figure—unlikely a mere generation earlier—as the Iranian sage Zoroaster. By Aristotle's death the world itself had changed. In the wake of Alexander the Greeks found themselves masters of a political empire that included, for the first time in the Hellenes' history, non-Greeks, those same *barbaroi* of the clergy-lands of Iran, Mesopotamia, Palestine, and Egypt. It should have been a moment of Hellenic triumph; it signaled instead the beginning of a period of profound and shattering self-doubt.

The progress of Hellenism into the vitals of the indigenous religious societies of Western Asia is not very well known, except perhaps in the case of the Jews, who recorded their own resistance to the new ideology. But the reciprocal changes that were wrought inside the Hellenic enclaves in the East can be traced in some detail. There were early turnings toward the occult within the Greek philosophical schools, in the growth of an astral theology, for example, but they did not at the outset destroy the faculties' conviction that philosophy was, and remained, a public and acquired good. There were signs of other, more portentous stirrings, however, notoriously the resurrection of a long-dead Pythagoras in the new guise of miracle worker and proponent of the occult. The historical Pythagoras may have been just that—we cannot tell with certainty—but the scholastic masters of the fourth century, Plato and Aristotle, preferred to think of and about him as a philosopher and a scientist.

In the end the Platonists, who were the chief survivors among the Greek philosophical schools, embraced the occult with a passion. Plotinus in the third Christian century stood almost alone in his resistance to what most of his philosophical contemporaries and successors judged to be an alternative, and superior, way to truth, a conning of the great oracular collections like the *Chaldean Oracles* in an attempt to extort and master the secrets of nature. The stars and planets, divinities all, were scanned and implored to work their wills benignly on men. Proclus, the head of the Platonic Academy at Athens in the fifth Christian century, fancied he might be the reincarnation of the Pythagorean numerologist Nicomachus of Jerash.[1]

It was not necessary to be a philosopher to indulge an interest in the occult in Late Antiquity. The Hellenic scientific establishment was likewise riddled with alchemists, astrologers, and a new breed of physicist who studied and manipulated the hidden powers of natural substances. Their work was generally under the patronage of the Greek god Hermes, who had begun his career modestly enough as a messenger for the other Olympian gods but now in his latest role as Hermes "Thrice Great" was crossed with the Egyptian deity Thoth and had become a latter-day Prometheus, the bearer of divine wisdom to the world of men. It was Hermes, the tradition ran, who built the pyramids, founded Babylonian science, and, finally, inspired the whole line of Greek sages. He was architect, alchemist, physician, and philosopher. And he was the Revealer.

There was no shape to Hermeticism, the body of teachings attributed to Hermes and whose literary expression is known collectively to modern scholars as the *Corpus Hermeticum,* just as there was none originally to Hermes himself. Some of its musings were constituted of thinly disguised Greek theological speculation placed at the service of a Hermetic revelation; some of it was science, Greek and Babylonian in the main; the rest was magical recipes, parlor tricks, sleight of hand. The whole was cast over with an elaborate veneer of Egyptian antiquity, and this cachet of oriental antiquity helped sell Hermeticism in a world that now revered rather than despised the eastern *barbaroi.* "From the East, light," it was said, to which one could add, "and wisdom and salvation." Isis not Aristotle was the name to reckon with in Late Antiquity.

The sixth-century Arabs were sublimely ignorant of all this. Some of the frontier tribes were Christian and served as mercenary auxiliaries for the Byzantines and Persians, but the greater number of the Arabs continued to live isolated from the high cultures of Alexandria, Antioch, and Seleucia-Ctesiphon as nomads within the Syrian steppe or as dwellers in the towns of the Hejaz. Their sciences had to do with survival, and their magic and demonology was that of a folk culture. By the eighth century, however, these same Arabs, now Muslims, were in possession of the great urban centers of the Near East by right of conquest and were already embarked upon the process of making the cultural goods of the Byzantines and Sasanians their own. Greek science and philosophy, Persian ethical and political ideals, Indian medicine and mathematics all quickly became part of the Arab intellectual experience.[2]

Absorbed by the Muslims with the rest of this prodigious inheritance was the later Greek fascination with the occult, as well as the object of that fascination, an unknown quantity of Hermetic literature. Indeed, as we shall see, the Arabs learned to be Hermeticists even before they learned to be philosophers. They were helped in their education by a peculiar community of people over whom the transforming wave of Near Eastern Christianity appears to have passed unavailingly, the so-called Sabians of the northwestern Mesopotamian city of Harran.

There were few outright and confessed Hermeticists in Islam. Such confessions were likely to prove dangerous in a professedly religious society such as Islam, but the ancient Greek sages from Empedocles and Pythagoras down to Apollonius of Tyana, the Arabs' "Balinus,"[3] had for some Muslim intellectuals both prestige and an attractive remoteness and so might serve the prudent believer as convenient candidates for attribution for his own thoughts. Some Hermetic devotees like Abu Ma^{c}shar and Ibn Wahshiyyah claimed that they were merely translators or exegetes of a rediscovered ancient tradition, while others like Jabir ibn Hayyan disappeared behind a cloud of legend as homegrown pseudepigraphomena. The "Brethren of Purity" wisely preferred to remain anonymous, as did the author who concealed himself behind the name of al-Majriti.

The result of this mystification is that it is as little possible to write the history of Islamic Hermeticism as it is to trace the career of its Hellenic prototype. In the four dense volumes of his *Révélation d'Hermès Trismégiste* Festugière undertook to disengage a number of the basic themes and motifs of Greek Hermeticism and to show their similarity to what was evolving in the philosophical schools of Late Antiquity. He did not, however, succeed in converting myth into history or in piercing the anonymity of the authors of the body of *Hermetica*. Hermeticism is in fact a historical mirage, and the body of science and near-science circulating under the name of Hermes Thrice Great was no different from what passed in Late Antiquity as the wisdom of Zoroaster or of Apollonius of Tyana.[4] One is confronted in fact only by a sprawling and amorphous tradition of disguised origins to which the later Greeks and Romans continued to add, but always in the name of other sages remote in time and space.

Nothing comparable to Festugière's work has been undertaken on behalf of Islamic Hermeticism.[5] Where probes have been made by Ruska, Kraus, Ritter, Massignon, Plessner, and Marquet,[6] Greek origins are invariably indicated, even though exact sources or routes of transmission are difficult to come by. There is no example to date of a forthright Arabic translation of a Hermetic work preserved in Greek. The fact is not remarkable, however, since where we do possess Arabic translations of Greek originals, it is generally a question of school books passing through some type of curricular channel, where teachers, students, and editors have all left their distinguishable marks upon the text. The Hermetic tract, on the other hand, deliberately effaced its birthmarks and circulated anonymously or pseudepigraphically, and often on a quasi-popular level.

Together with the mass of Hermetic lore the Arabs received a number of stories on the person of Hermes himself. They were taught by their Iranian informants that the original Hermes dated from antediluvian times, that he was in fact a grandson of Adam, and that one or the other of the Hermes known to them was a migrant bearing the wisdom of Babylon into Egypt (*Fihrist*, 351–52). That was the received version, but in the end Islam more comfortably synthesized Hermes into the already composite portrait of the Qur'anic Idris and the Jewish Enoch. It is not certain when this transmigration of Hermes into an Islamic setting took place, but as early as A.D. 845 Jahiz knew of the identification of Hermes-Idris (*Tarbi^c*, 55, Pellat), and Abu Ma^cshar writing about the same time confidently states that the Harranian sage Hermes was the grandson of the Hebrews' Adam and the Persians' Gayomart and so identical with the biblical Khanukh (Enoch) and the Qur'anic Idris.[7] Mas^cudi (*Muruj* I, 73) likewise says that Enoch-Idris is the same as Hermes and adds that this identification was made by the Sabians. If the Sabians were responsible for inserting Hermes into the Idris-Enoch complex, then it is likely that the identification began to be diffused at a time when, as we shall see, the *Dar al-Islam* took official notice of the Sabians of Harran, during the final days of the Caliph Ma'mun. Abu Sahl al-Fadl al-Nawbakhti, Harun's Iranian librarian, who was familiar with Hermes, knew nothing of the Idris association, at any rate.

In Ibn al-Nadim's *Fihrist* the sketchy description of the passage of the Platonic and Aristotelian school corpus into Islam is preceded by a series of somewhat disjointed narratives that provided the Muslim reader of the tenth century with an account of the origins of science and of Greek philosophy. The first and second of Ibn al-Nadim's narratives, those derived from Abu Sahl al-Fadl ibn Nawbakht (238–39/Dodge, 572–75),[8] and from Abu Ma^cshar (240–41/Dodge, 576–78), purport to return to the very origins of scientific knowledge. And though they were reporting on different parts of the story, both men drew from some common or complementary source.

According to their composite account, science originated in Babylon and passed thence into Egypt and India. The substance of this "science" was primarily cosmogonical, but its understanding was unaccountably blurred by some "original sin," and it was not until some later time that the true understanding of the origins of the universe was recalled and restored. Centuries afterward, during the reign of the King Tahmurath according to Abu Ma^cshar, there came to Babylon reports of a flood "in the west." Alarmed, Tahmurath ordered the construction of a repository on the citadel of Jayy near Isfahan and had concealed there the books of accumulated human wisdom.

This was not quite the Iranian version of events, as reported by al-Fadl and a parallel account in the *Denkart*: it was Alexander, so it was said, who destroyed most of the works of learning in Iraq and Iran, but only after having sent to Egypt translations of them in Greek and Coptic. The Persian kings had earlier been warned of some such catastrophe and had dispatched exemplars of these same books into India and China, whence the Sasanians retrieved them after their accession to power in A.D. 226.

In Abu Ma^cshar's narrative the Sasanians have nothing to do with the restoration of Iranian wisdom. The books concealed by Tahmurath at Isfahan were discovered quite by accident some years before Abu Ma^cshar's day (d. A.D. 866), and they formed the basis of his own astrologically oriented history, *The Book of Thousands*.⁹ There were further discoveries in A.D. 951 and again in 961 (*Fihrist*, 241/Dodge, 578–79).¹⁰ These books were seen in Baghdad; some of them were undecipherable, but others were in Greek.

Greece plays little or no role in this version of the origins of science, nor is there any reason it should. Ibn al-Nadim was using two sources who were both committed to a Babylonian and Iranian origin of learning. That the learning in question was chiefly astrological is no less obvious. Al-Fadl (d. 815), the older of the two authorities, was an Iranian who specialized in translations from the Pahlavi in Harun al-Rashid's "Treasure House of Wisdom" (*Fihrist*, 247/Dodge, 651), while his father had been the court astrologer of al-Mansur and had assisted in that capacity in laying out the city of Baghdad.¹¹ Abu Ma^cshar may have been somewhat more the Hellenophile,¹² but he too was an astrologer and relied far more earnestly on Iranian than Greek sources in his work.

However much these men inclined toward Iran, they both knew of at least one Greek sage, namely, Hermes. Indeed, Abu Ma^cshar knew three personages of that name, encouraged, doubtless, by the stereotyped epithet *trismegistos* applied to Hermes in the sources.¹³ The earliest of the three lived before the Flood. He was the first to study the sciences and— the practical element enters early—he constructed the pyramids of Egypt. The second was identical with the Hermes of al-Fadl's account of post-diluvian Iraq. A king called Dahhaq ibn Qay founded a city, likely Babylon, and constructed in it seven (or twelve) astronomical shrines for seven scholars, among them Hermes.¹⁴ The coming of an unnamed prophet shattered this golden age of learning in Iraq, and Hermes eventually left for Egypt where he became king. Later authors, who were obviously copying Abu Ma^cshar, Ibn Juljul and Ibn Abi Usaybi^cah, connected this Hermes with Pythagoras, one as the teacher and one as the student of Hermes.

The latest of the Hermes was the Egyptian sage associated with a body of Greek (and Latin) texts which bear his name, the so-called *Corpus Hermeticum*, the preserved Egyptian *summa* of gnosticism and alchemical science. This same Hermes was the sire of Asclepius, who passed his father's scientific and philosophical learning to the Greeks.

This view of intellectual history was put together in scholarly circles in the court of Harun al-Rashid (A.D. 786–809), well before the days of Hunayn ibn Ishaq and of al-Kindi, and so earlier than the full impact of scholastic Hellenism upon Islam. Earlier in ^cAbbasid times there was some interest in Greek philosophy, to be sure. Under Mansur, Ibn al-Muqaffa^c (d. 757) or his son was responsible for the first Aristotelian translations into Arabic.[15] The event was, however, isolated. Mansur was certainly interested in the "foreign sciences"—Jurjis ibn Jibra^{c}il ibn Bakhtishu^c came from Jundishapur to Baghdad as caliphal physician in 765—but that interest was neither entirely philosophical nor entirely Greek in its object.

Jurjis and his successors from the Bakhtishu^c family were Hellenically trained, but another family that came into prominence in Mansur's reign, the Nawbakhti, looked, as we have seen, in quite different directions. The founder of that line, Nawbakht, was an Iranian convert from Zoroastrianism to Islam and an astrologer of considerable influence at court. And it was from his grandson, Abu Sahl al-Fadl, likewise an astrologer and bilingual in Pahlavi and Arabic, that Ibn al-Nadim drew his account of the early history of science.

Harun too was interested in Greek science and philosophy. The Bakhtishu^c retained their position at court but were joined by another Jundishapur alumnus, Yuhanna ibn Masawayh, the Christian to whom Harun entrusted the task of translating the medical works discovered and confiscated during the various Muslim forays into Anatolia (Qifti, 380). Abu Nuh, the secretary of the Nestorian Catholicus Timotheus, edged forward the still relatively unsophisticated translation work on the Aristotelian logic,[16] and another obscure scholar, Sallam al-Abrash,[17] is alleged to have translated the *Physics* (*Fihrist*, 244/Dodge, 587).

Sallam probably had the patronage of the Barmacid family, but those recent converts from Buddhism to Islam had interests far more catholic than Greek science. Yahya ibn Khalid, the Barmacid who commissioned the translation of Ptolemy's *Almagest*,[18] was personally responsible for having Indian medical works translated into Arabic (*Fihrist*, 303/Dodge, 710, 826–27). Other scholars connected with either the Barmacids or Harun's *Khizanat al-hikmah* labored at turning both Sanscrit and Pahlavi works into Arabic (*Fihrist*, 244–45/Dodge, 589–90). Abu Sahl al-Fadl was among these latter; in the words of the *Fihrist* (274/Dodge, 651), "he was relied upon because of his knowledge of the books of Fars," which included (*Fihrist*, 239/Dodge, 651) works of "Hermes the Babylonian" translated into Pahlavi during the reign of Shapur.[19]

The Muslim savants of the late eighth century were well versed in Persian, Indian, and Greek astronomy, astrology, medicine, and alchemy, and this at a time when they knew Aristotle only in an epitome and apparently possessed no knowledge of Plato at all. Within a few years Ibn al-Bitriq, Ibn Bahriz, Ibn Na^{c}imah, and Theodore Abu Qurrah, all Christians, began the work of translating Aristotle, Plato, and the Neoplatonists.[20] This scholastic tradition, patronized by the Caliph Ma'mun, came into Arabic textually from Syriac or even Greek prototypes and without the notable Iranian contamination to which the stories told by al-Fadl and Abu Ma^cshar bear eloquent, if symbolic, witness. More, they underline an important element in the cultural development of Islam: Hermes Trismegistos and the works associated with him were domesticated in Islam a generation before either Plato or Aristotle found a firm base there, assisted, it would seem, by Iranian astrologers.

Scholastic philosophy did nothing to impede the growth and diffusion of Hermeticism in Islam. Indeed, their coming together was like the rediscovery of an old ally. The Greeks and Romans at the end of antiquity were persuaded of the identification of Hermes with the Egyptian god Thoth— the Theuth of Plato's *Phaedrus*—and were equally convinced that the works circulating in Greek under the name of Hermes Trismegistos were genuine reflections of a remote Egyptian antiquity. Not that those sunset Fathers of Hellenism had become antiquarians as such; it is rather more likely to think that their sapientalization of the past arose from their own failing confidence that they could add something new or true or certain to the sum of human wisdom. The philosophers of the European Renaissance embraced the Egyptian imposture with equal enthusiasm, though perhaps from different motives, and it was only in relatively recent times that western scholarship judged the *Corpus Hermeticum* as essentially the creation of late Greek learning and piety.[21]

The problems of analysis—and their proposed solutions—in that great age of religious syncretism reflect upon the search for the origins of parallel phenomena in Islam. The routes whereby Hellenic *scholastic* material passed into Islam are well marked in the *Fibrist*, and to go down them leads directly to Farabi studying the text of the *Metaphysics*. But the *occult* knowledge possessed by Farabi's contemporaries did not necessarily travel through parallel, albeit underground, channels. Indeed, much of what has been described as Hermeticism may have been on that same terrain long before Islam, in the hands of people like the Mandeans, Syrian Christian groups like the Daysanites, the theologians of the well-established Babylonian rabbinate,[22] the Hellenized pagan priesthoods which were still active in Babylon and elsewhere in the first Christian century,[23] or in later times the Hellenic and Hellenized philosophers at the court of Khusraw Anushirvan.

Of all these groups it is the Mandeans who are of most interest here since they too, like the formidable occultists of Harran, were known as "Sabians." They lived, and still uncertainly survive, in the marshlands of southern Iraq, whence they were also known as "Sabians of the marshes" (*Fibrist*, 340–41/Dodge, 811), or even as "Nabateans," another archaic denomination in Islam. According to modern estimates, these curious and

isolated marsh people almost certainly constituted a gnostic sect that had
its origins within later (though possibly pre-Christian) Judaism as an ascetic,
baptist society with its centers in the east Jordan, the former haunts of
the Nabateans. Some of these so-called "Nasorean Jews" may have been
absorbed within Judeo-Christianity, but another branch of the "baptizers"
(cf. the Arabic SBY, to immerse, baptize) migrated eastward sometime
before the destruction of the Jerusalem Temple in A.D. 70, and after passing
through Harran found their final refuge in the marsh areas of lower Iraq.

The Mandeans may well have been gnostics before they departed from
their camps in the Transjordan, but their preserved literature, at any rate,
dates from after their arrival in Iraq and testifies to the incorporation into
a very early form of Jewish gnosticism of ideas derived from both
Babylonian and Iranian sources, the importance of the seven planets, for
example, and the Mandean form of the gnostic savior myth.[24]

None of this painfully—and uncertainly—reconstructed history of the
Mandeans was evident to Ibn al-Nadim who contented himself with a few
brief comments on their practices and who seems to say that they were
originally Manicheans. The reality was, in fact, quite the reverse: there was
a Mandean sacred literature before 300, or in any event early enough for
Mani to have borrowed from it.[25] And it must surely have been the existence of those Scriptures that prompted Muhammad to include the
"Sabians" in the Qur'an (2:62; 5:69; 22:17) as "People of the Book."[26]

It would appear most unlikely that Muhammad had direct access to
the Sabian-Mandean Scriptures. Ibn al-Nadim credited them with no
specific titles, though he did know of other, more secular "Nabatean"
works, chief among them the *Nabatean Agriculture*,[27] a work purportedly
written by Ibn Wahshiyyah (*Fihrist*, 311–12, 358/Dodge, 863–65) but more
likely the creation of the Shiᶜite Abu Talib Ahmad ibn al-Zayyat (d. ca.
951). The purpose of the *Nabatean Agriculture* remains obscure, but it
is obviously Hermetic, and like the *Hermetica* in Greek, its pretended
antiquity—it claims to be merely a translation from the original Nabatean
(Aramaic) of the older Semitic learning from Babylonia—is largely a literary
fable.

Most of the material in the *Nabatean Agriculture* is, in fact, pre-Islamic,
though it does not return to the remote patriarchal times that the medieval
Muslims imagined.[28] Much of the material contained in it appears in fact
to be Greek, but there are also traces of Mesopotamian lore, a combination
that points once again to the besetting problem of Near Eastern syncretism.
In the five-odd centuries spanning the birth of Jesus, the Near East presents
a series of religious and quasi-religious movements compounded out of
motifs drawn from all over Western Asia. Gnosticism is one of them,
Mandeism another, and the typology can be multiplied through various

Jewish and Christian sects and the occult sciences like astrology and chemistry. Scholars' attempts at disengaging and assigning to their appropriate sources the various elements operating within these complexes have been only partially successful at best,[29] and least of all when they have attempted to speak with historical precision on the when and where of these obvious syncretisms.

The Arabs possessed, on the testimony of the *Fihrist*, a wide range of *Hermetica* which included versions of the Hermes myth as well as works of theology, cosmology, and physics that were the substance of the Hermetic "revelation." The extent of the latter may be measured in the alchemical Book Ten of the *Fihrist* (351–60/Dodge, 843–68) with its bewildering profusion of names and titles.[30] The major figures are Hermes—the Babylonian Hermes of Abu Sahl—Ostanes, Zosimus, Khalid ibn Yazid, Jabir ibn Hayyan, the Sufi master Dhu al-Nun al-Misri (d. 860), Muhammad ibn Zakariyya al-Razi (d. 925), Ibn Wahshiyyah (d. 904), his contemporary al-Ikhmimi, a Christian monk named Stephen, the ʿAlid Sufi al-Sa'ih al-ʿAlawi, Kindi's student Dubays, and the "extremist" Shiʿite al-Shalmaghani (d. 934).[31]

The list in the *Fihrist* points to some of the directions penetrated by Hermeticism in the late tenth century. The *Shiʿat ʿAli* consistently claimed the Hermeticist Jabir as one of their own (*Fihrist*, 255/Dodge, 853) and linked him with the Imam Jaʿfar al-Sadiq (d. 765), who was himself credited with alchemical works.[32] Jaʿfar's other companions are not, in fact, very well known except for what can be read on them in the Sunni heresiographers. Abu al-Khattab (d. 755) came to rest in those collections as an early example of the Shiʿite *ghulat* or "extremists" by reason of his divinization of both Jaʿfar and himself.[33] The *Fihrist* (186–87/Dodge, 462–63) connects two other famous members of the Imam Jaʿfar's circle with Abu al-Khattab, namely Maymun al-Qaddah and his son ʿAbdallah, the reputed founders of the Ismaʿili wing of the Shiʿah. Another man who belonged to the same group around Jaʿfar was the early Shiʿite *mutakallim* Hisham ibn al-Hakam (d. 795) (*Fihrist*, 175–76/Dodge, 437–38).

Whatever may be true of Jabir and Jaʿfar themselves, there is nothing to link any of the other followers of the Imam directly to the Hermetic tradition save a common belief in the transmigration of souls (*tanasukh*), a notion that had its supporters in ʿAlid circles as far back as Muhammad ibn al-Hanafiyyah (d. 700) and his champion al-Mukhtar. But unlike the Pythagorean theory of transmigration which was later thought to stand behind the views of men such as Thabit ibn Qurrah and al-Razi, the early Shiʿite *tanasukh* was actually *hulul*, the divine infusion into the Imam. The followers of Abu al-Khattab did believe, as Ashʿari explained, that they would not die, that is, that their souls would survive their passage from the body, much as the Pythagoreans held. But the heresiographers were far more interested in the Shi^cite theories of the Imamate, and so it was *hulul* that tended to usurp the center of their discussions of transmigration.

These alleged Shi^cite affiliations to Hermeticism carry us back to the marshlands of lower Iraq. The territory there occupied by the Mandeans-Sabians in the second or third Christian century was the breeding ground in the ninth of the Qarmatian wing of the Isma^cili Shi^cah. None of the earliest Isma^cilis, those associated with Ja^cfar al-Sadiq in the eighth century, were explicitly connected with the Mesopotamian Sabians, though Maymun al-Qaddah was accused of being an adherent of the Christian sect of the Daysanites who were once strong in those regions (*Fihrist*, 186–87/Dodge, 462–63). The charge appears somewhat unlikely. There was nothing in the Edessan theologian Bar Daysan (d. 222) of the *batin/gnosis* approach to knowledge, no spiritual emanations, no continuing revelation through an Imam.[34]

Whatever its claims to political and dynastic legitimacy, theoretical Isma^cilism was the creation of those obscure men connected in one way or another with the Imam Ja^cfar. None of their works has been preserved intact, but something of their theories can be put together from the heresiographers. Hisham, for example, was proposing a view of material being not unlike that of the Daysanites and the Stoa, and more than one member of the Isma^cili circle embraced the hypothesis of the transmigration of souls, though not, as has been noted, in the same manner as Pythagoras had preached that doctrine. Of Platonic metaphysics there is no trace in those quarters, but within the next century Isma^cili Shi^cism had drunk deeply of just such a system. The earliest Isma^cili literature was largely a dispute over the nature of the Imam, and the argument was pursued over the terrain of the history of prophetism. With Abu Hatim al-Razi (d. 933), the Isma^cili *da^ci* in Rayy and Jibal, Muhammad ibn Ahmad al-Nasafi (d. 942), his counterpart in Khurasan,[35] and then somewhat later, during the reign of Mu^cizz (953–79),[36] among the Fatimid Isma^cilis in Egypt, a new era begins: the Imam becomes a cosmic and transcendent figure as well as a historical one, a position henceforward supported by recourse to a type of late Platonic metaphysics.

The degree to which Neoplatonism invaded the preserves of Isma^cili Shi^cism in the mid-tenth century can be observed in the highly systematized theories of the "Brethren of Purity" at Basrah.[37] A quasi-secret society which sought to use philosophy for political ends, the Brethren, their true identity almost perfectly concealed, published their encyclopedic *Rasa'il* in the latter half of the tenth century. And though they could invoke Hermes on occasion, the greater part of the *Rasa'il* belongs to the *fal-safah* tradition rather than to Hermeticism.[38] There was, of course, a wisdom beyond what was revealed here, the wisdom of the prophets, but the entire project of the *Rasa'il* was one of *public* education, to support the revelation of Islam by an intellectually appropriate philosophy. Their society operated secretly, but the philosophy of the Brethren was open to all who had the ability to comprehend.

The main body of the philosophy and science propagated by the Brethren derives from the usual scholastic sources known to the medieval Muslims: Plato, Aristotle, Plotinus, Euclid and Ptolemy. Their occultism, on the other hand, comes, on their own admission, from the Sabians of Harran, who, according to the Brethren, were the teachers of the Greeks and a link in the chain of wisdom that began in Egypt and Babylon and ended in the Greek philosophical schools, or, rather, in the teachings of the Brethren themselves. Whether that first, more public strain of philosophy, a highly Neopythagoreanized version of the late standard mix of Plato and Aristotle, likewise passed through the hands of the Sabians, seems somewhat unlikely on the face of it since, as we shall see, the two groups did not share the same metaphysics.

For their part, the Brethren of Purity were exceedingly sparing in their citations of Greek philosophers, particularly the later ones. But a great deal of the Hellenic material can be identified, and if the *Rasa'il* were composed in the second half of the tenth century, as the few names supplied by al-Tawhidi seem to suggest, the Brethren already had available for their purposes the greater part of Greek philosophy and science that would eventually pass into Arabic. If, however, the nucleus of the collection goes back to the earliest Imams, as the Ismaᶜili tradition insisted it did—to ᶜAbdallah ibn Maymun, for example, who flourished early in the second half of the eighth century—then it would antedate most of the formal translation activity from Greek into Arabic. In this event the possibility of a Sabian intermediary for even the scholastic material would be a far more attractive notion.

How the Sabians of Harran could have passed to the early Ismaᶜilis a substantial body of Greek learning is not suggested by our sources, which are chiefly concerned with the scholastic *falsafah* tradition. But we obviously do not have the whole story. As we shall see below, Jahm ibn Safwan (d. 745), who lived even earlier than ᶜAbdallah ibn Maymun, apparently had access to some version of Neoplatonism, and others of the earliest *mutakallimun* show signs of Stoic influences. Sabian philosophical literature was almost certainly in Syriac, though it was not necessarily constituted on integral translations. The Sabians showed no interest in the purely scholastic accomplishments of Alexandria and Athens until certain of them moved into Islamic circles in Baghdad at the beginning of the tenth century. We must think, then, that they were drawing on syntheses rather than on the textual bases of an Olympiodorus or a Farabi. The Proclan Neoplatonism of Pseudo-Dionysius, available in Syriac, was one such synthesis, and the Greek *Corpus Hermeticum* was another. The encyclopedic system of the Brethren of Purity was far more ambitious than either of those collections, and so too was that of the Sabians, even though this latter can now be read only in Arabic summaries.

There were grounds enough for the Brethren at Basrah to dissemble their immediate associations with the pagan Sabians of Harran,[39] but their silence on their Greek sources may have arisen from a more genuine ignorance. They had inherited a synthesis rather than created one, and the artificers of that inheritance, like those of the pseudepigraphers of the *Corpus Hermeticum* and the *Corpus Areopagiticum*, were little inclined to reveal either their sources' or their own identity. The Brethren's theology and cosmology was not, however, identical with that of the Sabians. The former stood closer to late Platonic orthodoxy in positioning the two Plotinian hypostases of Universal Intelligence and World Soul, while they relegated the other spiritual beings, gods in the Sabians' eyes, to the acceptable Muslim status of angels.

The Brethren acknowledged the prophethood of Hermes, an admission rendered easier by the Sabians' prior identification of Hermes with the Qur'anic Idris. But the most overt expression of Hermeticism in the *Rasa'il* is reserved for the fifty-second and final *risalah* in our collection. It is here, in this assemblage of magic and theurgy, that the debt to the Sabians is explicitly confessed, the Sabians' connection with the Greeks asserted, and the ultimate origins of science traced, as they were in the various Hermes legends, to Egypt and Babylon.

The entire passage (*Rasa'il* IV, 295–306) is an important source on this still mysterious group of scientists and adepts at Harran who flourished, if only for a brief time, in Islam under the name of Sabians, and who left their profound mark on Ismaᶜili Shiᶜite and Sunni alike. In the first part of the ninth chapter of the *Fihrist* (318–27/Dodge, 745–73) Ibn al-Nadim has his own lengthy description of the sect. He names as his first source al-Sarakhsi (d. 899), who derived his account in turn from his teacher al-Kindi. This initial part of the narrative describes some of the rituals and taboos of the Sabians, but the hand of al-Kindi is most evident in the final equation of Sabian physics and theology with the contents of the Aristotelian school curriculum (*Fihrist*, 320/Dodge, 750).

After the Kindi-Sarakhsi account, Ibn al-Nadim proceeds to his other source on the Sabians of Harran,[40] including a Christian's narrative (320–21/Dodge, 751–53) of how Ma'mun first became aware of their existence. The caliph insisted upon the conversion of these obvious pagans, but the Harranians devised a way out of the impasse: they identified themselves as the Mandean "Sabians" mentioned in the Qur'an,[41] and so sought to move under the shelter reserved in Islam for the "Peoples of the Book." It was the same motive, doubtless, that brought Hermes into the orbit of the Qur'anic Idris.

There was a justice in this. The original invocation of both Hermes and Thoth in connection with the occultism of the *Corpus Hermeticum* was itself a subterfuge to convince the Hellenic reader of the impeccable eastern antiquity of what was actually the creation of the religious and intellectual sensibilities of late Greco-Roman antiquity. Just as Hermes-Thoth was used to conceal the true nature of the original philosophical-theosophical mélange, so now Idris was summoned to give Hermes a protective Islamic coloration by serving as a pseudepigraph for a pseudepigraph.

Enoch and Hermes were late Islamic arrivals at Harran. During the Greco-Roman period the spiritual founding fathers there were Hermes and Agathodaimon, to whose patronage the local ritual and, somewhat more successfully, the considerable Harranian skill in the theory and practice of alchemy and astrology was committed. The alchemy may have been a local growth; its constant and almost exclusive concern with minerals has suggested some kind of association with a metal-working guild.[42] The planet cult at Harran, of which authors such as Ibn al-Nadim, Mas͑udi, the Brethren of Purity, Shahrastani, and Dimashqi all produced detailed descriptions, was likewise very old there,[43] and its assimilation of the sophisticated techniques of Babylonian astrology could have occurred on either of two occasions when northern Syria and Babylonia were parts of the same political organization, during the rule of the Achemenians or, more probably, that of the Seleucids.

Ibn al-Nadim's description of the various rituals practiced at Harran has unmistakably to do with something exceedingly primitive, survivals from another age which managed to escape at Harran the oblivion which Christianity visited upon similar rites all across northern Syria and Mesopotamia. Hermeticism, on the contrary, was not, despite appearances and constant professions of antiquity, a primitive survival from a vanished world, and its mock antiquity stands in absurd contrast to the patently old cult practices at Harran.

Sabianism was far more than mere star worship; the Harranians possessed a physics and a theology as well. Kindi's account in the *Fihrist* reduced the Sabian philosophy to a somewhat too perfect image of Aristotelianism, but the Brethren's explanation of the philosophical premises of the Sabians' astrology, taken together with Shahrastani's report (*Milal* II, 662 ff.), with which it essentially agrees,[44] reveals something quite different. The Sabians believed in a creator God, remote in his transcendence. He is the One in his essence but is likewise present by infusion in other spiritual beings who are his creatures, whether the angels or the souls of men.

Seven of the divine spiritual beings who are not mixed with matter were assigned the direction of the planets. Although the Sabians called the planets the "temples" of spiritual beings, these divine beings did not inhabit them in the manner of souls or inherent forms but ruled them from without, while the planets in turn directed the rest of the material universe. The universe is the meeting place of the goodness of light—the One God was identified with Light by the Sabians—and the evil of darkness. The human soul is consubstantial with the divine beings but does not always realize its powers because of its mixture, as form with matter, with the material universe.

God has mercy on some men and these are the prophets. But for the rest of humanity a return to their homeland among the spiritual beings is attained only by a veritable Platonic *askesis*, the putting off of the influences of the lower part of the tripartite soul. How a man conducts himself in life determines his role in the next cycle of creation. In the Sabian view the species cease their reproduction at the end of a Great Year of 36,435 solar years. At that point begins a new cycle of material beings. The purified souls have since rejoined the spiritual beings on high, but those whose purification is incomplete must suffer another reincarnation, either as men, or, for the substantially impure, as lower beasts.

Although it is not stated explicitly, this body of cosmology, physics, and psychology probably constituted the esoteric teachings of the Sabians of Harran, what the Ismaᶜili Brethren of Purity called the "realities" (*haqa'iq*), while their elaborate rituals were designed for esoteric purposes. That the two were born at the same time or arose from the same religious sensibilities defies belief, however. We can only surmise that at some point which cannot at present be determined, but likely during Hellenistic times, the pagans at Harran fashioned for themselves a theology, that is, they attempted to explain their beliefs in terms of Hellenic rational discourse, albeit in a late, syncretized, and occult form of that discourse. The experiment cannot be judged a complete success. The old cult and the new theology sat uneasily together, uncomfortably enough for Shahrastani to deduce the existence of two Sabian sects, the "spirituals" and the "idolaters," the latter likely the original "Sabians" of Harran, and the former equally likely the product of a contact with Hellenistic piety and science.

Kindi was correct when he thought he could detect Aristotle through the outlines of Harranian theology, but only half so. What he did not understand was the highly syncretized nature of the Harranians'—and his own—philosophical inheritance. He says (*Fihrist*, 320/Dodge, 750): "The saying that God is unity, to whom no attribute applies and about whom no affirmative statement can be made, or any syllogism related, is similar to what is said in the *Metaphysics*." Kindi knew the *Metaphysics*—it had been translated for him by a certain "Astat" (Eustathius?)—and so too did his Sabian contemporary Thabit ibn Qurrah. But Kindi had before him another text masquerading as Aristotle which expressed sentiments far closer to the Sabian insights than was the *Metaphysics*, the abridgment of parts of Plotinus's *Enneads* known as the "Theology of Aristotle."

There existed another Arab tradition on the origins of the Harranian version of the *theologia negativa*. Saᶜid al-Andalusi's account of the history of Greek philosophy in his *Tabaqat al-umam* (22–26 ed. Cairo/Blachère, 57–62) opens with the remark, already seen in the *Rasa'il* of the Brethren of Purity, that the Greeks' religion was like the Sabians'. How this came about historically is revealed shortly after: the earliest Greek philosopher was Empedocles, who learned his wisdom in Syria from King David's vizier Luqman. Among Empedocles's successors Saᶜid mentions only Pythagoras, who was initiated into philosophy in Egypt by certain companions of Solomon who fled there, then Socrates and Plato, who were both students of Pythagoras, and finally Aristotle, the student of Plato but also in a sense of Pythagoras since his father Nicolaus was a student of Pythagoras.[45]

The Greeks' own view of that history reads quite differently, of course. Saᶜid or his source has reversed the correct chronology of Empedocles and Pythagoras to confer priority on the former. Later Greek lives of Pythagoras, like that in Porphyry's *Philosophical History*, do make him into an inveterate traveler over the Near East, and according to Porphyry, Pythagoras derived his wisdom from the Egyptians, Phoenicians, and Chaldeans, as well as from the Arabs and Jews who instructed him in the interpretation of dreams (*Vita Pyth.*, 22–23 Nauck). There are, however, no similar traditions in the case of Empedocles, and the tiny fragment preserved from Porphyry on Empedocles (*Vita Pyth.*, 7) does nothing more than state that he was a student and lover of Parmenides, the latter unknown to Saᶜid.[46]

Saᶜid's characterization of Socrates is another departure from the later Greek tradition. Despite the fact that later Platonists paid little or no attention to the ethical philosophy or political concerns of Socrates, he held nonetheless a central position in their understanding of the *history* of philosophy. Socrates was against, according to Porphyry, the "coryphaeus of the philosophers," an attitude that went back to the philosophers of the generation before Cicero, when the ethically oriented Stoics and Platonists came to regard Socrates as the founder of "modern" philosophy and claimed him as their own. That interest in ethics did not survive among the later Platonists, but the historical position granted to Socrates did.

Sa^cid was not, however, writing history but obscurely enunciating a philosophical attitude which had its origins in the east and located its Greek ancestry chiefly in the long-dead Empedocles and Pythagoras. According to Sa^cid, in Empedocles's own lifetime popular opposition forced his philosophy to go underground where it was cultivated by what were called in Arabic *batiniyyah*, that is, esotericists. In Islam the reappearance of this Empedoclean legacy was connected with the Spaniard Ibn Massarah (d. 931) and the early Mu^ctazilites,[47] who were, in Sa^cid's view, the chief beneficiaries of Empedocles's insistence on the unity of God and his denial of the reality of the divine attributes.

The historical Empedocles did attempt, by all accounts, to resist the current Greek anthropomorphism in the name of Parmenidean monism; but the interpretation of that stand by Sa^cid or his source is patently Neoplatonic. Aristotle, it appears, was not the only thinker used as a pseudepigraphical cover for Neoplatonism. Empedocles was cast in precisely that role in the Neoplatonic doxography preserved in Arabic under the title of *The Opinions of the Philosophers* and attributed to Ammonius.[48] And though he does not appear in the early Arabic literature on Harran, Empedocles does figure in Islam's most considerable piece of *Hermetica*, the *Ghayat al-hakim*, falsely attributed to Ibn Massarah's fellow Spaniard al-Majriti. Here the Sabians, Hermes, Empedocles, and the Hermetic Aristotle all have their places, and Aristotle the most prominent place of all.

The titles attributed to Hermes in the *Fihrist* are chiefly alchemical and astrological.[49] Similar works were earlier circulating under his name in Greek as well, but the *Corpus Hermeticum* published by Festugière and Nock is far more philosophical than occult in its contents, and its theology bears a marked resemblance to both Stoicism and Platonism.[50] None of the *Fihrist*'s titles points in that direction, however, but at the end of the already cited Kindi-Sarakhsi account of the Sabians, Ibn al-Nadim adds (320/Dodge, 750): "Al-Kindi said that he saw a book which these people [the Sabians] authorized. It was the *Discourse of Hermes on Unity* [*tawhid*], which he [Hermes] wrote for his son. . . . No philosopher exerting himself can dispense with them . . . and agreement with them."

The "Discourses on Unity" have been identified, without evidence, as the tract called "Poimandres" in our *Corpus Hermeticum*.[51] If we recall, on the other hand, that the information—and the editorial comment— comes from al-Kindi, a philosopher with known Mu^ctazilite leanings,[52] and that *tawhid Allah*, the unity of God, was *the* paramount Mu^ctazilite issue of the time,[53] we are no closer to locating the "Discourses" in the *Corpus Hermeticum*, but we have probably uncovered Kindi's motive in praising whatever he read in the "Discourses" and can perhaps conjecture what he did read there. In al-Kindi's bibliography we find among his controversial works (*Fihrist*, 259/Dodge, 622) various refutations of the Manicheans and other dualists, a work on *tawhid*, together with commentaries, and finally, a treatment of the differences that exist between the various sects on the subject of *tawhid*, and this despite the fact that they are all supporters of the divine unity.

Al-Kindi had already attempted, as we have seen, to locate Sabian theology in the context of the *tawhid* question by what must have been a highly Neoplatonic reading of the *Metaphysics*, just as Sa^cid al-Andalusi was to do with a similar reading of Empedocles. Sa^cid was far more explicit, however, in drawing the historical conclusions: the Empedoclean (read: Neoplatonic) version of Hermeticism had a direct influence on the theology of the Mu^ctazilite Abu al-Hudhayl (d. ca. 840–50). We do not know enough about the intellectual formation of Abu al-Hudhayl properly to comment upon Sa^cid's judgment,[54] except to note that the *kalam* formulated by Abu al-Hudhayl, who despite the date of his death belonged to the generation of thinkers before al-Kindi, had not yet been exposed to the scholastic tradition in philosophy.[55]

And yet the signs of exposure to some type of speculative theology on the Greek model are unmistakable, not, as might be expected, in the Mu^ctazilite pioneer Wasil ibn ^cAta', but in one of his contemporaries, Jahm ibn Safwan (d. 745). Jahm must be read through the mercies of his opponents, but it is difficult to believe that he was not meditating (Pseudo-) Empedocles or some other Neoplatonic source, the Hermetic "Discourses on *Tawhid*," for example, when he presented his own radical portrait of Allah as absolutely transcendent, beyond accidents, properties, or qualifications, and indeed, beyond being itself.[56]

Farther back in Islam it is impossible to go. Jahm antedates all the known translations of Greek *philosophica* into Arabic. He may have been relying upon Syriac rather than Arabic material, it is true, either Neoplatonizing Christian theologians—Pseudo-Dionysius had been available in Syriac since the sixth century in the translation of Sergius of Reshayna—or those of Harran whose God Kindi described as "*tawhid*, to whom no attribute applies and about whom no affirmative statement can be made or any syllogism related."

By all accounts the first of these Harranians to reach Baghdad and leave his mark there was Thabit ibn Qurrah (d. 901).[57] Again according to the *Fihrist* (272/Dodge, 647), Muhammad ibn Musa of the famous family of savants and patrons of learning found Thabit employed in Harran as a money changer, admired his style, and took him into his translation circle, which at that time included the celebrated Hunayn ibn Ishaq. Thabit trained with Muhammad, was eventually introduced to the Caliph Mu^c-tadid (892–902), and became the effective head of the Sabian community in Iraq.

Thabit was comfortable in Greek, Syriac, and Arabic and had an active scholarly life as a translator, epitomizer, and commentator of Hellenic scientific material, chiefly in mathematics, astronomy, and medicine. His interest in Aristotle centered on the *Organon*, but at least one Platonic study is cited among his works, "An explanation of the Allegories in Plato's *Republic*" (Qifti, 120, 7). It was not Thabit's only work on politics,[58] nor was it the last time that a member of the family wrote on the *Republic*. His son, the physician Sinan ibn Thabit (d. 942), wrote a world history which began, on the testimony of Mas^cudi's somewhat critical notice (*Muruj* I, 15–16), with a preface in the manner of Plato's *Republic*, that is, it proceeded from an analysis of the faculties of the soul to an understanding of the governance of the state.

The *Fihrist* does not make explicit use of information from Thabit ibn Qurrah for its account of the Sabians, but al-Qifti's bibliography of his works (116–20) credits Thabit with a number of tracts on the Sabians and their beliefs, mostly in Syriac. And even though al-Kindi belonged to the scholastic rather than the Harranian tradition in philosophy, it is possible that Thabit, who shared both traditions, the Harranian by birth and the scholastic through his contact with the Banu Musa, was the source of Kindi's philosophically oriented version of Sabianism.

It would be a mistake to characterize the entire Harranian tradition as Hermetic. In philosophy the line between Middle Platonism's flirtation with Neopythagoreanism and a full-blown Hermeticism was, in any event, a thin one. Pythagoras was extravagantly admired by his Neoplatonic biographers, and as much for his wondrous powers as for his philosophical perspicacity.[59] Indeed, Pythagoreanism had been closely linked with thaumaturgy since its revival by Nigidius Figulus in the late Roman Republic. By the first century of the Empire, however, Pythagoras represented a metaphysics as well as a *bios*, as the later Platonists were well aware. Its effects were already evident in Philo,[60] and both Porphyry (*Vita Pyth.*, 43–45 Nauck) and Simplicius (*In Phys.*, 230–31) cite long extracts from Moderatus of Gades, a Pythagorean of the first Christian century, whose theses, if they are his,[61] anticipated positions generally characterized as Neoplatonic.

One of the most remarkable features of Moderatus's theory as described by Simplicius is the immediate derivation of matter from the One by the latter's "withdrawing" or "contracting" itself and so producing, from its own substance as it were, a "quantity" without form, distinction, or figure. Iamblichus knew of this theory but attributed it not to Moderatus but to the Egyptians (*De Myst.* VIII, 3), a judgment which by the time of Proclus (*In Tim.* I, 386) was more precisely credited to Hermes Trismegistus.[62]

Moderatus was unknown to the Arabs, and so too was this peculiarly Pythagorean theory of the creation of matter; Muhammad ibn Zakariyya al-Razi, who was thought to have taken his inspiration from both the Harranians and Pythagoras, held a very different view on the subject (see below). Thabit did know the work of another pre-Plotinian Pythagorean, Nicomachus of Jerash, whom the Arabs fairly consistently confused with Aristotle's father. Nicomachus's *Arithmetical Theology* was apparently unknown to the scholars of the tenth century (*Fihrist*, 272/Dodge, 643), but his other major work, the *Introduction to Arithmetic*, which became a standard textbook in the later Platonic schools,[63] was translated into Arabic by Thabit. And in its introduction he could read the familiar philosophical premises of Middle Platonism, the preexistence, for example, of the Platonic *eid*, here numbers, in the mind of the Creator God (18 Kutsch; 12 Hoche).

Thabit's scientific interests are well attested;[64] assessing his work as a philosopher is considerably more difficult. His bibliography shows that he devoted a great deal of attention to Galen, one of the chief routes whereby scholastic philosophy passed into Islam. Galen's *On Demonstration*, which had been translated into Syriac by a certain Ayyub and then into Arabic by Hunayn ibn Ishaq and his assistants, was given close study by Thabit (Qifti, 118, ll. 6–7).[65] Only a few years later an otherwise unknown philosopher of Mosul, Abu Bakr ibn abi Thawr, was exercised by the same tract and wrote against it. There are strong Platonic reminiscences in Abu Bakr al-Mawsili, and yet the only post-Islamic *faylasuf* he cites is Thabit ibn Qurrah.[66] On the face of it both Thabit and his son Sinan had an abiding interest in ethical and political questions, an interest that went back, through Galen as seems likely, to a study of Platonic psychology.

Thabit's son Sinan (d. 942) enjoyed an equally prestigious position in Baghdad, where he was in charge of the licensing of physicians for the practice of medicine in the capital. Despite his closeness to both Muqtadir (908–32) and Qahir (932–34), Sinan's Sabianism provoked difficulties. He resisted the importuning of Qahir, even to the point of fleeing to Khurasan, but Sinan ended his days as a Muslim. Others of his coreligionists were feeling the same pressure. The *Fihrist* (326/Dodge, 768–69) has preserved a list of "headmen" at Harran reaching from the time of ʿAbd al-Malik (685–705) down to the beginnings of Ibn al-Nadim's own lifetime, when the succession appears to grow somewhat uncertain. From another source we learn that the last head of the Sabian community died in 944,[67] though his position, and that of his immediate predecessors, may not have been official. There was a temporary respite in 965 when a prominent Sabian, Abu Ishaq Ibrahim ibn Hilal (d. 995), became the chief secretary of the Buyid *diwan* and used his influence on behalf of his confreres.[68] By Ibrahim's day the chief Sabians were cultivating the perhaps safer domain of belles lettres and history: both Ibrahim and Thabit ibn Qurrah's grandson, Thabit ibn Sinan (d. 975), were literary men rather than scientists, the latter a historian of some distinction and with a marked Hellenic cast to his work.[69]

What was the impact of the Sabians upon Islam? As is the case in the parallel instances of the Manicheans and the Daysaniyyah, we do not possess the books of the Harranian sect nor even their history but must rely on what can be read in the oblique *testimonia* of Mas'udi, Ibn al-Nadim, the Brethren of Purity, Shahrastani, Maimonides, and Dimashqi, all of whom, with the exception of the sympathetic Brethren, regarded the Sabians as a manifestation of a somewhat exotic paganism given to the worship of planets and idols. Individual Sabians, by way of contrast, operated within the intellectual circles of tenth-century Islam with what appears to be considerably greater freedom than contemporary "zindiqs," those suspected of some clandestine form of Manicheanism.

Ibn Hazm (*Fasl* I, 137) ranked the Sabians among the *thanawiyyah* or pluralists. The characterization may have been technically correct as argued by Ibn Hazm in the pages of a heresiography, but by all appearances the Sabianism described in the Muslim sources was a myth, a *roman* as Massignon called it, founded upon the historical survival in northern Mesopotamia of a pagan sect whose antiquity was obvious but not historically identifiable by the Muslims. Trading on this ignorance, the Harranians managed to associate themselves with the Mandeans of Iraq, who themselves had no greater claim to antiquity but who had the inestimable advantage of being accepted, on the testimony of the Qur'an itself, as "People of the Book." Thus both groups, Harranians and Mandeans, were drawn into the biblical complex of Enoch and Abraham, and by linking Enoch, Idris, and Hermes, the Harranians could assume the role of possessors of a wisdom that was both patriarchal and attractively Hellenic.

One philosopher who accepted the historical claim but not the conclusions to be drawn therefrom was Maimonides. He had seen, he tells us, the Sabians' books and found them interesting in that they provided the precise pagan context against which the precepts of the Torah were revealed. The *Guide* (III, chap. 29) dwells upon a number of those books: a defense of the community of the Sabians and a book of their rituals by a certain Ishaq the Sabian, a clutch of Hermetic Aristotelian pseudepigraphs, and particularly the *Nabatean Agriculture* of Ibn Wahshiyyah.

Maimonides was little interested in the speculative side of Sabian Hermeticism; his obvious intent was to connect Sabian cult and ritual with the theurgic practices that rendered the Sabian reprobate to the Jew. Earlier Muslim authors such as Ibn al-Nadim and Mas^cudi were less concerned with drawing a moral than in describing what was a received element of ancient history, an element that had curiously survived in living form into the tenth century: the Hermes of whom the Muslims' Greek and Iranian sources spoke was represented in contemporary Baghdad by the Sabians from Harran.

The most notorious product of Sabian influence was the already cited philosopher-physician Muhammad ibn Zakariyya al-Razi (d. 925), the director of a hospital at Rayy who also spent at least part of his life in the medical circles at Baghdad.[70] Razi identified his own philosophy as Platonic, at least as it concerned his famous dialogue with the Isma^cili da^ci Abu Hatim al-Razi who in Muhammad ibn Zakariyya's view was holding the Aristotelian, and incorrect, view of time.[71] Razi did not subscribe, it appears, to one of the most cherished myths of later scholasticism, the essential agreement of Plato and Aristotle.

That Razi's physics derived from some later version of Platonism is beyond reasonable doubt.[72] Each one of his five eternal principles—the demiurge, soul, matter, the void, and eternity—had Platonic antecedents which find their origins in Plato's *Timaeus*. The *Timaeus* was read in a variety of ways in the later Platonic schools, to be sure, but the only commentator explicitly connected with Razi's understanding of that dialogue is Plutarch of Chaeronea,[73] a partisan, no less than was Razi, of the creation of the world in time.

Razi's position on the temporal creation of the universe, an attitude which ranged him with Plutarch and John Philoponus—and the Qur'an—against the main body of the later Platonists, was not the result of Islamic piety nor a desire to do justice to the Qur'anic account of creation; for Razi, God's creation of the world was necessary, not willed, and it came about in a specific moment of time by reason of the freely willed choice of the soul to bind itself to matter.

The most elaborate description of Razi's cosmology is provided in a late work by al-Katibi (d. 1276) who says that it is identical with the teachings of the Sabians of Harran.[74] Katibi was by no means the first to connect Razi with the Sabians. The charge appears as early as Mas^cudi who cites (*Muruj* IV, 68) Razi as the author of a work on the Sabians, and far more explicitly in Sa^cid al-Andalusi (*Tabaqat*, 33) who derives Razi's belief in transmigration (*tanasukh*) from the same Sabians. Ibn Hazm (*Fasl* I, 76–77) likewise mentions Razi among the partisans of *tanasukh*, a group that includes the Mu^ctazilite Ahmad ibn Habit[75] and Abu Muslim.

Transmigration had well-known antecedents among the Indians, but in the case of Razi the inspiration was felt to be Greek, not Empedocles but another thinker who held, as we have seen, an important and well-defined position within later Platonism, Pythagoras. Indeed, Mas^cudi describes (*Tanbih*, 122) how the Christian Yahya ibn ^cAdi (d. 974) studied the theology of Razi as a prime exemplar of Pythagoreanism.

The Sabians, Manicheans,[76] Brahmans, Plato, and Pythagoras were all charged by Muslim authors with the responsibility of having shaped the irreligious and heterodox philosophy of Muhammad ibn Zakariyya al-Razi. Many of the source attributions were provided by Razi himself and may in fact have been intended to deflect readers down an antique path. Islam knew other instances of putting difficult or unlikely doctrines into the mouth of an alien tradition.[77]

Razi's Platonism was real enough, however. Its most curious ingredient is doubtless the atomism which was central to his physics. Despite Pines's suggestion that Razi may have acquired it from his reading of Galen, its origins remain obscure.[78] A Middle Platonist like Plutarch of Chaeronea might still be concerned with the influence of Epicureanism, but Razi stood, for all his atomism, remote from the tradition of Epicurus. His God was both demiurge and provident, and the human intellect for Razi was no mere conglomeration of atoms but part of the divine substance,[79] all of them propositions recognizably Platonic and infinitely remote from the mind of Epicurus and his followers.

Its atomism apart, Razi's Platonism, with its five eternal and hypostatic coprinciples, was not that of Plotinus, Porphyry, or Proclus. To cite a single obvious example, in Razi there is no intellectual hypostasis corresponding to the *nous* of Plotinus,[80] nor does his version of the "fall" of the soul—a consequence of its lust (*ladhdhah*) for matter—bear any but the most superficial resemblance to Plotinus's *tolma*.[81]

But for Razi, no less than for his Platonic predecessors, the soul did in fact fall. But not irremediably. At the heart of Razi's philosophy is a paradoxical and abortive soteriology. The Creator, he explains, was moved with pity for the fallen soul and provided it with the means for its salvation, a part of the divine substance whereby the soul might remind itself of its origins. At first view the attitude appears gnostic in the manner of the Manicheans, but upon investigation Razi's cure for mortality is not a secret *gnosis* but the public *falsafah* available to everyone according to his abilities.[82] Neither an elitist *gnosis* nor an Islamic prophet are necessary to restore the soul to its spiritual homeland.

Razi's denial of the need for prophecy brought him into conflict with Sunni and Shi^cite Muslims alike,[83] but it makes him equally remote from the oracle-ridden theology of Proclan Platonism. And yet Razi stood athwart a similar tradition that sought to relate philosophy not to oracles but to the occult powers of nature. He was undoubtedly an alchemist (*Fihrist*, 358/Dodge, 863), and he defended its study as a necessary propaedeutic to philosophy. It was not, however, alchemy that brings a man to that "other world" but rather philosophy, the supreme science. Proclus ventured into the *Chaldean Oracles* after theology (*Vita* XXVI); for Razi the quest for wisdom and salvation ended in speculative theology.

Razi's resistance to prophecy, whether in its usual Judeo-Christian-Islamic form of a public and social revelation or in its esoteric Shi^cite manifestation in the person of an Imam, held him close to a naturalistic theory of knowledge. The Platonist Farabi developed a theory of naturalistic prophecy out of late Peripatetic speculation on the imaginative faculty, but the Platonism of Razi was tethered far too closely to physics to permit such development. More, Razi denied the basic propositions governing the greater part of the Greco-Islamic "wisdom" literature. The first was that God (or the gods) could be summoned earthward to take up residence in an idol, or, as the Islamic Hermeticists preferred, in a "temple" (*haykal*). The theme is a common one in Greek Hermeticists like Iamblichus, and it must stand in one form or another behind Shahrastani's detailed exposé of Harranian idol worship. The second possibility of descent from above is that which directs itself not into idols but into living men, the divinely inspired sages, poets, and philosophers of the Greek tradition, the prophets of Sunni Islam, and the Imams of Shi^cism.

Razi acknowledged the sage but denied the prophet. His wise man was not, however, the divinely inspired bard or the oracles so highly praised by later Platonism but the intellectual "striver" (*mujtahid*), in short, a Plato or an Aristotle whose accomplishments were the result of investigation and not inspiration. Although gravely heterodox in Islam, Razi's position would not have been unseemly among the pagan but ostentatiously secularist schoolmen of fifth-century Alexandria. No one there was teaching Razi's brand of physics, not on the philosophy faculty at any rate, though we cannot speak with the same assurance about the Alexandrian physicians. More likely Razi was an original: the material was Greek, principally Platonic, in its inspiration, but his use of it was his own. The late Greek Platonists took their physics from Aristotle, just as Ibn Sina and the Brethren of Purity did, but Razi had other perceptions. But to call them Sabian is, in the present state of our knowledge, to say nothing.

Like the Judaism of the first century, the late philosophical tradition was a more mottled creature than its scholastic rabbis permit us to apprehend. Syncretism was constantly and pervasively at work, and if its effects are so visible at Athens and Alexandria where *Urlagepietät* was at its strongest and most protective, we can perhaps grasp the complexity of the peculiar mutants that were thrown up elsewhere. Many, like Gnosticism, were suppressed by Christian orthodoxy and pinned, like so many exotic butterflies, to the pages of the heresiographies, but for others of the religio-philosophical hybrids the more relaxed—and less historically sophisticated—climate of Islam brought respite and even rejuvenation. The Sabians of Harran, the Mandeans, Daysanites, Isma'ilis, Jahm, Hisham, Razi, and the Brethren of Purity all had access to philosophical sources, themselves already hybridized as seems likely, about which we can only guess. Farabi, the good scholastic, explicitly linked himself with the masters of the schools; the others, each in his own degree alien to the scholastic tradition of Late Antiquity, acknowledged only Hermes as their father.[84]

Notes

[1] This final stage in the history of Greek philosophy is traced in my *Harvest of Hellenism* (New York, 1970), 671–81.

[2] I have described the process in my *Allah's Commonwealth* (New York, 1973), 286–331.

[3] See M. Plessner, "Balinus," *The Encyclopaedia of Islam*. New edition (hereafter *EI²*), 1:994–95.

[4] A. J. Festugière, *La révélation d'Hermès Trismégiste*. Vol. I: *L'astrologie et les sciences occultes*, third edition (hereafter *Révélation* I³) (Paris, 1950), 355–56.

[5] Much of what follows I have already sketched in *Allah's Commonwealth*, 271–86, though without reference to either the sources or the secondary literature on the subject.

[6] Julius Ruska, *Tabula Smaragdina. Ein Beiträge zur Geschichte der hermetischen Literatur* (Heidelberg, 1926); Paul Kraus, *Jabir ibn Hayyan. Contribution à l'histoire des idées scientifiques dans l'Islam*, 2 vols. (Cairo, 1941–42), esp. 2:270–303; Helmut Ritter, "Picatrix. Ein arabisches Handbuch hellenistischer Magie" in *Vorträge der Bibliothek Warburg* (1921–22), 94–124; Louis Massignon, "Inventaire de la littérature hermétique arabe" in *Révélation* I³, 384–99; Martin Plessner, "Hermes Trismegistus and Arab Science," *Studia Islamica* (hereafter *SI*) 2 (1954): 45–59, "Hirmis" *EI²* 3:463–65, and *Vorsokratische Philosophie und griechische Alchemie* (Wiesbaden, 1975); Yves Marquet, "Sabéens et Ikhwan al-Safa," *SI* 24 (1966): 35–80, and 25 (1966): 77–109.

[7] The account is preserved in Ibn Juljul, *Tabaqat al-atibba* (Cairo, 1955), 5, written in the same year as the *Fihrist*.

[8] The citations from the *Fihrist* are from Fluegel's edition; the parallel passages from Bayard Dodge refer to his English translation based on an improved manuscript collation: *The Fihrist of al-Nadim*, 2 vols. (New York and London, 1970). Abu Sahl's account is interrupted by a brief excerpt from an anonymous source and is followed by an equally brief citation from a certain Ishaq the monk who is cited elsewhere (15/Dodge, 28, 594) on questions of chronology concerning Socrates and Plato.

[9] See David Pingree, *The Thousands of Abu Ma^cshar*, (London, 1968), 2n4.

[10] On parallel stories from other sources, see Pingree, *Thousands*, 1n3.

[11] al-Mas^cudi, *Muruj al-dhahab*, ed. Charles Pellat (Beirut, 1965–), 8:290; al-Khatib al-Baghdadi, *Ta'rikh Baghdad* (Beirut, 1966), 1:67. His son Timadh may have played a similar role in the same proceedings; cf. Yaqut, *Mu^cjam al-buldan* (Cairo, 1936–38), 1:684.

[12] Earlier in his life Abu Ma^cshar had been a rather conservative student of hadith and a critic of al-Kindi's penchant for philosophy. He underwent a "conversion" to philosophy at the latter's instigation, however, but in the end Abu Ma^cshar gave himself over to astrology. *Fihrist*, 275/Dodge, 656.

[13] Pingree, *Thousands*, 14–18, and M. Plessner, *SI* 2 (1954): 56–57.

[14] Two of the others, "Tinkalus" and "Tinqarus," probably refer to the same Greek astronomer, Teucros; see Pingree, *Thousands*, 11, and cf. Dodge, 643.

[15] P. Kraus, "Zu Ibn al-Muqaffa^c," *Rivista degli studi orientali* (hereafter *RSO*) 14 (1933): 1–14. But the question remains an open one; cf. S. M. Stern in *Journal of Semitic Studies* 7 (1962): 236 ff. and particularly the studies of Mario Grignaschi in *Bulletin d'études orientales* 19 (1965–66): 7–83 (hereafter *BEO*) and *Le Muséon* 80 (1967): 211–64, where he makes the case for an Umayyad translation of some of the pseudo-Aristotelian *Letters to Alexander*. Grignaschi's choice of translator, Salim Abu al-^cAla' (*Fihrist*, 11/Dodge, 257–58), is based on highly circumstantial evidence, but if true, requires a serious revision of the history of the Arabic translations from the Greek; F. Sezgin, *Geschichte des arabischen Schrifttums* 4: *Alchemie-Chemie, Botanik-Agrikultur* (Leiden, E. J. Brill, 1971), 24. By a somewhat curious coincidence, this alleged oldest translation from Greek into Arabic would also be the earliest known piece of *Hermetica* to come into Arabic; cf. Grignaschi, *BEO* 19 (1965–66): 49–51. Here too the argument is circumstantial rather than explicit.

[16] For his work, see P. Kraus, *RSO* 14 (1933): 11–13. Dodge's identifications systematically confuse him with a later translator, Ibrahim ibn al-Salt.

[17] Kraus, *RSO* 14 (1933): 11n3.

[18] According to the *Fihrist*, 268/Dodge, 639, Yahya received his instruction on the *Almagest* from "Salm, the director of the *Bayt al-hikmah*." This cannot be correct since both Salm and the "House of Wisdom" date from Ma'mun's reign. Possibly the reference is to Sallam al-Abrash. On Salm see note 57 below.

[19] Another Greek author who came into Pahlevi during the same period was "Dorotheus the Syrian." One of al-Fadl's contemporaries, ^cUmar ibn al-Farrukhan, who served both Harun and Ma'mun, was responsible for the Arabic version of Dorotheus's *Pentateuch* (*Fihrist*, 268/Dodge, 641). The Arabic text has been edited with an English translation by David Pingree, *Dorotheus Sidonius Carmen Astrologicum* (Leipzig, 1976).

[20] See F. E. Peters, *Aristotle and the Arabs: The Aristotelian Tradition in Islam* (New York, 1968) and "The Origins of Islamic Platonism: The School Tradition," in P. Morewedge, ed., *Islamic Philosophical Theology* (Albany, 1979), 14–45.

[21] See Festugière, *Révélation* I³, 81–88.

[22] See the remarks of J. Neusner, *History of the Jews in Babylonia* (Leiden, 1969), 4:316–17, on the extremely private quality of the esoteric theological

learning of the rabbis, and cf. 2:183–84 on the gnostic "style" of those same Iraqi rabbis.

²³ See K. Rudolph, "Probleme einer Entwicklungsgeschichte der mandaischen Religion" in U. Bianchi, ed., *Le Origine dello Gnosticismo* (Leiden, 1967), 304–5.

²⁴ On these Babylonian and Iranian elements in Mandeanism, see G. Widengren, *Handbuch der Orientalistik* 8 (Leiden, 1961), 92–96.

²⁵ See Widengren, *Handbuch*, 96–97.

²⁶ See K. Rudolph, "Entwicklungsgeschichte," 588, and Widengren, *Handbuch*, 97.

²⁷ C. Brockelmann, *Geschichte der arabischen Literatur* (Leiden: E. J. Brill, 1953), 1:280–81; Supplbd. 1:430–31; L. Massignon, *Révélation* I³, 396.

²⁸ Masᶜudi, *Muruj* I, 78.

²⁹ To cite but two well-known examples, see the remarks of Neusner, *History of the Jews*, 4:423–25, on the possibility of Iranian influences on Palestinian Judaism, and K. Rudolph, "Zum Problem: Mesopotamien (Babylonien) und Gnostizismus," in Bianchi, *Le Origine*, 302–6.

³⁰ For some of the identifications, see Johann Fück, "The Arabic Literature of Alchemy According to Ibn al-Nadim," *Ambix* 4 (1951): 81–144.

³¹ On Dhu al-Nun and Ibn Wahshiyyah, see S. K. Hamarneh, *Catalogue of Manuscripts on Medicine and Pharmacy at the British Museum* (Cairo, 1975), 26–31, 57–64. Shalmaghani, who appears in the *Fibrist*, 147, 176/Dodge, 323, 340, belonged to an intellectual circle which included, not always on friendly terms, Thabit ibn Qurrah and two later members of the Nawbakhti family, Abu Sahl Ismaᶜil and his nephew al-Hasan ibn Musa.

³² The attribution was earlier denied by Julius Ruska, *Arabische Alchemisten* (Heidelberg, 1924), 2:40, but now compare Sezgin, *GAS* I, 529.

³³ Ashᶜari, *Maqalat al-Islamiyyin* 1:10–11; cf. M. Hodgson, *Journal of the American Oriental Society* 75 (1955): 7–8.

³⁴ There was, however, among Bar Daysan's followers, though not perhaps in Bar Daysan himself, a belief in the "Father and Mother of Life," who by their sexual union brought forth either two daughters or seven sons; H. J. W. Drijvers, *Bardaisan* (Assen, 1965), 131 ff. These mythical expressions derive from either astrological or agricultural motifs—the Father and the Mother are identified with the sun and the moon and the two daughters with the earth and the sea—but are in no way similar to the Ismaᶜili asexual emanation system descending from a single, transcendental power.

Bar Daysan is not to our eyes a very clearly defined figure. Some of that obscurity may have arisen from the shifting positions of those who claimed his name over the following eight centuries. Though interested in theology, he was not, it appears, part of the occult Hermetic tradition associated with the city of Harran. Bar Daysan was a Christian and so his myth was a Christian and not a Hermetic one, even though it was invaded by the sensibilities of his highly syncretized milieu. The knowledge of the doctrines of Bar Daysan must have arrived within Islam though Syrian Christian channels, even though the Muslim heresiographers preferred to associate him with Mani because of their own preoccupation with the problem of dualism. Ibn al-Nadim appears not even to have been aware that he was a Christian.

[35] See S. M. Stern, "The Early Isma^{c}ili Missionaries in North-West Persia and in Khurasan and Transoxania," *Bulletin of the School of Oriental and African Studies, London* 23 (1960): 56–90.

[36] See W. Madelung, *Der Islam* 25 (1960): 87–101.

[37] See Y. Marquet, "Ikhwan al-Safa'," *EI*^{2} 3:1071 ff.

[38] Their attempt at concealing their rationalism behind the veil of a divinely revealed *shari^{c}ah* is precisely the charge leveled against "the Brethren" by the contemporary *faylasuf* Abu Sulayman al-Sijistani and reported by Tawhidi, *Imta^c* (Cairo, 1939–49), 2:6ff.

[39] Marquet, *SI* 25:107–8.

[40] Among them (*Fihrist*, 327/Dodge, 772) a Syriac book about the Sabians which the Qadi of Harran, Harun ibn Ibrahim (d. 940), found there, had translated and sent to the vizier ^{c}Ali ibn ^{c}Isa.

[41] On these and other varieties of Sabians, see Carra de Vaux, "Sabi'a," *Shorter Encyclopaedia of Islam*, ed. by H. A. R. Gibb and J. H. Kramers (Leiden: E. J. Brill), 477–78, and Dodge, 922–23, with the older literature cited there. Other etymologies are proposed for the name by Marquet, *SI* 25:109n1.

[42] See J. Lindsay, *The Origins of Alchemy in Graeco-Roman Egypt* (London, 1970), 313–22.

[43] See note 33 above and Marquet, *SI* 25:77–103.

[44] See Marquet, *SI* 24:62–80.

[45] Sa^{c}id's source has likely confused Aristotle's father with Nicomachus of Jerash, the Neopythagorean mathematician of the Roman Empire.

[46] And almost so to Ibn al-Nadim. The name Parmenides appears in the *Fihrist* only in a list which comes from John Philoponus and which names the most famous physicians before Galen: *Fihrist*, 286/Dodge, 675.

[47] Ibn Massarah's connection with the eastern Mu^{c}tazilites was probably through his father ^{c}Abdallah (d. 899) who had earlier spent some time in Basrah; see M. Cruz Hernandez, *Historia de la Filosofia Espagnola* (Madrid, 1957), 1:221–22.

[48] See S. M. Stern, "Anbaduklis," *EI*^{2} 1:483–84; and for a later Gnostic reading of Empedocles by a Christian heresiographer, H. Diehls, *Die Fragmente der Vorsokratiker*, sixth edition by W. Kranz (Zurich, 1952), 356–57.

[49] They are analyzed by L. Massignon in A. J. Festugière, *Révélation* I³, 390–92.

[50] On the Stoic themes in the cosmic religion of the *Corpus*, see Festugière, *Révélation* II: *Le Dieu Cosmique*² (Paris, 1949); and for its version of the transcendent One of the Neoplatonists, *Révélation* IV: *Le Dieu Inconnu et la Gnose* (Paris, 1954).

[51] H. Corbin, *Histoire de la philosophie islamique* (Paris, 1964), 1:180.

[52] See R. Walzer, *Greek into Arabic* (Cambridge, Mass., 1962), 176 ff.

[53] Compare the tendentious dream of Ma'mun reported by Ibn al-Nadim (*Fihrist*, 243/Dodge, 583–84), where Aristotle appears to the caliph and advises him to appreciate *tawhid*, that is, support the Mu^{c}tazilites.

[54] See A. S. Nyberg, *EI*^{2} 1:128.

55 As represented in the first instance by the syllogistic method expounded in the Aristotelian *Analytics*. The pre-Ash^{c}arite *mutakallim* reasoned dialectically rather than syllogistically; see J. van Ess, *Die Erkenntnislehre des ^{c}Adudaddin al-Ici* (Wiesbaden, 1966), 19–22, and for the identification of *kalam* and *dialexis*, 57–59.

56 See the analysis, set against the parallel passages in Plotinus, in R. M. Frank, "The Neoplatonism of Jahm ibn Safwan," *Le Muséon* 78 (1965): 395–424. In drawing the parallels Frank does not mean to suggest that Jahm's theology was derived immediately from Plotinus (398).

57 The *Fibrist* (cf. 243/Dodge, 584) does speak in a number of places of a certain Salm (or Salman) who was in charge of Ma'mun's "House of Wisdom" and was an associate of Sahl ibn Harun (120/Dodge, 262–63), the Iranian specialist who did translations from the Pahlevi and who was in charge of the library. Salm, who was one of those sent by Ma'mun into Byzantine territory in search of Greek manuscripts, is described in one of them (Beirut ms. St. Joseph 338) as a "Harranian." This may have been so, but Ma'mun inaugurated his *Bayt al-hikmah* sometime about 830 and did not "discover" the Sabians until his own final expedition into Byzantine territory somewhat later. If Salm was a Sabian as well as a Harranian, he kept the knowledge exceedingly private; cf. P. Kraus, *RSO* 14 (1933): 11.

58 Cf. al-Qifti, *Ta'rikh al-hukama'* (Leipzig, 1903), 120, 4.

59 The Arabs, on the other hand, knew Pythagoras chiefly as a moralist, as the author of the *Golden Verses* which found their way into a number of Arabic gnomonological collections like Miskawayh's *Al-Hikmah al-Khalidah* (225–28 Badawi). On the other appearances of the *Golden Verses* in Arabic, see Badawi's edition (Cairo, 1952), 44–46 of the introduction.

60 See P. Boyance, "Études philoniennes," *Revue des études grecques* 76 (1963): 64–110.

61 See E. R. Dodds, *Classical Quarterly* 22 (1928): 129–42, and P. Merlan in A. H. Armstrong, ed., *The Cambridge History of Later Greek and Early Medieval Philosophy* (Cambridge, 1967), 94.

62 On the possibility of the theory's appearing in the *Poimandres*, see Festugière, *Révélation* IV, 40–42 and, more generally, 36–40.

63 It was commented upon by Iamblichus, Philoponus, and Proclus, the last of whom considered himself the reincarnation of Nicomachus (*Vita* XXVIII).

64 *GAL* I², 241–44; Suppl. 1:384–86; M. Ullmann, *Die Medizin im Islam* (Leiden, 1970), 123–24; Hamarneh, *Catalogue of Arabic Manuscripts*, 46–48.

65 Another student of both science and things Sabian, Muhammad al-Razi, likewise interested himself in Galen's treatise, and his refutation is still extant; cf. R. Paret, "Notes bibliographiques," *Byzantion* 29–30 (1959–60): 425n2.

66 See S. Pines, "La doctrine de l'intellect selon Abu Bakr al-Mawsili" in *Studi orientalistici in onore di Giorgio Levi della Vida* (Rome, 1956), 2:350–64; cf. R. Paret, *Byzantion* 29–30:434–36.

67 See L. Massignon in *Révélation* I³, 385–86.

68 On his fluctuating political position, see H. Busse, *Chalif und Grosskönig. Die Buyiden im Iraq* (Beirut, 1969), 301–3.

[69] On Thabit as a historian, see M. S. Khan, "Miskawayh and Thabit ibn Sinan," *ZDMG* 117 (1967): 303–17. The historiographical tradition in the family actually began with Sinan who was commissioned by Mu^{C}tadid to write a world history for the education of the caliph's two sons; see F. Rosenthal, *A History of Muslim Historiography* ^{2} (Leiden, 1968), 48; and for Mas^{C}udi's criticism of the work, 507–8. The relationship between this history and the *History of the Kings of Syria* mentioned among Sinan's works by Qifti (195) is unknown.

[70] Ibn Juljul, *Tabaqat*, 77–78 (Sayyid) and n3 on the incorrect connection of Razi with the ^{C}Adudi *bimaristan* there. On Razi as a physician, see Ullmann, *Die Medizin im Islam*, 128–36.

[71] P. Kraus, *Razis Opera Philosophica* (Cairo, 1939), 305; cf. S. Pines, *Beitrage zur Islamischen Atomenlehre* (Berlin, 1936), 69.

[72] See Pines, *Beiträge*, 60–78.

[73] Ibid., 69, 73n2

[74] P. Kraus, *Opera Philosophica*, 203 ff.

[75] Cf. n127 in the Nyberg-Nader edition of the *Kitab al-intisar* (Beirut, 1957).

[76] Cf. Pines, *Atomenlehre*, 69.

[77] See J. van Ess, *Die Erkenntnislehre des Ici*, 260; Pines, *Atomenlehre*, 67.

[78] Pines, *Atomenlehre*, 74n2. The atomist physicians Erasistratos and Asclepiades both figure as adversaries in Galen, and his fellow Platonist Plutarch directed a treatise against the earlier Epicurean atomist Colotes. Later Platonism remained, nonetheless, generally unconcerned with Epicurean physics, and if the reputation of Colotes was still alive in Porphyry and Proclus, it was only because of his attack on Plato's use of myth; cf. R. Westman, *Plutarch gegen Colotes* (Helsinki, 1955), 37. On Erasistratos in Arabic, see Ullmann, *Die Medizin im Islam*, 69.

[79] Kraus, *Opera Philosophica*, 285.

[80] Shahrastani, *Milal* (Cairo, 1899), 2:95 ff. does, however, enumerate the five Sabian principles as Creator, intellect, soul, space, and void.

[81] See Armstrong, *Later Greek Philosophy*, 242–45, and H. Corbin, *Étude préliminarie pour le "Livre" réunissant les deux sagesses* (Teheran and Paris, 1953), 132 ff.

[82] Kraus, *Opera Philosophica*, 285.

[83] Cf. the controversy on the need for prophets that went on between him and the contemporary Isma^{C}ili *da^{C}i* Abu Hatim al-Razi. Kraus, *Opera Philosophica*, 295–316.

[84] The later history of Hermeticism in Islam is still only imperfectly known, but the materials are all available to the scholar; cf. F. Sezgin, *GAS* IV, and M. Ullmann, *Die Natur und Geheimwissenschaften in Islam* (Leiden, 1972).

IV

12

WHEELER M. THACKSTON

Department of Near Eastern Languages and Civilizations
Harvard University, Cambridge, Massachusetts

Treatise on Calligraphic Arts: A Disquisition on Paper, Colors, Inks, and Pens by Simi of Nishapur[1]

THE PAPERS of all countries have been tried, and the best paper for calligraphy is produced in Baghdad, Damascus, Amul, and Samarqand. The paper from other places is generally rough,[2] blotches,[3] and is impermanent. It is better to give paper a slight tint because white is hard on the eyes and the master calligraphic specimens that have been observed have all been on tinted paper.

There are many various colors.[4] Some noncompound, simple colors are: yellow, dark red, light red, blue, verdigris, natural, and straw. A few compound colors are: blackish, green, rose, dark green (?), and orange. Now the method [of making] each of these will be explained.

For a yellow color (*zard*), separate one from another the strands of a bit of unadulterated saffron that is very bitter and yellow in color, and put them in a glass [vial]. For every mithcal of saffron mix in five seers of pure water and seal tight the top of the glass. Put it in the sun for three days, until the liquor is completely steeped and the strands of saffron are like straw. Then strain it through a piece of fine cloth and store it in a china vessel until it is nice and clear. Then pour it into a large flat dish and dip the paper in it, letting it remain [in the dye] so that the color affects equally all parts of the paper. Hang a piece of muslin on a line, drape the paper over the muslin, and let it dry in the sun. Afterwards polish it.

Red color (*surkh*) is made by boiling brazilwood in water, or by boiling anemone flowers, or from mulberry juice. However, these colors have no permanence and turn yellow and fade. They also make paper coarse and brittle. However, if it is made from lac[5] color, it is extremely good and cannot be faulted. For every five seers of lac color, boil in a stone vessel one maund of water plus half a seer of *lutr*[6] until [it is reduced to] ten seers. Strain it, tint the paper in it, and let it dry as previously explained.

For a light red color (*al*), place a quantity of safflower on a clean piece of cloth. Little by little sprinkle some water on it until the yellow liquor in it has all dripped out. For every maund of safflower, sprinkle two seers of powdered sal ammoniac on it and rub it with the hands for an hour. Then sprinkle a little warm water on it so that the color comes out. Afterwards put a little sour apricot juice, orange or lemon juice, sour pomegranate juice, green-grape juice, or vinegar into it until it is clear. Then immerse the paper in the color and let it sit for a day or a night, after which it may be removed and left to dry as explained before. Much care must be taken, for this is the most difficult color of all [to obtain].

A dark blue color (*kabud*) can be made from pure, first-rate indigo or from an infusion of blue flowers, but it is not approved of. The best method is to gather a quantity of sunflower seeds during winter, stain a piece of cloth with the extract [of the seeds] and let it dry in the sun. Do this three times. Afterwards, moisten a bit of earth with ammonia and spread the earth over the dyed cloth for an hour, or until it takes on a bluish color, then let it dry. When desired, sprinkle a bit of that blue powder into cold water, strain it, and tint the paper with it. This is not permanent either, for the original color will fade and turn purple.

In a china bowl pound with vinegar some good verdigris made from copper leaf and vinegar, until no solids are left. Then for every seer of verdigris mix in ten seers of water and let it sit for twenty-four hours with the lid sealed so no dust can get in. Afterwards tint the paper in the strained dye.

For natural dye (*khwadrang*), take a few leaves of pure henna,[7] free of dust and dirt, that have not been pulverized, and put them in warm water for a day or a night. Afterwards strain it and color the paper in it. Use ten seers of water for every seer of henna. If more water is used it will turn a cotton color. This color has been the choice of most [calligraphers].

For straw color (*kahi*), take a little of the yellow extract of safflower, strain it well, dye the paper in it, and let it dry in the sun.

In mixed colors, two colors are mixed to produce a different color.

A blackish dye (*ᶜudi*)[8] is made from a bit of lac mixed with some blue powder [discussed above], and with this paper is dyed. The mixture of colors depends on the taste of the calligrapher. As one dye [or the other] is increased, a change will appear in the [resulting] hue, and this can be controlled by the individual.

For green dye (*sabz*) mix together a bit of blue powder and a little yellow extract, strain it, dye the paper in it, let it dry, and then repeat.

For a rose color (*gulgun*) mix together a little lac and saffron, and then dye the paper in it. The more saffron there is, the better.

For a dark green (*faresa*)[9] dye mix together a little gall water (*ab-i mazu*) and blue powder. Let it sit for a day until it is clear, then dye the paper in it.

For an orange dye (*naranji*) mix together a bit of saffron and the first water of safflower extract. Put the paper in it for half [the normal time?], and then let it dry in the shade. It is better to dye the paper light red first and then in saffron.

Several [other] various types of colors have been invented on which writing turns out very well. A little henna, saffron, and blue powder are mixed together and the paper is dyed therein. Another is a little black mixed with saffron and green-grape juice, and the paper is dyed with that.

Another is [made by] immersing marshmallow seeds in water for twenty-four hours. It is then strained and the paper is dyed in it. This is extremely choice and pleasing, for it makes the paper soft and calligraphy looks good on it.

Another is [made by] cooking and straining a bit of fine starch powder,[10] dipping the paper in it, and letting it dry. Two pieces of paper can also be bonded together with the starch so that the two become as one. It can then be polished and written on, and the writing will be extremely legible and beautiful, as good as on *sultani* paper.

Another is [made by] letting white fish glue sit in pure water for three days and nights. It is then warmed over a slow fire. Strain it, dip the paper in it, and dry it carefully, after which it can be polished and written on.

By means of other things flimsy paper can be reinforced so that the tufts that are raised and prevent the pen from moving swiftly can be removed.

Clarify the mucus of fleawort seed and let the paper sit in it for a while. Then let it dry.

Another method is with sweet-melon juice, the liquid of cucumber and muskmelon seeds, molasses of seedless grapes, nonoily rice paste, gum arabic, or the like. [These things] reinforce paper and make it [as smooth] as a mirror. All of these methods are tried and true.

Dyes have been explained because these days people are naturally inclined to grace and elegance, and letters written to various parts are not without ornamental elaboration. Some paper is tinted, coated,[11] and flecked. It is now correct for what is written from sultans to various places, or from nobles to rulers, to be written on white paper and better not even to be polished. However, among friends and acquaintances any amount of ornamentation is all right.

[Gilts and suspensions.]

Gold gilt. After the goldsmiths have rendered one mithcal of twenty-four-carat gold into a hundred leaves, take a few of those leaves. Melt a bit of black glue and put a little in a china bowl. Then, one by one, put the gold leaf into the bowl. Wash your hands with warm water and pure soap and then with the forefinger and middle finger rub [the contents] around from right [to left] until you know that it is mixed well. Put a lot of pure water in the bowl, rinse your fingers and the bowl well. Taking care to protect it from dust and soot, put it aside until all the gold has settled to the bottom of the bowl. Then pour out the excess water, take a brush, load it with the gilt, and write with it. When it has dried, polish it very slowly with a jasper stone or a polished Arabian shell. If you can, outline it with a very fine black line.

Silver suspension is made into a solution in the same manner as gold, or it can be suspended in thick gum arabic or clarified honey. When you finish writing and there is gold or silver gilt left over, pour out the water left in the bowl and dry it up over a flame, for if it is left standing a long time in water it will turn dark. When you want to resume writing, rub the gold or silver a bit between two fingers with resin or glue and then you can write as before.

Bronze or copper suspension. Rub a bit of bronze or a sheet of pure copper over a stone until it has been triturated. [Rinse and] pour off the [excess] water. Rub it with black glue, as you did the gold and silver, and write with it. If polished with an Arabian shell it will look nice.

Lapis lazuli (ultramarine) suspension. [Lapis lazuli] is obtained from the mountains of Badakhshan and then pulverized and washed. [The particles] that float on the top are collected, and that is called *shamt*. What remains is extremely colorful and brilliant. Then, when you want to use it, you must first knead it with resin and rub it well in the bottom of the bowl. After that, keep adding a solution of water and pure resin until it becomes suitable for writing.

A practical ultramarine can be compounded of first-rate raw indigo, ceruse [white lead], and resin water. The indigo should be rubbed on a stone with water. The ceruse should be washed and the soft part added to the indigo. When it has stiffened, pound it with the resin water and use it. Writing [done with this substance] lasts a long time.

Cinnabar[12] comes originally from sulfur and mercury, [which are put into] a vessel made from lute [mud cement] and heated very slowly over a flame. The best type [of cinnabar] is made in Europe. It is widely used by calligraphers. Extreme care must be taken in pulverizing it. It should first of all be rubbed on a stone until it is good and soft. Then, it can be pounded little by little with some sour pomegranate juice until no solids are left. With warm water wash [it off] the stone and your hands into a receptacle and let it sit for two hours. Then pour off the yellow water that will have collected on the top and spread the residue onto a newly baked unglazed (*abnarasida*) brick so that it will dry quickly. Then knead a bit of it with resin water and write with it.

For verdigris, take a bit of polished copper and put it in a vessel. Mix in an equal amount of vinegar and suspend it in a well for a period of forty days. When taken out, it will have acquired verdigris. Sift a bit of it through a piece of cloth and pulverize it in a china bowl with some balsam infusion and write with it. If a little saffron is added to it, it will turn pistachio green. However, after a time it will eat holes in the paper and cannot be counted on to last.

Talcum is derived from a stone found in earthen mounds on large mountains. There are two varieties. One comes in sheets, one on top of the other like mica, and from this bathhouse tiles are made. The other variety comes in sheets that are extremely fine, light, flimsy, pure, and shiny. Of the second variety a bit is put into a bag made of muslin. Pieces of ice are put into the bag, and it is rubbed with the hands over a bowl. The water is allowed to drip little by little into the bowl until the ice is completely melted. Then more ice is put into the bag, and it is pulverized in a like manner a few times. It is then left overnight, and then the excess water is poured off. [The residue] is dissolved in resin water and used to write on colored paper. If a little saffron is added to the water it will look like gold. If a bit of cinnabar is added, it will look like silver fleck. If used to write on light red paper and polished with Arabian shell, it will look like gold and silver. This is called "milky" talcum. If the talcum can be dissolved, many remarkable and wonderful things can be done with it.

Arsenic suspension is also of two varieties, leaf arsenic and nugget (*kulukh*) arsenic. Leaf arsenic is more colorful and shinier. Take a bit and soften it by rubbing it on a stone. Then sift it through a piece of muslin, pulverize it in cold water, knead it with resin, and use it to write with and it will look almost as beautiful as lapis lazuli on dark blue, black, or red paper.

Hurmuz clay (*gil-i hurmuz*) is obtained from the bottom of the sea. When it collects on the bottom, people gather it and dry it. Take a bit and put it in water. Then pour it back and forth from one vessel to another, pouring each time what comes to the surface of the water into another vessel until finally all is put into an ink pot. Mix in a bit of sifted powder, and it will be blackish.

Ceruse is made from tin. Take a bit and rub it until it is soft and make it into a paste with resin water. Then put it into a large quantity of water until a little is dissolved. Pour this back and forth from one vessel to another, collecting the lead particles, which are called *rub*.[13] When it has settled, pour off the excess water and mix it with resin water and use it for a pleasing medium for writing.

"Doll-baby red" (*ᶜarusak*)[14] is made from the first water of safflower. Put a bit of safflower infusion in a vessel and add a chunk of ice until liverlike flecks appear. Then, with a little excess water [in the vessel], comb out a bit of wool and place it on the lip of the vessel and tip the vessel over so that [the water] will drip out. Then add a bit of pulverized resin to [the residue], smear it over a reed [mat], and let it dry in the shade. When needed, dissolve a little of it in warm water and use it for writing. If it remains in water overnight it will turn dark.

Rulings can be made from all of the colors that have been mentioned. If rulings are made from gold gilt they will be very elaborate and ornamental. By analogy one should know in what places and for what persons such things are suitable.

An explanation of how to make ink.

If you want a shiny, free-flowing black ink, and you attach great importance to such a thing, it would appear imperative for you to make your own ink, and the ancients have left tried and tested, choice recipes for making ink. The very best and easiest is as follows:

Take a bit of unadulterated linseed oil. Twist a thick wick of unprocessed cotton, moisten it a bit and put it in a lamp, fill it with oil, and place it in a protected place where there is no draft and light it. Break off a piece of the top of an unglazed (*abnarasida*) pot and suspend it over the top of the lamp until some soot gathers. Collect the lampblack from the pottery with a chicken feather, spread it on a piece of paper and wrap it up tightly, and bury it in some dough and put it in a hot oven until it is well cooked. Then, when the grease contained in the essence of the lampblack is burned off from the high heat, take it out of the oven. Measure out ten drams and put aside. Take twenty drams of white gum arabic so pure that if a ball is put in the mouth it will dissolve in the saliva with no solid particles left, and put it for three days and nights in boiled water that has been allowed to cool until it is completely dissolved. Then strain it forcefully through muslin. Put the lampblack in a mortar and knead into it resin water. Pound it well until the two are completely disintegrated. Afterward, heat fifteen drams of some ripe gallnuts that are not full of holes, like [the size of?] barley and wheat; let it stay in water for five days, then put it in the sun until the essence (*shira*) has been completely extracted.

Strain it through thick muslin and pour a little bit of this gall water (*ab-i mazu*) at a time into the lampblack and pound it in a mortar until the gall water is completely mixed in with it. Spread five drams of Turkish vitriol (*zag-i turki*)[15] on an iron or copper plate and hold it over a flame until the sulfur in the vitriol burns away completely. Rub until soft and pour it little by little into the black. Pound it in a mortar for a few days until all the ingredients are completely mixed together. Add to the black a little henna water, myrtle-leaf water, woad-indigo (*wasma*) water, a bit of rose water and narcissus liquor, saffron water and powdered aloe, crystalline salt, a little pulverized pearl and coral, musk and whitish ambergris, gold and silver, copper and bronze gilt, cinnabar, and lapis lazuli, for each of these gives its own property and peculiar characteristic. This amazing combination will never change on account of climate and will last immutable for countless years and centuries in the face of the vicissitudes of the impermanent world. It is called "peacock ink." It does not soon coagulate, but if, with the passage of time and fluctuations in temperature, it should thicken slightly and not flow easily, it can be rectified by adding a little sea froth, resin, and powdered sandarac to the ink pot to make it thicker. Then pour a little rosewater into it to reconstitute it as before.

Now, if you are not able to perform all these steps or acquire all these ingredients, a simpler variety can be made, according to the recipe versified by a learned person for quick memorization:

Take two drams of lampblack from a dry lamp.
　　Put four drams of gum arabic into it.
Three drams of gall, half a dram of vitriol
　　And pound them together to make ink.

Another variety, summarized by Mawlana Sadr al-Shariᶜa,[16] is as follows:

Equal in weight to lampblack, vitriol; equal to
　　both, gall;
Equal to all three, resin. Then muscle power.[17]

For another variety, crush a bit of gall and let it sit in water for three days. Then put the strained water into a stone vessel and heat it slowly over flame until it thickens enough so that when written with on paper it does not run. Then mix in pure desulfured vitriol and earth and strain. It makes a nice ink, but it must be kept away from dampness lest it splotch and the pages stick together.

Another variety, also simpler than the other, is made by putting a quantity of starch in an iron pan and heating it over a high flame until it is scorched and catches flame. Then dissolve it in rosewater and write with it.

On the best type of reed pen.

The indication of a good reed is that the color of the skin is translucent and red, it feels heavy, is long and straight, and the inside is extremely white. No reed should be used whose skin is yellow or white, which is raw and light in weight or the middle of which is dark or without pulp, or which is short or crooked, for the line will not turn out as the writer desires. And God knows best.[18]

Notes

[1] The text of this treatise has been twice published, based on different manuscripts: "Risala-i khatt dar bayan-i kaghadh u rangha-yi alwan," edited by Parwiz Adhka'i in *Hunar u mardum* 85 (1348): 51–57, an edition based on Tehran, Kitabkhana-i Majlis-i Shura-yi Milli MS No. 6150; and "Yak risala-i nafis u kuhansal-i hunari," edited by Ahmad Gulchin-i Ma^{c}ani in *Nashriyya-i Danishkada-i Adabiyyāt-i Tabrīz* 14 (1341): 287–303, edition based on Tehran, Majlis MS No. 2459. The two texts are very similar in content and have only minor discrepancies.

The authorship of this treatise has been demonstrated by Yves Porter, "Un traité de Simi Neyšapuri (IXe/XVe S.), artiste et polygraphe," *Studia Iranica* 14 (1985): 179–98. The treatise forms an extract from Simi's *Jawhar-i Simi*, manuscript copies of which are found in (1) the British Library, Or. 7465, foll. 38b-49b, in which the date of completion is given by the author as 1433/837, (2) Oxford, Bodleian, Ouseley Add. 69, foll. 344a ff. (Sachau-Ethé catalogue No. 1241, 32nd text), (3) Tehran, Kitabkhana-i Malik, *majmu^{c}a* No. 526, 8th text. The printed texts lack the beginning and end of the British Library MS, which in turn lacks the end of the Bodleian MS. A table of collation for the various manuscripts may be found in Porter, "Un traité,[6]" 197. Of Simi, who was a librarian at Mashhad and expert in the arts of the book, the scant information available derives from Dawlatshah Samarqandi, *Tadhkirat al-shu^{c}ara*, ed. E. G. Browne (London and Leiden, 1901), 412–17.

[2] Or brittle (*shikananda*): he may mean either that the paper itself is liable to crack or that it is rough and prevents the pen from flowing smoothly.

[3] Or is flimsy: *nushu-kunanda* in Gulchin-i Ma^{c}ani's text; Adhka'i's text has *nashr-kunanda*. In the *Burhan-i qati^c* the word is given as both *nushu* (4:2146) and *nasu* (4:2140), while in line 70 of Sayrafi's poetic version of this treatise, *Gulzar-i safa* (ed. Muhammad-Taqi Danish-pazhuh, *Hunar u mardum* 93 [1349]: 30–42), it must be read as *nashw* to rhyme with *hashw*.

[4] All of the "colors" described by the author are meant for dyeing paper. Most will also produce paint if bound in the proper medium.

[5] Lac is derived from a resinous incrustation on certain trees and yields a lustrous dark red.

[6] So vocalized in both edited texts. Gulchin-i Ma'ani (293n2) quotes from the *Farhang-i Shalimar*: "*lutr*: skinned it has no use in Iran except in compounding with various dye stuffs '*kashnil*' (?) which they imagine picks up color." In *Farhang-i Mu^{c}in* and *Burhan-i qati^c* the word *latar* is given as equivalent to half a Tabriz *man* or 300 *mithqals*. Neither meaning is satisfactory. The recipe given

by Sayrafi in *Gulzar-i safa* (lines 98–100) mentions no additive: he boils five seers of lac in one and one-half maunds of water until it is reduced to ten seers.

7 Henna is the Egyptian privet, *Lawsonia inermis*.

8 This color is defined as the hue of aloeswood, or blackish. The mixture of colors given by the author could result in a dark violet, depending on the proportions. See Porter, "Un traité," 189.

9 In the *Burhan-i qati^c* (3:1483) the word *fares* is given as a variant of *farez*, defined as "a plant, extremely green and succulent, from eating which cattle get fat." Another variant of the word is *farej*, which is defined as a plant called "Turkish aloes" (*agar-i turki*), and *farir* (a misdotting of *farez*), which, among other things, is said to be the plant called *gawzaban* and *lisan al-thawr*, bugloss or alkanet, the root of which yields a red dye.

10 The text edited by Adhka'i has: *qadr-i nishasta-i ahar-i tanuk bi-zanad u bi-palayad*; Gulchin-i Ma^cani's text has: *qadr-i nishasta-i ahar-i nik tanuk pazand u bi-palayand*. Sayrafi's *Gulzar-i safa* (line 226f.) has *tab^c-kun shira-i gandum bisyar/pas bi-palay u bi-bar baz ba-kar*; if we read *tabkh* for *tab^c*, Gulchin-i Ma'ani's and Sayrafi's texts would be in agreement.

11 *Mayda*, defined in the *Burhan-i qati^c* (4:2075) as "twice sifted wheat flour" and as a confection made of grape juice thickened with starch and flour and boiled until quite stiff and known by the Turkish name *basduq*. The author must intend one of the starchy coatings that would take a high polish.

12 Or vermilion, mercuric sulfide (HgS).

13 An Arabized form of the Persian *roy*, "brass."

14 ^c*Arusak* is given in the *Farhang-i Mu'in* as equivalent to *kaknaj*, wintercherry or nightshade, "a reddish plant."

15 In the *Burhan-i qati^c* (2:998) five varieties of *zag* (alum or vitriol) are given: (1) red vitriol, called *qalqand* (χάλκανϑον) in Greek, (2) yellow vitriol, called *qalqitar* (χαλκιτάριον) in Greek and "cameltooth alum" in Persian (*zag-i shuturdandan*), (3) green vitriol, called *qalqidis* (χαλκίτης or χαλκῖτις) in Greek, (4) white vitriol (zinc sulfate), called Yemenite alum (*shabb yamani*) in Arabic, and (5) black vitriol, called "shoemakers' alum" (*zaj al-asakifa*) in Arabic (undoubtedly the same as Bar-Bahlul's *kalqōs sqōpāyōs* [1:898, line 21], defined as "burnt copper," and χαλκός κεκαυμένος [1:858, line 14]). In his Syriac *Lexicon* (1:899), quoting from Bar-Sroshoe, Bar-Bahlul says that when χαλκίτης gets old it becomes χαλκιτάριον. *Kalqdis* (= χαλκίτης [1:898, line 25]) is defined as "burnt white copper" (*nḥāšā ḥewwārā mawqda* = *nuḥās abyaḍ muḥraq*), and according to Bar-Sawma it changes to χαλκιτάριον. What "Turkish vitriol" is has not been ascertained. In Greek, χάλκανϑον is the normal word for copper sulfate, the vitriol used in inks and shoemaker's black, and χαλκῖτις is defined as rock-alum. In a note in the *Burhan-i qati^c* (2:998n7), quoting from Nasir Khusraw's *Jami^c al-hikmatayn*, we read: "And it is a characteristic of alum (*zag*), which is an earthy mineral, and gall, which is borne by trees, that when the two are mixed together, even though both are yellow, they turn very black." In modern terms red vitriol is cobalt sulfate, blue vitriol is copper sulfate, green vitriol is iron sulfate (also called copperas), and white vitriol is zinc sulfate.

¹⁶ Jamal al-Din ᶜUbaydullah Bukhari, a polymath who died in Bukhara in 1349–50/750, see Adhka'i, "Risala," 56n53, quoting from *Rayhanat al-adab*.

¹⁷ The proportions in this recipe are the same as those given by Sultan-ᶜAli Mashhadi in his treatise on calligraphy, *Sirat al-khutut*, photo reproduced and translated into Russian by G. I. Kostygova, "Traktat po kalligrafii Sultan-ᶜAli Meshkhedi," in *Trudy Gosudarstvennoy Publichnoy Biblioteki imeni M. E. Saltykova-Shchedrina* (Leningrad, 1957), vol. 2, part 5, lines 89–100. He adds that *zamma* (white vitriol, zinc sulfate) is superior to alum/vitriol (*zāg*), which he considers harmful in ink.

¹⁸ Gulchin-i Maᶜani's text ends here; Adhka'i's treatise ends with an explanation of *khatt-i awhal*, a simple cipher in which the following pairs of dotless letters are substituted for each other: K-M, Ṣ-lāmalif, alif-W, Ḥ-Ṭ, D-R, S-ᶜayn, L-H. Dotted letters remain as they are unless a word consists entirely of dotted letters, in which case the order is reversed.

13

LOUISE MARLOW

Department of Religion, Wellesley College
Wellesley, Massachusetts

The Peck *Shahnameh*: Manuscript Production in Late Sixteenth-Century Shiraz

IN 1983, the Princeton University Library received an illustrated manuscript copy of Firdawsi's *Shahnameh*.[1] The acquisition, a bequest of the late Clara S. Peck, sister of Freemont C. Peck (Princeton, Class of 1920), is a major work of the late sixteenth-century Shirazi school. It is in excellent condition; moreover, unlike so many manuscripts of its kind, it is intact, and thus can still be appreciated in its original form. In this article I will describe the Peck *Shahnameh* and consider its early history in the context of the commercial aspects of manuscript production in the late sixteenth century.

The Peck *Shahnameh* is a bound volume of 474 folios (984 pages). As has been noted by an unknown hand on the back of the last folio (474v.), the manuscript contains fifty paintings. Although none of the paintings is signed, the calligrapher recorded his name on the last line of the last folio, where he wrote: "The humble servant of God, Qivam b. Muhammad Shirazi, wrote this in the year 998 of the hijra [November 10, 1589–October 29, 1590]." The manuscript was therefore completed early in the reign of Shah ᶜAbbas I.

The date, size, and style of the Peck *Shahnameh* identify it as a late sixteenth-century Shirazi work. Similar manuscripts include copies of the *Shahnameh* in the British Library (Or. 27257),[2] and the India Office Library (ms. 3540),[3] a copy of Sultan Husayn Mirza's *Majalis al-ᶜushshaq* in the India Office Library (ms. 1138),[4] and a copy of Nizami's *Khamseh* at the University of Pennsylvania.[5] This group of manuscripts, to which several others could certainly be added, represents the work of a discrete school, distinct in style from the schools of Qazvin and Isfahan, the Safavid capitals.

Shiraz had a long history of cultural, as well as political, importance. Under the Timurids, it had been second only to the capital Herat as an artistic center. The two cities catered for the sophisticated tastes of the court, and at the same time produced artifacts for commercial purposes in their several workshops. After 1452, when Shiraz passed from Timurid control to that of the Turkman confederations, the "Timurid style" was perpetuated in the east at Herat, while in the west, a new style emerged, now commonly referred to as the "Turkman style."[6] This style was associated with the new Turkman capital, Tabriz (held by the Qaraqoyunlu from 1408 to 1468, and by the Aqqoyunlu from 1468 to 1501). Shiraz was influenced by both the Timurid and the Turkman schools, but eventually developed a distinct artistic identity of its own. This became especially clear in Safavid times, when a synthesis of the two dominant traditions took place in the capitals, while Shirazi painting remained separate.

Shiraz was held as an appanage by members of the ruling dynasties, Qaraqoyunlu, Aqqoyunlu, and finally Safavid. Its importance as a provincial center is suggested by the fact that in 1590, the year in which the Peck manuscript was made, the governorship of the city was held by Muhammad Khudabandah, the previous shah and father of the reigning Shah ᶜAbbas. Although the leading regional artists had consistently made their way to the Safavid courts (Tabriz, Qazvin, and from 1598 Isfahan), such royal governors and local notables still provided generous patronage in the provinces. In addition, Shiraz continued to flourish, as it had in Timurid times, as a commercial center for artistic production. A considerable number of illustrated manuscripts, as well as single-page paintings, were made in the many large workshops of the city. Some of these remained within Iran; others, the Peck *Shahnameh* among them, traveled elsewhere: to the Ottoman Empire, the courts of the Indian subcontinent, and the Uzbek khanates of Central Asia.

Thanks to the high productivity of the Shirazi workshops, a relatively large number of manuscripts made there survives. This abundance makes it possible not only to identify the Shirazi style but also to trace its development. The most important study of sixteenth-century Shirazi painting is still that of Grace Guest, who compared a large number of manuscripts in her *Shiraz Painting in the Sixteenth Century*. Like other art historians, however, Guest is concerned primarily with the work of the first half of the century, and accordingly she devotes particular attention to a copy of Nizami's *Khamseh*, dated 1548, in the Freer Gallery, Boston. The work of this period, she finds, is derived mainly from the Timurid style, and owes little or nothing to contemporary trends at the Safavid capital.[7] After about 1560, Guest detects a "growing eclecticism" in Shirazi art,[8] but does not thoroughly explore this later work, of which she writes: "When recognised at all, it is apt to be dismissed as lifeless and conventional, or to be committed to that limbo of uncertainty presided over by the question mark."[9]

Among the conventions of later Shirazi works are elements of composition and color, as well as specific motifs, such as facial types, animal, tree, and rock forms.[10] It is largely by virtue of such recurrent features that sixteenth-century Shirazi painting can be identified as the work of a distinct artistic school. Moreover, Guest's comments above notwithstanding, these conventions did not necessarily inhibit the production of exceedingly fine manuscripts; in the best examples, they were "but the scaffolding on which the individual masters built their interpretations."[11] The Peck *Shahnameh* demonstrates how such devices could be manipulated successfully in the realization of the painters' conceptions.

The Peck *Shahnameh* opens with a frontispiece, composed of two paintings placed facing one another on opposite folios (ff. 1v., 2r.). Both paintings depict scenes of enthronement, but, like the paired paintings of the corresponding endpiece (ff. 473v., 474r.), they are not illustrations from Firdawsi's text. The frontispiece is followed by a prose introduction, the "Baysunghur" (ff. 2r.–12r.). This introduction, which describes the history of the *Shahnameh*'s composition, is the work of an unknown scholar at the court of the Timurid prince Baysunghur at Herat. It was written to accompany the *Shahnameh* "edition" commissioned by the prince through the collation of the many manuscripts in his library. There is no indication that the Baysunghur "edition" became a model copy; its companion introduction, however, was frequently attached to the beginning of future manuscripts. In the Peck *Shahnameh*, it covers ten folios, of which the opening pair are richly illuminated (plate 1). The date of its original composition is given here as 829 (A.D. 1425–26).

Firdawsi's epic begins on folio 12v. of the volume. The calligrapher, Qivam, son of Muhammad of Shiraz, is probably related to (or otherwise associated with) Muhammad Qivam, a calligrapher of the same city, several of whose manuscripts survive.[12] Some of these manuscripts are dated, the earliest having been finished in 1536 and the latest in 1552. Our own calligrapher, who completed the Peck *Shahnameh* in 1589–90, belongs to a later generation. He may have been less prolific; at any rate, fewer of his works survive. Those extant include copies of two *masnavi*s by Sanaᶜi in the India Office Library,[13] Saᶜdi's *Kulliyyat*, and Hafiz's *Divan*, both in the Topkapi Sarayi Library.[14]

Plate 1

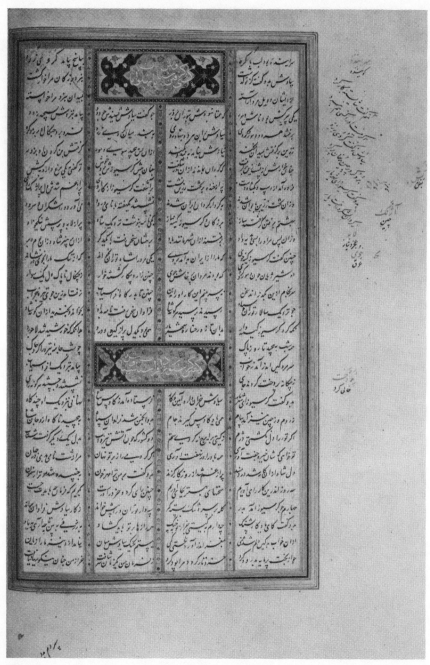

Plate 2

Plate 2 shows a typical page of text in the Peck *Shahnameh*. On each page, a frame of gold and colored lines, measuring nearly 2 cm. in width, has been drawn. Within this frame, twenty-nine lines of calligraphy appear. Each line consists of two full *bayt*s, which should be read continuously across the three vertical shafts marking the division of the four *misra*^cs. Two ^c*unvan*s, or illuminated "chapter headings," can also be seen here. Such ^c*unvan*s appear on almost every page and serve to guide the reader/viewer through the continuous text of the epic. They are always centered horizontally, but appear at varying heights, which do not necessarily coincide exactly with the beginning of the new "chapter." While the epic itself is written in black ink and in *nasta*^c*liq*, the ^c*unvan*s appear in white *naskh*. Probably they are not the work of the main calligrapher but of a specialized craftsman, the illuminator.

An interesting feature of the Peck *Shahnameh* is the presence of numerous notations in the margins outside the frame. Several examples are seen on this representative page. Individual words appear written in red and marked with full vocalization, in some cases perhaps to clarify the rhyme scheme. It is likely that the calligrapher, acting here as an editor, singled out certain linguistic items and glossed them for the benefit of the reader in 1590, to whom the vocabulary employed by Firdawsi nearly six centuries earlier was no longer readily comprehensible. Other definitions may have been added by later readers. Forgotten Persian words are often given their Arabic equivalents: on this page, the old Persian word *khuy*, meaning "sweat," is defined in black by the Arabic word ^c*araq* which superseded it. Sometimes, the notations are poetic usages, such as *sarayandeh*, explained here by the more usual *guyandeh*. Elsewhere in the manuscript, personal and place names are similarly glossed. Such obscure items are often defined each time they occur, even within the space of a few pages, for the benefit of the casual reader.

The Peck *Shahnameh* contains approximately 45,000 *bayt*s. On almost every page, however, at least one *bayt*, written in standard black ink, has been added in the margins. Three such additions can be seen in the margins of this typical page. One is marked by a small sign in red, which indicates that it should be inserted at the corresponding point in the text and was forgotten in the copying. The other two verses, added either by the calligrapher himself or by a later reader, are unmarked. Their position in the margin reflects uncertainty over their authenticity.

Firdawsi's poem is a continuous whole. Leading from the universal to the specifically Iranian, the work moves through the realms of cosmology, myth, legend, and history. The miniatures in the Peck *Shahnameh* occur at specially significant points in the narrative, and encourage the reader/viewer to pause and respond there. Although the notation at the end of the manuscript announces a number of fifty paintings, the exact number of pictures depends on the method used for counting them. The number fifty may be reached by counting the frontispiece and endpiece each as two separate paintings, and the double-page miniature which occurs within the text itself as a single picture.

Other than these three paintings, all the miniatures in the Peck manuscript occupy the whole of a single page and face a full page of text. When the manuscript is opened to a miniature, the two opposite pages of text and picture form a unit which cannot be divided, since each image is planned in conjunction with its facing page of text.

The scene depicted in plate 3 might be entitled "Rustam and his Brothers in the Throes of Death." Rustam, identifiable by the familiar motif of his leopard-skin headgear, is caught in the pit of spears on the lower left. His envious half-brother Shaghad is the figure seen behind the tree in the center of the miniature. Before this scene, Shaghad, who, with the duplicitous king of Kabul, plotted to kill Rustam, had lured the latter to the locale represented here, a hunting ground in the vicinity of Kabul. As a trap for the unsuspecting huntsman, Shaghad had arranged for deep pits to be dug, lined with poisoned spears, and concealed with branches. Rustam, though mortally wounded, is determined to exact his final revenge for Shaghad's treachery. The lines on the miniature tell the story:

> Seeing this, Rustam raised his arm. Wounded though he was, he released his arrow from the bow, and stitched his brother to the tree. At his moment of passing, his heart was kindled with joy. Shaghad groaned, but Rustam restrained him, and said: "God be praised! I have always been cognizant of Him, and now that my soul has risen to my lips, not two days have passed before I exacted my revenge. You gave me strength, so that before death I sought vengeance from this faithless one." As he said this, his soul rose from his body. Everyone broke into weeping and lamentation over him. Not one horseman, great or small, remained.

Not only Rustam and Shaghad, but also Rustam's full brother, Zavareh, is represented in the picture. According to the text, he dies in a nearby pit, as depicted here in the lower left-hand corner. In the reprisals which follow these deaths, still more members of the Sistani house lose their lives. The spectators express their grief and astonishment by biting their index fingers.

Since the miniature occupies a larger area than that filled by the text on a standard page, the boundaries of the frame here are pushed outward into the margins. Nevertheless, a ghost of the original frame is still discernible; its four corners are marked by the two boxed sections in which the text appears. The last line of text visible on the miniature reads: "Not one horseman, great or small, remained." The designer of the book carefully calculated the arrangement of the double-page unit so that this dramatic last line would coincide with the foot of the miniature, where the reader and viewer would naturally linger before turning the page. The patterning on the facing page of text shows how this was plotted.

On an ordinary page of text in the Peck manuscript, such as that in plate 2, a set twenty-nine lines of calligraphy appear. In this example, however, eleven full lines are written horizontally; but the calligraphy then takes different forms. Three lines, separated from each other by two more horizontal ones, appear diagonally across the page. Without omitting any lines, this manipulation of the text reduces the total number of lines on the page from the standard twenty-nine to a mere twenty. This ensures that the chosen passage falls on the page of the miniature itself.

The sparser concentration of words in this geometric patterning also serves to highlight a section which appeared specially important to the maker of the book. In this case, the lines written diagonally express Firdawsi's conception of a random, impersonal fate, a theme which pervades the *Shahnameh*. Having perceived the perfidy of Shaghad and his patron, the ruler of Kabul, Rustam meditates:

> A man may enjoy abundant life, but time will still forestall him; no living being escapes the turning of the heavens. My lustre is not greater than that of Jamshid, whose enemy sliced him in two; nor than that of Faridun or Kay Qubad, great monarchs of illustrious lineage; nor than that of Siyavash, whose throat, when his hour came, was slashed by the dagger of Giruy Zireh. They were all sovereigns of Iran; in battle, each was a ferocious lion. They have departed, yet we abide longer; like enraged beasts, we have remained on the path.

When Rustam meets his undignified end as the dupe of his half-brother, it is a demonstration of fate's indifference to mortal affairs. The accentuation of this theme here prepares readers/viewers for the miniature and influences the way in which they will respond to it.

Contact continued between the artistic centers of Shiraz and the Safavid capitals. Some artists of the royal atelier had trained at the old center of Shiraz; others, who lost the patronage of the court, might move there in search of alternative employment, just as they might travel further afield to the Ottoman Empire or the courts of the Indian subcontinent. Moreover, it is almost certain that the Shirazi painters sometimes received royal commissions. When the royal atelier had more demands than it could meet, for example, it might pass on assignments to the masters of the Shiraz workshops. This may well have been the case with the present manuscript.

Plate 3

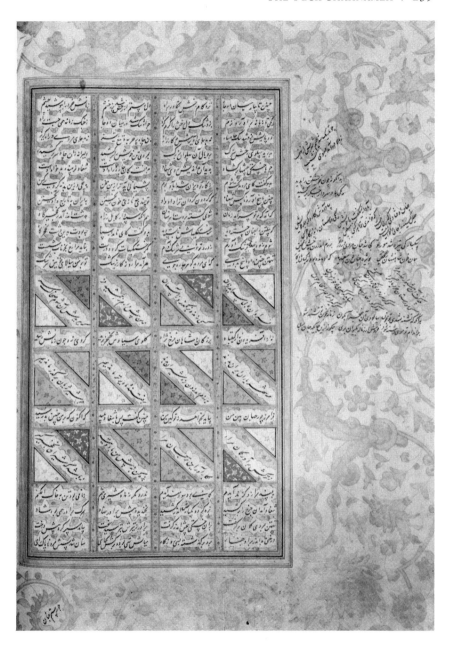

Although no patron is named in the Peck *Shahnameh*, some information about its early history can be obtained from an inscription added on the back of the last folio (f. 474v.). This inscription is not a formal colophon, but the anonymous contribution of an as yet unidentified "owner and possessor." The text reads as follows:

> This book, the *Shahnameh*, was purchased by the illustrious and exalted Khayrat Khan. He had come to the capital Isfahan on an embassy from cAbd Allah the Qutbshah, Zenith of the Sovereign Mighty Heavens, Center of the Glorious and Prosperous Sphere. At the foot of the throne, similar to that of God Himself, [Khayrat Khan] paid homage to His Exalted Majesty Shah Safi, the world-upholding Shadow of God. During his stay, [the envoy] bought this book for the sum of fifty-five silver tumans, from the daughter of Khan-Ahmad Khan of Gilan. She had been the honorable wife of Shah 'Abbas, who now dwells in the Elysian Fields. This took place in the venerable month of Rajab in the year 1040 of the hijra [February 1631].

In other words, an envoy from the Qutbshah cAbd Allah, who ruled at Golconda from 1626 to 1672, came to the court of Shah Safi, who had acceded on the death of cAbbas in 1629. In 1631 this ambassador bought the Peck *Shahnameh* from a widow of Shah cAbbas I, daughter of the Gilani ruler Khan-Ahmad Khan II. This lady is the first known possessor of the manuscript.

Born around 1586, the Gilani princess (whose name is not recorded in the chronicles or local histories of the period) was related on her mother's side to the Safavid ruling dynasty. Khan-Ahmad II had married an aunt of cAbbas, Maryam Sultan Begum, in 1578,[15] and his daughter was therefore cAbbas's cousin. She was originally betrothed to be married not to cAbbas, but to the shah's eldest son and heir, Muhammad Baqir Mirza, commonly known as Safi Mirza. It is possible that the Peck manuscript played a part in the negotiations leading to this betrothal.

At the beginning of 1591, a year after the Peck *Shahnameh* was completed, cAbbas requested that Khan-Ahmad send his daughter, then aged five, to Qazvin, in order that she be engaged to Safi Mirza, aged four. Khan-Ahmad, whose rebellious activities against the Safavids had already resulted once in his deposition and lengthy imprisonment,[16] was again threatening central authority. Since his territories lay on the unstable Ottoman-Safavid border, his loyalty was particularly necessary to the shah, who hoped that the conclusion of a marriage between the Kar-Kiya and Safavid families might secure it. cAbbas therefore sent an embassy to Khan-Ahmad's capital, Lahijan, led by prominent figures from the court and laden with royal and magnificent presents.[17] Although these gifts are not described in the sources, the coincidence of the date and the possession of the Peck manuscript by Khan-Ahmad's daughter in later years suggest that it may have been one of them. A fine copy of the *Shahnameh* was a particularly appropriate gift on such occasions as betrothals, marriages, and accessions; furthermore, Khan-Ahmad had a reputation as a keen patron of the arts. At his court he supported calligraphers and artists, including the famous ᶜAbd al-Jabbar Astarabadi;[18] poets, musicians, and composers, doctors, astronomers, wrestlers, sword players, conjurers, and lion tamers were also among his entourage.[19] Evidence of his patronage is still visible in a painting of a dragon in the Houghton *Shahnameh* which bears the inscription: "Done by this humble servant at the Court of Heavenly Resort of His Excellency, Khan-Ahmad Husayni."[20] Khan-Ahmad was also a poet and talented musician in his own right, and was considered an authority on music, philosophy, and astronomy.[21] Such a prominent cultural figure would have been a particularly appreciative recipient of the Peck *Shahnameh*.

The party in charge of negotiations arrived in Lahijan in the spring of 1591. Khan-Ahmad at first refused the request, but eventually acquiesced in the plans for the betrothal of his daughter. ᶜAbbas then immediately sent a group of leading religious officials from the capital to conduct the ceremony. The Gilani princess was formally betrothed to Safi Mirza on August 2, 1591.[22]

Contrary to the shah's hopes, the betrothal did nothing to improve his relations with Khan-Ahmad. The Gilani ruler had already harbored certain enemies of state in 1588.[23] He had also sent his vizier to Istanbul, with the intention, apparently, of concluding a military alliance with the Ottomans; this was at a time, moreover, when ᶜAbbas himself was endeavoring to negotiate a peace treaty with the Ottomans to end the war which had lasted for nearly a decade.[24] Finally, in his struggle to assert authority over the warring factions within his dominions, the shah diverted some of his troops from the Ottoman front to Gilan. Khan-Ahmad's army was defeated in battle against the shah's forces in 1592. He then fled by sea to Shirvan and abandoned his wife and daughter, who were taken to the capital, Qazvin.[25] Perhaps the Peck *Shahnameh* was transferred to Qazvin among the possessions of the princess. Khan-Ahmad was received at the court of the Ottoman Sultan Murad III in January 1593, and never returned to his hereditary dominions. He died in 1597.[26]

Khan-Ahmad's daughter spent her childhood as the companion of the Safavid heir to whom she had been betrothed. In 1601, when Safi Mirza reached the age of fifteen, ᶜAbbas made preparations for the wedding. To his surprise, however, his son raised violent objections to the marriage. It seems that, as children, the princess had tormented her younger playmate, and the prince had never outgrown his resentment. Eventually, ᶜAbbas agreed to marry his heir to a daughter of Ismaᶜil II instead. Since this left the Gilani princess in need of a suitable husband, the shah decided to add her to his own small number of official wives. This marriage took place on September 1, 1602.[27]

According to the inscription mentioned above, the Peck manuscript changed hands a second time a generation later. It appears that the princess remained in Isfahan, the capital, after the death of her husband, the reigning shah, in 1629. Her status and means were undoubtedly much diminished after this date; perhaps the hardship of an aging widow accounts for her sale of the Peck *Shahnameh* to the Qutbshahi envoy in 1631.[28] In any event, as a result of this sale, the manuscript was transported to Golconda, a major artistic center. It is well known that several artists, calligraphers, and poets made their way from the Safavid courts to those in the Deccan; the Peck *Shahnameh* is an example of an actual artifact which traveled from one royal court to another. Furthermore, all the details of the transfer are supplied: the identity of the purchaser, the sum of money exchanged, and the date of the sale.

Notes

[1] Portions of this article appeared in "A Persian Book of Kings: The Peck *Shahnameh*," *The Princeton University Library Chronicle* 46 (1985): 192–214.

[2] Charles Rieu, *Catalogue of the Persian Manuscripts in the British Museum* (London, 1879–83), 536. Cf. Ivan Stchoukine, *Les peintures des manuscrits de Shah ᶜAbbas 1er à la fin des Safavis* (Paris: Institut Français d'Archéologie de Beyrouth, Bibliothèque Archéologique et Historique, 1964), 135–36 and passim, pls. 1, 2, 3, 4, 5; N. M. Titley, *Miniatures from Persian Manuscripts: A Catalogue and Subject Index of Paintings from Persia, India, and Turkey in the British Library and British Museum* (London: British Museum Publications, 1977), 47–48.

[3] Hermann Ethé, *Catalogue of the Persian Manuscripts in the Library of the India Office* (Oxford, 1903–37), 2992. Cf. B. W. Robinson, *Persian Paintings in the India Office Library: A Descriptive Catalogue* (London: Sotheby Parke Bernet, 1976), 124–36; Stchoukine, *Shah ᶜAbbas*, 136–37, pl. 7.

[4] Ethé, *Catalogue*, 1871. Cf. Robinson, *Persian Paintings*, 138–44.

[5] See Grace Guest, *Shiraz Painting in the Sixteenth Century* (Washington, D.C.: Smithsonian Institution, 1949), 62, pls. 48, 49; Ivan Stchoukine, *Les peintures des manuscrits safavis de 1502 à 1587* (Paris: Institut Français d'Archéologie de Beyrouth, Bibliothèque Archéologique et Historique, 1959), 12; Basil Gray, *Persian Painting* (Geneva: Skira, 1961), 154, pl. 153.

[6] On the Turkman style, see Martin B. Dickson and Stuart Cary Welch, *The Houghton Shahnameh* (Cambridge: Harvard University Press, 1981), 1:15–26, and B. W. Robinson, "The Turkman School to 1503," in Basil Gray, ed., *The Arts of the Book in Central Asia, 14th-16th Centuries* (Boulder, Colo.: Shambhala/ UNESCO, 1979), 215–47.

[7] Guest, *Shiraz Painting*, 25.

[8] Ibid., 31.

[9] Ibid., 25.

[10] On the characteristic features of Shirazi painting, see ibid., 25, 30, and passim; Robinson, *Persian Paintings*, 79–145; Gray, *Persian Painting*, 151–54.

[11] M. G. S. Hodgson, *The Venture of Islam* (Chicago, 1974), 2:517.

[12] See Mahdi Bayani, *Ahval-o Athar-i Khushnivisan* (Tehran: Danishgah-i Tehran, 1969/1348), 3:814–16; F. E. Karatay, *Farsça Yazmalar Kataloğu* (Istanbul: Topkapi Sarayi Müzesi Kütüphanesi, 1961), 7 (R. 327), 75 (H. 407), 161 (H. 756), 197 (R. 933), 272 (R. 1549); E. G. Browne, *A Catalogue of the Persian Manuscripts in the Library of the University of Cambridge* (Cambridge: Cambridge University Press, 1896), 355; Robinson, *Persian Paintings*, 100, 136.

[13] Ethé, *Catalogue*, 917.

[14] Karatay, *Farsça Yazmalarğu*, 188 (H. 741), 218 (H. 1009).

[15] Iskandar Beg Munshi, *Tarikh-i ʿalam-ara-yi ʿAbbasi*, ed. Amir Kabir (Tehran, 1955–56/1334–35), 1:135, 227 (hereafter *TAAA*); ʿAbd al-Fattah Fumani, *Tarikh-i Gilan* (ed. B. A. Dorn, *Mohammadanische Quellen zur Geschichte des kaspischen Meeres* [St. Petersburg, 1857–58]), 46.

[16] *TAAA*, 1:110–14; *Tarikh-i Gilan*, 31ff., 45–46.

[17] *Tarikh-i Gilan*, 99–100.

[18] *TAAA*, 1:175–76.

[19] Ibid., 1:168, 191; cf. Nasr Allah Falsafi, *Zindigani-yi Shah ʿAbbas-i Avval* (Tehran: Danishgah-i Tehran, 1955/1334), 3:153–54.

[20] Dickson and Welch, *Houghton Shamaneh*, 1:239n2, 256n1.

[21] Falsafi, *Zindigani-yi*, 3:153–54.

[22] Ibid., 2:171–72.

[23] *TAAA*, 1:418.

[24] *Tarikh-i Gilan*, 124; Cf. Falsafi, *Zindigani-yi*, 3:135.

[25] *TAAA*, 1:450, 135–36; *Tarikh-i Gilan*, 102.

[26] *TAAA*, 1:529.

[27] Falsafi, *Zindigani-yi*, 2:212–13.

[28] Khayrat Khan's embassy is described in Iskandar Beg Munshi, *Khuld-i Barin* (*Dhayl-i Tarikh-i ʿalam-ara-yi ʿAbbasi*), ed. Suhayli Khwansari (Tehran, 1938/1317), 28–29, and the Qutbshahi chronicles Ahmad Saʿidi Shirazi, *Hadiqat al-salatin*, ed. ʿAli Asghar Bilgrami (Hyderabad, 1932/1350), 67–71, and Mir Abu'l-Qasim Shushtari Mir ʿAlam, *Hadiqat al-'alam*, ed. M. ʿAli Shirazi (Hyderabad, 1310/1892–93), 1:314.

Index

جمال نومان